Positivism in Mexico

The Texas Pan American Series

POSITIVISM
in MEXICO

BY LEOPOLDO ZEA

Translated by Josephine H. Schulte

UNIVERSITY OF TEXAS PRESS, AUSTIN & LONDON

The Texas Pan American Series is published with the assistance

of a revolving publication fund established by the

Pan American Sulphur Company.

Library of Congress Cataloging in Publication Data

Zea, Leopoldo, 1912–
  Positivism in Mexico.

  (Texas pan-American series)
  Bibliography: p.
  1. Positivism. 2. Philosophy, Mexican. 3. Mexico
—Intellectual life. I. Title.
B1018.P6Z413   199′.72   74-549
ISBN 0-292-76413-8

Translated from *El positivismo en México*
Copyright © 1968 by Fondo de Cultura Económica

CONTENTS

PREFACE TO THE ENGLISH TRANSLATION

This is the first part of my study entitled *El positivismo en México*. It analyzes the antecedents and birth of the philosophy used by the Mexicans after the triumph of the liberal Reform movement led by Benito Juárez. Once colonial conservatism was conquered, the French Intervention over, and Maximilian of Hapsburg executed, the reformers wanted to create a new national order to replace the Spanish colonial one. The victorious liberals immediately tried to achieve what their leaders called "mental emancipation," a kind of second independence, which would abolish the habits and customs imposed on Mexicans by three centuries of colonialism. They expressed the need for a philosophy to replace the one that had introduced into colonial Mexico habits of subordination and servitude.

The Mexican Reform, expression of this liberal ideology, had fulfilled its mission; it had combatted and destroyed the colonial system. A new ideology, one of order rather than combat, was to provide the basis for a new system. As you will later detect in this book, the new system would rest on the philosophy of Auguste Comte. The second part of my study, *El apogeo y decadencia del positivismo en México* [The apogee and fall of positivism in Mexico], examines this new ideology, which was supported by positivist interpretations of John Stuart Mill, Herbert Spencer, and Charles Darwin. It was necessarily a provocative ideology, inasmuch as it justified the domination and exploitation of marginal social groups—a domination and exploitation in no way different from that imposed by the former colony—on the basis of a supposedly scientific language.

The Comtian motto, Order and Progress, adopted by the social group that Justo Sierra called the "Mexican Bourgeoisie," merely served to maintain colonial forms of exploitation and, at the same time, to create new ones that were peculiar to the neocolonialism that the great nations of western Europe and North America imposed on other peoples. These leaders of progress prevailed upon Mexico to adopt the positivist philosophy. The so-called Mexican bourgeoisie would collaborate in that neocolonialism by accepting the role of intermediary and amanuensis in the new empire. The conflict between exploited social groups, on the one hand, and foreign interests and a middle class on the margin of an oligarchy, on the other, brought about the movement known as the Mexican Revolution. The revolution tried to correct the errors that had prevented the fulfillment of the dreams of the great liberal leaders of the nineteenth century who strived to make Mexico a modern and progressive nation. Their model of progress was the great nations, which, at their height, had given origin to neocolonialism. They wanted Mexico to become a part of modern progress and a Mexican nation rather than a dependency. The present essay describes this experience. The men of the revolution were not going to repeat the errors of Mexican liberalism, which, during the Porfiriato, was transformed into order by the acceptance of a new kind of subordination.

This book, now translated for the English reader, is not unknown to the United States student of Mexico and Latin America. On the contrary, it has received special attention, which includes criticism as well as interpretation. The same applies to the rest of my works that deal with the study of Latin American ideas, thought, and philosophy. Various friends of mine in the United States, including those who have made possible the publication of this work in English under the auspices of the University of Texas Press, suggested that I make special reference to the criticisms and interpretations of this book by United States scholars. Having summarized the contents of the book, I will now mention these interpretations, for which I am grateful, inasmuch as they have stimulated me to continue this work, which has its natural limitations.

I will refer, specifically, to three United States scholars of Latin American and Mexican thought who have been concerned with this book and have related it to the rest of my works. They are Professors Harold Eugene Davis of the American University, Charles A. Hale of the University of Iowa, and William D. Raat of Moorhead State College. To begin with, I wish to emphasize a general observation that refers to everything that has not been treated in this book and in my other published works. Naturally, I accept it and—remembering my teacher, José Gaos—I believe that there is no limit to my ignorance, except for what I have already written. Along these lines, the universally known work on Latin American thought by Harold Eugene Davis analyzes certain aspects that were not included in my perspective, but from now on they will be treated by future scholars or by anyone who wishes to learn more about Latin American thought. In addition, Charles A. Hale has written a book on José María Luis Mora, and I understand that he is now writing another book concerning new interpretations of Mexican thought that I did not include in my study of positivism. He will complete, with additions, what I have been expounding. A more persistent and sharper critic is William D. Raat. His work on positivism in Mexico, as I understand it, includes aspects that escaped my research. In this sense, it gives me satisfaction to know that one of my books has aroused further interest in the subject and that new interpretations have come out.

The interpretation of facts seems to me to be the most important aspect on which the above-mentioned scholars focused their attention. The same historical reality can be considered from different angles, depending on the historian who analyzes it. Therefore, my interpretations will not always coincide with those of my critics. To begin with, it was indicated that I do not write intellectual history, properly speaking, but rather that I am preoccupied with the formulation of a philosophy of the history of America. José Gaos had already pointed this out to me, though not in a critical way. In contrast, William D. Raat directly and concisely criticizes my focus on historical reality, which preoccupies both of us. He says, "For Zea, the importance of his work on positivism is found in relation to a larger context and concern, that of the philosophy of the history of the New World." What is the reason for this concern? Raat answers:

Now the Mexican as an American can universalize from his particular Mexican situation to develop a New World philosophy which

can be shared with all humanity. American philosophy will save
Occidental culture from the spiritual crisis of our times and turn
the tide of dehumanization.

This, then, is Zea's grand scheme and hope for the future. It has
been argued that philosophy of history is poor philosophy and bad
history. All I can claim is that in the final analysis Zea's speculation
about history is beyond the realm of ordinary historical analysis. It
is metahistory, not intellectual history.[1]

Charles A. Hale, on the other hand, maintains that "the North
Americans consider the presuppositions from which the Mexicans
depart to be entirely different from those that should be made by
a historian in the strict sense of the word. . . . What makes Zea's
work unsatisfactory from a historiographical point of view is the
impossibility of separating the philosopher from the historian."[2]
Harold Eugene Davis accepts Zea's metahistorical preoccupation in
a broader sense, even though he has not accepted his interpretation. He says, "We owe a large debt to Zea for his interpretation
of the nineteenth century, even while not accepting all of Zea's
dialectic."[3]

Where is the problem? According to what we have said, it
would be in the scholar's situation or historical perspective.
From this viewpoint it seems that my colleagues in the United
States feel that they can write a history that is not their own more
objectively and that they are less apt to fall into the same snares as
those who interpret their own reality. Zea's philosophical suppositions, says Hale, "impose certain limitations on the reliability of
his work as intellectual historian. If the historian must become
totally involved in the past, and if his principal concern is the future, how can he help but distort the historical matter he is
studying."[4] And Raat says, "Unwilling to detach history from
present or future concerns, viewing his role of a philosopher-savior
who will direct Mexico's destinies toward a genuine historical con-

[1] William D. Raat, "Ideas and History in Mexico: An Essay on Methodology," in *Investigaciones contemporáneas sobre historia de México*, p. 696.

[2] Charles A. Hale, "Sustancia y método en el pensamiento de Leopoldo Zea,"
Historia Mexicana 20 (October–December 1970): 286, 301.

[3] Harold Eugene Davis, "La historia de las ideas en Latinoamérica," *Latinoamérica anuario de estudios latinoamericanos*, vol. 2.

[4] Hale, "Sustancia y método en el pensamiento de Leopoldo Zea," p. 300.

sciousness in the Hegelian sense, Zea's subjective histories invite honest criticism."[5] This is a difference in interpretation, which both Hale and Raat will end by presenting as a difference in methods. This is a point of departure for a criticism of North American scholars, for it appears that some have accepted this philosophical interpretation. North and Latin Americans are invited to reconsider both their viewpoints and their method of interpretation so that they can write a more objective intellectual history of Latin America.

It is in relation to this supposed objectivity, not contaminated by historicism, sociology of culture, and other philosophies, that the method of Arthur Lovejoy is presented as an example. Raat says: ". . . historical understanding requires transcending the biases of the present. . . . The task of the historian was not to bring certainty, but to approximate objectivity." For Lovejoy, "to confuse a present idea with the past events to which it refers violated the basic canons of temporalism."[6] Hale, however, although in passing, refers to the impossibility of a similar interpretation among Latin American and United States historians. He admits that the latter have more of a possibility for objectivity because United States historians are farther away from the problem peculiar to the Latin American historian of Latin American ideas, as in my own case. Foreign historians have no limitations regarding nationality. He says: "Here the foreign historian has an opportunity that is unique and worth mentioning. Inasmuch as he is not directly affected by patriotic sentiments, he probably has greater freedom to relate ideas to their proper historical perspective. . . . In other words, perhaps it is easier for the outsider to make a critical and comparative study than it is for the native historian."

Thus, regarding the objectivity of United States historians of their own history, great as well as lesser known ones, we simply would have to cite Albert K. Weinberg's book *Manifest Destiny*, in which he expounds on the philosophy of United States history that has to justify the expansion of that country at the expense of other peoples. Latin America is necessarily part of that world which he includes in his history.

[5] Raat, "Ideas and History in Mexico," p. 694.
[6] Ibid., p. 697.

With respect to Latin American historians, they would have to refer to the history of the United States, and therefore it would be difficult for them to maintain the objectivity that United States historians supposedly have when they write about Latin America. When the Latin American historian writes about the United States, he must refer to the present, past, and future of his own history, making impossible the objectivity required of the historian. Hale mentions this lack of objectivity when he refers to my work: "The United States represents for Zea the 'simplistic' modernity which has even relegated Europe to the status of marginality attributed to the Hispanic world. Yet, there is still an ambivalent note in Zea, for it appears that his fundamental antagonism toward the United States is not toward its values per se, but toward North American imperialistic resistance to the realization of these values by other peoples."[7]

Now the question with respect to the objectivity of United States historians toward Latin America must be inverted. The opposite, we insist, is practically impossible for Latin Americans, because the history of Latin America is deeply immersed in the history of the United States. Thus, in my books *América como conciencia*, *América en la historia*, and *Dialéctica de la conciencia americana*, I have insisted on giving the word *dialectic* two different meanings, the Latin and the Saxon, to define this unavoidable relationship. Thus, does it mean that a United States historian of Latin American intellectual history cannot relate Latin American history to his own if he wants to be objective? Would not such supposed objectivity be the best expression of this unavoidable interdependence? Would not such a relationship also explain the concern about supposed contagion that some United States historians of Mexico and Latin America suffer by accepting the interpretations of their Latin American colleagues? The criticism to which we have referred, the need for a more objective methodology, originated in this concern. Harold Eugene Davis says, "A number of North American scholars, consciously or unconsciously, were inspired to write on Latin American positivism in Zea's

[7] Hale, "Sustancia y método en el pensamiento de Leopoldo Zea," pp. 297, 302.

terms."[8] Mexican historians of positivism since Zea have been, says Raat, with a few exceptions, dependent upon Zea's method- ologies. "English-speaking writers have shown even less inclina- tion than their Mexican counterparts to question Zea's method and conclusions."[9] It is precisely a matter of seeing history more objectively, free from presentism and futurism. It would mean the revision of a study that is considered the only one of its kind in this period. But, let us repeat the question. Can the United States scholar separate his own history from the history of Mexico and Latin America? Can he obtain objectivity without falling into futurism and without justifying his own relations with Latin America?

Characteristic of the problem of objective comprehension is one of the criticisms of the pivotal interpretation of all my works, in- cluding my philosophy of positivism in Mexico. Charles A. Hale points out two tendencies in my work: On the one hand, he says, Zea appears as a liberal, interpreting Latin American history as a progressive effort toward the "mental emancipation" of the Latin American from the Spanish colonial regime; but, he adds, on the other hand, "he is in search of cultural identity in historical reali- ty," which is affirmed in that same past that denies the liberal position. Thus, he is in rebellion against liberalism. He adds, "It is ironic that Zea is in reality looking to the Spanish reform tradition in his search for Latin American cultural identity in the modern world." And elsewhere he says, "Contrary to what Zea thinks, we think it can be demonstrated, for example, that the mental emancipator, José María Luis Mora, was far from rejecting the Spanish heritage. Rather, he was prepared to turn to the inspira- tion of the Bourbon and Cádiz reformers."[10]

The key interpretation of my work, including *El positivismo en México*, concerns the situation and consciousness of man's de- pendence in Latin America as well as the efforts he has made and is making to end this dependence. In order to complete the desired

---

[8] Davis, "La historia de las ideas en Latinoamérica."

[9] William D. Raat, "Leopoldo Zea and Mexican Positivism: A Reappraisal," *Hispanic American Historical Review* 48 (1968): 3.

[10] Hale, "Sustancia y método en el pensamiento de Leopoldo Zea," pp. 288– 289, 300–301.

political emancipation of Mexico, he affirmed the necessity of "mental emancipation" from Iberian colonialism. By accepting positivism, Mexico strove to break completely with its colonial heritage, which had imposed habits and customs that prevented it from becoming incorporated into the world of progress led by England, France, and the United States. The acceptance of positivism was an attempt, as Justo Sierra picturesquely describes it, to Saxonize Mexico, that is, to convert the Mexicans into "Yankees of the South." Something similar was attempted by the Argentinian Domingo Faustino Sarmiento when he proposed a United States of South America. Why did the generation of Justo Sierra wish to make the Mexicans Yankees of the south? One very important reason was to prevent Mexico from again becoming subordinate or dependent. Mexico should not fall under another insatiable colossus of the north.

In other words, to reject one type of colonialism while refusing to accept another is not, nor can it be, contradictory. On the contrary, this is a natural attitude of an association of people, like the Latin Americans, who become conscious of their existence under the emblem of subordination. Liberalism and positivism, as opposed to Iberian colonialism, were instruments to abolish the habits and hereditary customs that prevented Latin America's incorporation into the world in a nonsubordinate way. And opposed to the new type of subordination, which was peculiar to the founders of liberalism and positivism, it was also natural that the Latin American search his own history, denied only as it justified the old dependence, for instruments to prevent the justification of a new kind of colonialism. It was the purpose of the Mexican Revolution to confront this two-fold subordination, that is, the old and the new, or Porfiriato, which sought its justification in positivism. José María Luis Mora was the prototype of this meaning. He repudiated, on the one hand, expressions of the colonial period, such as "mania for holding public office," which created Mexican attitudes of servility, because they prevented Mexico's incorporation with the past. On the other hand, he looked into that same past, which was also Spain's past, for a liberal and reform doctrine of which Spain herself had given great examples. He searched in the past for Iberian values that did not contradict the efforts and desires of the Mexican to become as capable as the Saxon so that he could control his natural world and use its wealth as the basis of his own development. He wanted progress that would not be in the hands of foreigners.

The history of positivism in Mexico as well as in Latin America is the expression of an experience that terminates in a dead-end alley. Despite the spirit of this doctrine, and their supposed assimilation of it, Mexicans did not transform themselves into "Yankees of the south." Nor was South America converted into the United States of the south. If one form of subordination was destroyed, another was immediately created by the formation of Latin American societies hardly different from those created by three centuries of Iberian colonialism. A new colonialism was created by nations who were the leaders of progress. Mexican positivists became tools in this new order. Their social preeminence was patterned after Iberian colonial exploitation.

Then where is the contradiction? The attitude is the same for both Mexican and Latin American liberals who tried to abolish colonial habits and customs. They tried to solve the problem with doctrines that they thought might eliminate former feelings of subordination and dependency. They adopted liberal institutions and educated the people to habits of work that would allow Mexico and Latin America to exploit their own wealth. One and the same is the attitude of the Latin American nationalist, who looks to his own past for forms, doctrines, and experiences capable of forging a feeling of unity, and refuses to accept new kinds of subordination, such as becoming an instrument of foreign progress. It is purely and simply a matter of selecting past values that can help realize possible future values. Are we once again falling into a metahistorical interpretation? Of course, if at the same time we accept the impossibility of the objectivity that should be proper to intellectual history.

But how can the same United States historian be objective when he writes about Latin America? Charles A. Hale, like his colleagues who have already been mentioned, explains how this supposed intellectual and objective history of Latin America should be written. This history, he says, "will allow us to surmount the sterile debate over whether Latin American thought is original or imitative. Though it has obsessed Zea and others, it is a debate the outside intellectual historian need not enter into. We can reject the distinction between 'Western' and 'Hispanic' and begin with the simple assumption that Latin America, like Spain, has always been intellectually a part of the West. Our question is why certain currents of thought were significant and why others were not."[11]

Thus, the debate on the originality and imitation of Latin American thought is not, nor can it be, sterile, inasmuch as it concerns the Latin American historian's feelings toward subordination and dependency in his history. For my part, I have looked in the so-called imitation of foreign philosophies for expressions of a certain originality, that is, the form in which these philosophies are applied to problems that are peculiar to Latin America. Another of my concerns is to know Latin America's place in Western culture. Therefore, the central theme of my works is *América en la historia*.

One of the main concerns of Latin American intellectuals is how their societies can form part of Western culture without accepting dependency. That is why Latin America has incorporated certain aspects of Western thought into its own and not others, trying not simply to repeat them, but to make them a vital part of their own being. This incorporation is expressed as awareness of originality.

Is Latin America part of the West? Relatively, yes, but in what way? It is unwilling to continue to be subordinate to the West or to any other power. This coincides with the struggle of the non-Western peoples of Asia, Africa, and Oceania, who also struggle like Latin America to become an active part of Western culture, refusing to be its tool by accepting a dependent status. The assimilation of a philosophy peculiar to this culture has always occurred in relation to this concern, which has given rise to the debate mentioned by Hale, a debate which cannot be considered sterile.

Then, can the United States historian, who is an active part of a culture whose values have become universal, maintain objectivity as if he had nothing to do with the extension of those values and with the demand made by non-Western peoples for the recognition of those values in themselves? Is it not this awareness that caused, in the United States, the great moral crisis that now afflicts its people? Are not the people of Southeast Asia fighting for the recognition of those same values? Is this not the essence of the intellectual history of Latin America since its political independ-

[11] Ibid., p. 304.

ence from the Iberian world? The history of the United States, like that of the Western world, is an essential part of the history of Latin America. And it is with reference to this interdependence that problems of dependency and limitation continue to arise. In this sense, cannot United States historians retrace Latin American history as the history of the third-world countries is now being retraced and show the relationship between their history and Latin American history? Is there not a connection between the sense of dependency and underdevelopment and the sense of dominion, colonialism, and development? I understand that such an interpretation would necessarily have to transcend pure historical fact, no matter how objective the world might seem. The past and the present would have to be interpreted in relation to what is desired for the future. Metahistory? Philosophy of history? I do not believe that is important. What is important, however, is a better understanding of the man who makes history, independent of his situation, so that he can transform it.

In concluding this preface, I wish to express my appreciation to Dr. Stanley R. Ross for his interest in the publication of this book in English, as well as to the University of Texas Press, which has made it possible. I am also grateful to my translator, Dr. Josephine Schulte. This subject is one in which she herself is a specialist, as she demonstrated in my seminar entitled "The History of Ideas in Latin America," which was offered in the Department of Philosophy and Letters at the National and Autonomous University of Mexico in 1966, which she attended while she was in Mexico researching certain unstudied aspects of the topic with which this book deals.

LEOPOLDO ZEA
Mexico, 1973

INTRODUCTION

I. Philosophy and Its History

§ 1. *The Problem*

This study, positivism in Mexico, deals with a problem that concerns all philosophies. It is the problem of the relationship between philosophy and history, that is, the relationship between ideas and their reality. Like many other philosophical systems, positivism is a body of ideas that claim to possess universal validity. These philosophical systems assert their ability to solve man's problems, whatever his situation—spatial, temporal, geographical, historical.

Starting with this hypothesis, that is, the universal validity of a method or a philosophical doctrine, one must discuss positivism from a purely conceptual point of view. One must abstract it from every spatial and historical relationship; one must abstract it from reality in its highest sense. One must speak of positivism in Mexico just as one speaks of positivism in France, Germany, England, or any other country. Mexican positivism would be then an imitation of the original. It would not differ from European positivism.

If this be true, then we should analyze the ideas of the great philosophical systems and abstract these ideas from their men, creators, and "heroes," as Wilhelm Windelband did in his *Historia de la filosofía*.[1] We could speak then of only one valid posi-

---

[1] Wilhelm Windelband, *Historia de la filosofía*, vol. 1.

tivist philosophy, that "discovered" by such "men," or, rather, *instruments* of culture, of whom the most important were Auguste Comte, John Stuart Mill, and Herbert Spencer. What Mexican positivists have done would not be too important. It would have been necessary for them to make some "discovery" in the field of positivist ideas that would serve as a universal concept, valid everywhere for everyone.

In fact, that is what Mexican positivists attempted to do. They believed that they had a philosophical method to which everything could be submitted. They felt that they possessed the truth valid for all men, and they attacked all truths that did not conform to theirs. History, for them, was the path that led toward positive truth. Man had to be a positivist—*complete* or *incomplete*. Not man himself, but his ideas were what counted. Horacio Barreda, son of Gabino Barreda, felt that it was impossible to call the positivists Comtians, because Comte himself could not be a complete positivist, if in the exposition of his ideas he departed from the positivist method. Complete positivists, said Horacio Barreda, are those who apply the positivist method to all their research; incomplete positivists are those who use nonpositivist methods.[2]

According to this philosophical concept, by positivism in Mexico we mean Mexican contributions to positivism. To discuss these contributions would be a very interesting and important labor, of course. We would have to examine the Mexican positivists and point out those who merit a place in what Windelband called the "realm of the permanent and absolutely valid." We must demand a place for those ideas in the history of universal philosophy, but only the ideas, not their discoverers. Since they are universal ideas, they cannot be called Mexican. The culture that molded their discoverers is merely an instrument in the service of this permanent and absolutely valid realm. The biography of these men, that is, the history of the culture that molded them, is of little interest. It is merely an insignificant anecdote. Had they not discovered these ideas, others would have. Like stars, these ideas would have wandered through the heavens awaiting some observer to discover them. And in the discovery the fact that the observer was a being that lives and dies, rejoices and suffers, would not matter; what was

[2] Horacio Barreda, "La enseñanza preparatoria ante el tribunal formado por el Bonete Negro y el Bonete Rojo," *Revista Positiva* 9 (1909): 473.

important would be the instrument used by him. By instrument is meant the tools, such as the astronomer's telescope and the methodology that he uses in his calculations, as well as the methodology used by the philosopher in his research. Both are instruments of a mechanical nature.

Thus, the fact that a Mexican made a contribution to positivist philosophy is not important. Men of other countries could very well have made these contributions. But it would be a grave matter if we should discover that Mexican positivists did not contribute anything that deserved to belong to the realm of the absolutely valid. That would be the case if Mexican positivists merely repeated, that is, imitated, the positivist ideas expounded by other thinkers, or even worse, if these ideas were often a poor imitation; that is, if they were poorly interpreted by Mexican positivists. We would find that Mexicans, instead of contributing ideas to the realm of the absolutely valid, borrowed ideas from this realm and gave them a relative value, which was valid only for Mexicans in a specific period of Mexican history.

Is this not enough to make one lose interest in examining these ideas? I do not think so. I think that it is this limitation, that is, the limitations of Mexican positivists, that makes a study of Mexican positivism important. The perfect or good imitation does not concern us; one can go to the original for that. The contribution of Mexican positivists to universal positivism, if there is such a thing, must be found in the personal way that Mexicans interpreted positivism. Thus, the purpose of this study, as the title of the book indicates, is to deal with positivism in Mexico. We must see positivism in a very special relationship, in a partial relationship, in relationship with a circumstance called Mexico. There are problems that pertain only to Mexican circumstances in certain moments of its history. We must not consider positivism from a universal point of view, because then the work of the Mexican positivists cannot be understood.

§ 2. *Ideas about the History of Philosophy*

The problem posed by Mexican positivism is the same as the one posed by contemporary philosophy: the relationship between philosophy and its history. José Ortega y Gasset in some of his works, especially in his prologue to *Historia de la filosofía*, by

Émile Bréhier, has posed this problem.[3] The history of philosophy, according to this Spanish thinker, has been only the history of abstract ideas detached from their originators. But a history of philosophy in which philosophical ideas are removed from their thinkers and their circumstances cannot be history, because the abstract has no history. Only human life has a history. To detach ideas from their circumstances is to remove philosophy from its history. "A *history of philosophy*, as a chronological exposition of philosophical doctrines," said Ortega, "is neither history nor history of philosophy."[4]

Ortega said that there are no absolute ideas. They are merely relative. An idea is a form of reaction by a certain person to his circumstances. Thought exists only as a dialogue with circumstance. The philosopher addresses himself to his circumstances and asks them to tell him in human terms what they are. Philosophical formulas, namely, methods, are merely verbal expressions, that is, human terms, of man's relationship with his circumstances, his dialogue with his circumstances. Juan David García Bacca explained very well a dialogue between a Greek and his circumstances: ". . . the Greek, through his vital structure, 'said' in a loud voice what things silently 'were.' "[5] Those things could not say what they were; it was man who asked himself what they were and who then repeated the answer in a loud voice. "Nature," said Heraclitus, "loves to conceal itself."[6] But, he continued, "like the king whose oracle is in Delphi, it neither talks nor is silent; it makes signs."[7] It is up to man to interpret these signs, that is, translate them into human language. To say aloud what things are is what the Greeks called philosophy.

What can be said of Greek philosophy is true of all philosophy. Philosophy tries to say in a loud or human voice what it stumbles across in its circumstances; until he can say them, the things he has stumbled across are problematic, obscure, and, therefore, dangerous. The history of philosophy is a search for enlightenment,

---

[3] José Ortega y Gasset, "Ideas para una historia de la filosofía," prologue to *Historia de la filosofía*, by Émile Bréhier.

[4] Ibid.

[5] Juan David García Bacca, *Introducción al filosofar*.

[6] Heráclito, *Fragmentos*, frag. 10.

[7] Ibid., frag. 11.

that is, a clarification of the circumstances that man stumbles across, so that he may not stumble again.

Thus, if in a history of philosophy one of its protagonists disappears, that is, if a history of philosophy speaks only of ideas, words, and the symbols that man has used to interpret his circumstances, abstracting these symbols from their circumstances and from their creators, then, as Ortega correctly states, "it is neither history nor history of philosophy." To understand the meaning of philosophy it is necessary to consider it in relation to its circumstances, that is, its history. Philosophical methods in themselves are worthless. Only their content, which always depends on their historical circumstances, has any value.

Ortega said that "an idea is an act that man performs in view of predetermined circumstances and a definite end."[8] Here his ideas concerning the relationship between history and philosophy, between thought and action, coincide with those of Benedetto Croce. According to Croce, all concrete knowledge, as historical judgments, must be tied to life and action.[9] History cannot exist without philosophy and vice versa. Every philosophy is the work of a human being, and, as such, arises at a definite time and place, and this work is the cause of its historical condition. Every philosophy possesses truth proportionate to reality, provided this reality is historical rather than permanent. It is impossible to jump the fence of history. When history changes, philosophy, too, has to change, since it is a philosophy of reality, which is historical. Thus, it is impossible to separate history from philosophy, or philosophy from history. Every history has its philosophy, that is, some type of conceptual expression that is proper to it. And every philosophy has its history, that is, a content or reality that is proper to it.

§ 3. *Absolute and Circumstantial Truths*

The problem of the relationship between philosophy and history is intimately tied to the problem of truth. The idea of the relationship between philosophy and history depends on one's concept of truth. If one conceives of truth as absolute, then the relationship between philosophy and history will be purely accidental. The

---

[8] Ortega, "Ideas para una historia de la filosofía."
[9] Benedetto Croce, *La historia como hazaña de la libertad.*

truths of philosophy will not be dependent on any historical reality. On the other hand, if one conceives of truth as circumstantial, then the truths of philosophy are dependent on a specific time and place. Truth is historical.

A philosophy that holds that its truths are absolute will find solutions in these truths for every possible time and place. One can speak of Philosophy with a capital letter—a Philosophy opposed to the truths of other philosophies. The real problem is this: every philosophy claims to be the Philosophy; it claims to have the Truths. It views other philosophies in lower case; it views their truths as simply accidental truths—blindness, error, ignorance, and incapacity to attain absolute truth, the only Truth.

A philosophy that claims to possess absolute truths denies that any other philosophy exists. There can be only one Philosophy; the others are philosophies, that is, errors. The error lies in the circumstantial, in the historical, in that which changes. The absolute is beyond history and circumstances. According to this criterion, the history of philosophy is merely the history of major or minor philosophical errors, depending on how closely they approach the philosophy of the author of the history. Every history of philosophy will center around the philosophy professed by the historian of philosophy, and each is considered true according to how closely it resembles the philosophy considered to be the true one. If the true philosophy is viewed dynamically, as is the case with positivism and Hegelianism, the historical and circumstantial are merely inevitable steps toward absolute truth. Every philosophy is only a step toward the philosophical truth that is professed. The other philosophies, those that coexist with the true philosophy without recognizing it as such, are only anachronic philosophies, philosophies that refuse to recognize the fact that their time has passed. These philosophies, which refuse to recognize that their truths depend on the development of the true philosophy, are seen as obstacles to the true history that must be eliminated. We will see this in the philosophy professed by Mexican positivists in their struggle against the philosophical doctrines that contradict theirs.

The ambition of every philosophy to be the only possible philosophy, to be the only one that possesses the truth, has made the history of philosophy a history of philosophical contradictions. If the historian of philosophy professes a particular philosophy, he will try to use his doctrine to point out the errors of other philosophies. He will praise those doctrines that most resemble his, and he will disapprove of those doctrines that least resemble his.

Modern philosophy, conscious of its contradictory nature, has tried to solve the problem of truth, a problem that is proper to philosophy. The conclusion reached is that such contradictions do not exist. What seem to be contradictions are merely different solutions given in different situations. Philosophical truths are not absolute in the eternal sense. They are absolute in a circumstantial sense; that is, they are absolute for a given circumstance. The problems posed by man originate in his circumstances; thus, the solutions are also circumstantial. Philosophical truths seem to be contradictory because they want the solutions to the problems of determined historical circumstances to be good for any circumstances. The confusion of absolute truth with relative truth results in contradictions. To judge, rather, to characterize every truth in the history of philosophy as absolute, is to deny other philosophies and to consider all other philosophical truths as errors.

Unfortunately, this seems to be inevitable. By avoiding contradictions and by holding that philosophical truths are circumstantial, contemporary philosophy is affirming a series of truths that it considers absolute. By denying that absolute truths exist, it affirms a truth held to be absolute and, therefore, becomes involved in a polemic with another concept of philosophy. This polemic has, in fact, begun, opposing those philosophies that affirm their truths to be absolute and eternal to those that affirm no less absolutely that philosophical truths are circumstantial.

§ 4. *The Historical Method in Philosophy*

This thesis does not deal with the problem of truth, although it is important. We will consider this problem when we study the Mexican positivists and their polemics relating to ideas opposed to theirs. The present thesis concerns the method of philosophy that holds that truths are relative. It is the historical method of interpretation.

According to this method, one puts the philosophical truth or truths that he wishes to interpret into their historical circumstances. They are considered in their historical basis rather than as abstract, absolute philosophical ideas. Instead of dealing with abstractions, one connects these ideas with the culture in which they appear. Concepts and philosophical truths are considered as expressions of a certain view of the world in which all types of cultures participate. Bernhard Groethuysen said in respect to philosophy, "What the philosopher sees and interprets is, in fact, the world that he and his fellow men inhabit: their spiritual fatherland."[10] There exists a world that is prior to all philosophical interpretation. This world is presented under diverse forms, one of which is philosophy. Philosophy is a way of understanding the world, that is, of understanding the feelings of certain men. If one wishes to understand a philosophy, he must understand the background of which it is the conceptual expression. It is necessary to ask oneself how the authors of a certain philosophy lived, that is, their feelings, their desires, their dreams, and their difficulties.

Therefore, contrary to the usual interpretations of philosophy, it is not the ideas and methods, but the authors of these ideas and methods, that are important to this interpretation. Philosophy is a way to interpret man. Man is a being with many activities, including philosophy. Thus, to understand man, that is, to understand what kind of being he is, it is necessary to interpret his different activities and to understand why he does some things and not others, and among these things is philosophy.

Philosophical concepts in themselves are not important; what is important is the "why" of philosophical concepts. This "why" is found in history. It is necessary to look for the philosophical "why" of certain men in the history of their civilization and in their own biographies. Hence, it is necessary to apply the historical method to philosophy. Philosophy should be treated like other forms of cultural expression, such as art, religion, politics, and language. Philosophy is understood within its historical perspective.

The historical interpretation of philosophy has explained the contradictions encountered by the historians of philosophy. What appeared to be contradictions have been presented as diverse stages in a cultural development. The contradictions that one finds in the same thinker have been presented in the light of the historical method as the natural result of diverse vital stages of the philosopher. A philosopher can suffer and, in fact, does suffer the influ-

[10] Bernhard Groethuysen, *El origen de la burguesía.*

ence of diverse circumstances; these circumstances cause the changes in his thinking. If one takes a philosopher as a whole and his philosophy as a unity, he naturally finds many contradictions. Sometimes he says yes and sometimes he says no. But this will not happen if those yeses or noes are put into their proper historical perspective. Then they can be analyzed in view of the circumstances that provoked these affirmations and negations.

The operation that is carried out by the historical method regarding a thinker or a doctrine in both the general and the particular aspects of the history of philosophy is also carried out in the particular concepts of philosophy. Those concepts are apt to have the same form in the history of philosophy, but completely different contents. If one compares the methods used by two or more different civilizations, one discovers that the contents of those philosophical concepts change, although verbally they are the same. Many have carried out studies of this kind. Groethuysen compared the different meanings that the same concepts have acquired in the Christian and the bourgeois civilizations of the eighteenth century.[11] Paul Hazard pointed out the crisis suffered by the European conscience at the end of the seventeenth and the beginning of the eighteenth century.[12] The Spanish philosopher Xavier Zubiri also made an interesting study of the different meanings of philosophical concepts in his work "Sobre el problema de la filosofía"[13] by comparing the different meanings of the word *truth* in Greek and Christian philosophy. In various studies, Ortega compared the problems of what is called modern civilization with those of our own civilization.[14]

Max Scheler used this same type of interpretation. He called it *sociología del saber* [sociology of knowing].[15] Karl Mannheim also used it. He called it *sociología del conocimiento* [sociology of knowledge].[16] Through these methods of interpretation they pointed out the different meanings of an idea. These different meanings

[11] Ibid.

[12] Paul Hazard, *La crisis de la conciencia europea.*

[13] Xavier Zubiri, "Sobre el problema de la filosofía," *Revista de Occidente* 11, nos. 115 and 116 (1933).

[14] José Ortega y Gasset, *Tema de nuestro tiempo y la rebelión de las masas,* and others.

[15] Max Scheler, *Sociología del saber.*

[16] Karl Mannheim, *Ideología y utopía.*

were explained by historical facts, that is, by the different ways of life of those who held these concepts. The same concept could have different meanings in the same cultural atmosphere. The differences would depend on the different social situations of the groups that held the concepts, their education, their beliefs. When various men or social groups could not agree on the meaning of a word, this difference of opinion originated from their different situations. Each group, said Mannheim, will interpret a certain concept according to its own interests. Those who hold social power will understand the word or concept of liberty differently from those who do not.[17]

The application of this method to this study will better clarify positivism in Mexico. We will see how Mexican thinkers interpreted positivism. We will see why and how positivism was introduced into Mexico. Positivism may be a doctrine with universal appeal, but the form in which it was interpreted and applied by the Mexicans is Mexican. To understand the Mexican interpretation of positivism, it is necessary to examine Mexican history, that is, the history of those who used positivism to justify their interests, which were not the same as the interests of the founders of positivism.

[17] Ibid.; idem, *Libertad y planificación social.*

II. Positivism in Mexican Circumstances

§ 5. *The Mexican Interpretations of Positivism*

Positivism has been interpreted in Mexico as a universal philosophy detached from its circumstances. However, this is the least common interpretation. It was used by the positivists themselves as a defense against those who attacked positivism in Mexico. The Mexican positivists also held that their philosophy was universal and eternal. They believed that positivism and its method were the true philosophy and method, while other philosophies were the product of enslaved consciences, but this product will be one of the themes of this study. Generally, and this seems to be peculiar to Mexico, Mexican positivism tends to be interpreted in non-abstract, concrete terms. One could almost say that it is interpreted in terms of militant politics.

This can be explained by the fact that one is dealing with a doctrine that was purposely brought to Mexico to serve the interests of a particular political or social group. Positivism was not just studied in the schools. One cannot study positivism with the same serenity as one studies Platonism or Kantian philosophy. Positivism was not introduced into Mexico as a new doctrine that had to be studied in order to understand the culture. Positivism was a doctrine to be discussed in public rather than in academic circles. Since it was a philosophy that served a particular political and social group, it is impossible to separate positivism from that group. The Mexican positivists were very conscious of the instrumental nature of their philosophy. When they affirmed the universality of their philosophy they were conscientiously affirming the social preeminence of their class. Perhaps this is one of the few examples of philosophy being less disguised and more open about its purpose.

The fact that positivism in Mexico was openly associated with a social group that had political ambitions affected its political interpretations, which were determined by the social, political, and religious position of its interpreters. There was a "rightist" interpretation that was almost always hostile to Mexican positivism, and a "leftist" interpretation that agreed with positivism on many points. Because of this, there were interpretations, such as the one of Emeterio Valverde Téllez, that were extremely critical of Mexican positivism.[18] Leftists, especially Gabino Barreda, defended positivism. In a more recent study of positivism, José Fuentes Mares gave an excellent critical interpretation derived from his political ideas.[19] It can be seen that we are dealing with a philosophy that is still alive, one that still arouses passions.

§ 6. *The Positivist Generation*

Various political and religious groups in Mexico violently attacked positivism. They included the Jacobins and the Catholics. We will discuss in detail the polemic sustained by the Mexican positivists against these two groups. There was another group, educated in positivism itself, that opposed Mexican positivism. This group consisted of young men who felt confined within the limits of positivist philosophy. They gave up the positivist doctrine in which they had been educated and searched for new horizons. They were a self-taught generation who had to search outside of their own cultural circumstances for a new way to perceive life. This group was called the generation of the "Athenaeum of Youth."

[18] Emeterio Valverde Téllez, *Bibliografía filosófica mexicana*, vol. 2.

[19] José Fuentes Mares, Prologue to *Estudios de Gabino Barreda*. Alberto Bremauntz, in *La educación socialista en México*, presents the educational reform of Barreda as an antecedent of the socialist school.

"The positivism of Comte and Spencer," said José Vasconcelos, one of the leaders of this group, "could never contain our aspirations; today, since positivism disagrees with scientific data, it has no vitality or reason, and it seems that a weight has been lifted from our consciences and that life has been amplified."[20] This group viewed positivism as no longer useful. It felt that positivism had accomplished its mission. This group wanted to participate in the cultural life of the nation, but its members were hindered by their former positivist teachers. Antonio Caso, the most brilliant and most active polemicist of the group, considered positivism a philosophy for mediocre and irresponsible people. He referred to it as a doctrine that "saves thinking." Caso said that the Jacobins, those revolutionaries who preceded the positivists, were idealists who committed the sin of extreme idealism. They wanted to give Mexico a series of absolute rights, a perfect government, an ideal republic, and a utopia, but they forgot that "they legislated neither for eternity nor for the incorruptible archetypes of Plato, but for Mexicans."[21] This group of idealists was succeeded by a group of serene realists, whose policy was based on social induction. This was the positivist group.

Positivism formed prudent, poised, judicious, and humble men. "The positivists," Antonio Caso said, "formed a generation of men hungry for material well-being and jealous of their economic prosperity, men who collaborated for thirty years with the political labor of Porfirio Díaz."[22] Alfonso Reyes, remembering the epoch in which his generation confronted the positivists, said that "the positivist generation in the latter Díaz era detained history; our positivist leaders were afraid of evolution, of transformation. . . . Mexico was a mature country that was not capable of change."[23] According to the interpretation of the generation that followed the positivists, Mexico passed from an era of struggle, transformation, and ideals into an era of conformity, mediocrities, and reaction.

The importance of this interpretation is the relationship between positivism and social reality. It was not so much positivism but

---

[20] José Vasconcelos, "Don Gabino Barreda y las ideas contemporáneas," in *Conferencias del Ateneo de la Juventud.*

[21] Antonio Caso, *Filósofos y doctrinas morales.*

[22] Ibid.

[23] Alfonso Reyes, *Pasado inmediato.*

the expression of positivism that was attacked. Positivism was a doctrine that saved a group of mediocre men the trouble of thinking. It was a doctrine that protected their interests. Rather than a philosophical doctrine, it was a political doctrine that served a political faction. When one attacked positivism, it was not so much the doctrine that he attacked, but rather the political group behind it. Porfirismo and the political group called the Científicos used positivism as their ideological basis.

Positivism, according to the generation of the Athenaeum, was the ideological tool used by a particular social class to justify its social and political prerogatives. "The old type of scientific writers and educators," said Vasconcelos, "frequently expressed the opinion that our people, especially the Indian and the working class, constituted an irredeemable caste. . . . They affirmed that this oppressed population was totally incapable of overthrowing the military and political despotism of Porfirio Díaz. And, nevertheless . . . the revolution and life itself mocked the positivist doctrine that progress fatally produces a privileged class which, by being better endowed, represents the fittest and hence has the sacred right to exploit and maintain its dominance over the unfit."[24] The social group that professed this doctrine used Spencer and Darwin to justify its social position and the means it had used to gain it. On the basis of social Darwinism, said Vasconcelos, the people were denied the right to hold their own opinions and to defend their own interests. Anything that contradicted the laws of the survival of the fittest was condemned. According to Darwinism, the fittest always survived in the struggle for life.[25]

Such was the view of positivism of the generation closest to it. It was an interpretation of positivism by a group that was dissatisfied with its circumstances. Its nonconformity was complete. It accepted either all or nothing; hence it accepted nothing. This generation not only refused to conform with positivism in an abstract sense, but also refused to conform with everything that positivism represented. The nonconformity was cultural; hence, in its attacks, this group could not dissociate the doctrine from social

[24] José Vasconcelos, speech published in *La Revista del Maestro* (1922).
[25] See the work of Vicente Lombardo Toledano entitled "El sentido humanista de la Revolución Mexicana," *Revista de la Universidad de México* 1, no. 2 (December 1930).

reality. It saw the relationship between positivism and the Mexican cultural atmosphere. Samuel Ramos effectively pointed out that the generation of the Athenaeum attacked everything about positivism not attacked by the Jacobins and Catholics.[26] And it was this generation that made the revolution against the social and cultural aspects of Porfirismo.[27]

§ 7. *Mexican Positivists Defend Their Doctrine*

The interpretation of positivism by the generation of the Athenaeum was refuted by the Mexican positivists themselves. They exposed the errors that were committed by those who attacked positivism, confusing positivism with Porfirismo. In defense of their doctrine, they said that the political group known as the Científicos were not true positivists. In the last four volumes of the *Revista Positiva*, the editor, Agustín Aragón, published various notes in which he condemned the fallen Porfirist regime. And in one of his many works on Gabino Barreda, he pointed out how the positivism of Barreda differed from Porfirismo. Gabino Barreda, he said, wanted the "progressive and complete independence of education from public power whether it be civil or political."[28] And elsewhere he said that Gabino Barreda was exiled to Europe through the despotism of Porfirio Díaz.[29]

Another positivist, José Torres, openly stated that positivism was not responsible for the social misery brought about by Porfirismo. Referring to the attacks made by Antonio Caso, he said that Caso blamed positivism for the social misery and revolutionary crisis. "Malicious speculation transformed the philosophical problem into a political faction and aided the triumph of the new school by giving the disputed question a false and deceptive appearance."[30] Revolutions and social misery, said Torres, are something that we have lived with since our independence. "We have tolerated bad

[26] Samuel Ramos, *Historia del pensamiento filosófico en México.*

[27] This theme will be contained in a later study. Concerning Porfirismo, see José C. Valadés, *El porfirismo.*

[28] Agustín Aragón, "Gabino Barreda y sus discípulos," speech read before the Mexican Athenaeum on March 8, 1938.

[29] Note commemorating the death of Gabino Barreda, *Revista Positiva* 14 (1914).

[30] José Torres, "La crisis del positivismo," a study that was given to me by Professor Samuel Ramos.

governments and ignominious tyrannies, and before 1867 positivism was unknown in the Republic. The national disaster should be
attributed to the psychology of our race, to our social evolution,
to the class struggle and not to a philosophical doctrine that has
never penetrated the consciousness of the masses . . ."[31]

Professor Torres quoted Mr. Ramón Pardo, then director of the
Institute of Arts and Sciences in Oaxaca. Pardo gave a report in
March 1923 in which he defended positivism as foreign to the
social movement of 1910. He said: "A privileged class, profoundly
conservative and full of the prejudices born of privilege and Ro-
man intolerance, and an inferior class, frustrated in its destiny,
reproached and humiliated, can explain those terrible convulsions
that upset the equilibrium. In this background [of the revolution]
one does not find a philosophical doctrine, but a historical past
of insurmountable power."[32] Torres said that it is unfair to say
that the government of Porfirio Díaz was based on positivism. He
said that the philosophers who adopted the ideas of Comte merely
accepted his method and the concrete and practical results of his
ideas; but very few of them adhered to positivist politics. He continued, "Barreda was not a politician but an educator who dedicated himself to the positivist organization of national education."[33] The complete positivist program, including the political
order, could never be carried out, because the historical moment
in Mexico had not arrived. "But Gabino Barreda did not attempt
any experiment that would have required a complete social transformation."[34] To demonstrate his thesis, José Torres examined
the positivist politics of Auguste Comte. He pointed out that these
politics had nothing to do with the development of Porfirian politics. "In the positivist organization," according to Torres, "the
military, politicians, and every type of adventurer and parvenu
are irrevocably eliminated from the government."[35]

Furthermore, Torres pointed out that, even though positivist politics were only an ideal that should not be confused with the corrupt politics of Porfirismo, this did not mean that the laws dis-

[31] Ibid.
[32] Ibid.
[33] Ibid.
[34] Ibid.
[35] Ibid.

covered by positivist science were ineffective. He particularly referred to José Vasconcelos's attack on social Darwinism. The triumph of the revolution was merely the survival of the fittest. A government as corrupt and decrepit as Porfirismo in its latter years had to be replaced by a young and vigorous government. "The inevitable law of nature prevailed," said Torres, "and the triumph of the fittest and strongest signified the fall of a government weakened by the old age and torpidity of its directors. The triumph of the revolution once more confirmed the truth of the positivist doctrine of social Darwinism."[36] A plutocracy of former proprietors was replaced by a plutocracy of former proletarians. "A new military caste acquired the prerogatives of Porfirian militarism, and each of the two groups that sought public posts formed a privileged class that shared the absolute dominion of the country."[37] The revolution and life itself, concluded Torres, once again confirmed the positivist doctrine that progress inevitably produces a privileged class.

José Torres distinguished between the theoretical and the practical aspects of positivism. He tried to prove that the attacks against positivism by the generation of the Athenaeum were false, because they confused theory with practice. Torres, like other positivists, said that the positivist doctrine was independent of the reality to which it was applied. The new generation attacked a reality that should not be confused with the positivist idea. Therefore, the doctrine was not blamable for the impossibility of its realization. Torres said: "Positivism, like all the previous philosophies, has been limited to the purely theoretical and abstract. Positivism cannot, as Mr. Caso believed, reach the masses and orient their moral criteria; it is well known that in our country the people have always lived outside the intellectual movement and the renascent philosophical disciplines."[38] One should not confuse the practical and theoretical aspects of positivism. The defects attributed to positivism in its practical aspect, that is, how the positivists put the doctrine into practice, had no connection with the theoretical aspect of the doctrine. The ideals of a doctrine have nothing to do with reality, that is, with the impossibility of the material realiza-

36 Ibid.
37 Ibid.
38 Ibid.

tion of the doctrine. "In alluding to the common and incorrect meaning of practical positivism, Mr. Caso," said Torres, "deliberately confused it with its corresponding philosophical acceptance and applied a meaning to abstract criteria that belongs only to a totally practical condition that is foreign to all philosophy."[39] The knowledge of positivist ethics made it impossible "to derive from its principles the immoral attitude of those, like practical positivists, who do not subordinate their conduct to any moral ideal."[40]

§ 8. *The Interpretation Pursued in This Study*

As already mentioned, this study will stress the interpretations of positivism in this circumstance called Mexico. The political interpretation, which has been mentioned, unifies all the interpretations. All its interpreters tried to demonstrate either the political aspect of positivism or its opposite. Mexican positivists who pointed out that the positivist doctrine differed from positivism in practice tried to redeem the doctrine from its political failure. Mexican circumstances, they said, prevented the realization of the political ideal of positivism. Mexico's political problems were not caused by positivism, but by its historical reality.

In fact, neither positivism nor any other doctrine causes social well-being or social misery, but rather this social well-being or social misery expresses itself in a doctrine. We have seen, by analyzing the relationship between history and philosophy, how philosophies were merely expressions of specific social realities. The exponents of the generation of the Athenaeum understood this. In 1867 there was introduced into Mexico a doctrine that attempted to solve its social and political problems. A few years later this doctrine was unable to solve the problems that continued to come up. Its incapacity was demonstrated by new social disturbances.

It is true that the positivist ideal and its failure to be fulfilled were two different things, but it had been proven that the application of this ideal, which was also attempted in other countries, could be realized. And this realization supposedly could take place in spite of all the obstacles. Positivism as an unattainable ideal could very well stay in its ivory tower, but not positivism as a practical thing, that is, as something that Mexicans felt in multiple

[39] Ibid.
[40] Ibid.

and diverse forms. Positivism was untouchable as long as it was an ideal, but when it became practical it interfered with particular circumstances and one had to pass judgment. And this judgment could not be passed on theoretical positivism, but on positivism in practice. Therefore, I believe that the generation of the Athenaeum justly attacked the problem, although I do not defend the justness of their actual attacks. This study concerns the justice or injustice of those attacks rather than the attacks themselves.

Torres and those positivists who thought like him went off on a tangent. To say that one thing is theoretical positivism and another thing is practical positivism implies a lack of intellectual responsibility, which is characteristic of our century. It is like hiding the hand that throws the rock. The purpose of every theory is to put that theory into practice. The theory is responsible for the practical effects of the theory. In fact, the purpose of the theory of a particular individual or group is to change their circumstances. This person or group is responsible for the practical results of the theory. In other words, one deals with the human and personal responsibility of man's acts, a responsibility from which the human side of the doctrine cannot escape. Only when one supposes that a doctrine is foreign to man, that is, foreign to historical reality, can one believe that a doctrine is not responsible for its practical results. Only when one considers theory as the work of a superhuman being, of which man is only a receptor, can one say that theory is not responsible for its practical results. According to this thesis, nothing can be said about positivism that was not said by its creators in Mexico and elsewhere. One could criticize positivism only from its purely theoretical point of view. In fact, many criticisms have been made in this sense, but always abstracting from men and social circumstances. It is merely a matter of the conflict between two sets of ideas in an area where each claims to be right. This type of interpretation makes Mexico and all the Mexican positivists look like poor interpreters of a doctrine whose contributions are unworthy of universal attention.

But, on the other hand, if we believe that every doctrine is the expression of particular circumstances, that is, the expression of the desire of a certain group to get something, then we can speak of positivism in Mexico and say that this is what some Mexicans who called themselves positivists wanted. They claimed that the positivism that they professed was scientific. They devised an educational plan based on positivism. The different ministries at their disposal worked in accordance with the doctrine of positivism. One must consider positivism independently of the fact that these men may have been charlatans who used positivism to justify themselves or to gain trust. One must understand that positivism was introduced into Mexico not simply as a theory, but to resolve a series of social and political problems. Its theory may have been unknown to the Mexican masses, but not its practical results. They were felt in different ways both by those who understood the doctrine and by those who did not understand it.

This brief outline will explain what is Mexican in this interpretation of positivism. One must distinguish between its theoretical and its practical results. For example, Torres interpreted it as an ideal or an unrealizable utopia; politicians used it to justify their abuses; educators like Gabino Barreda tried to adapt it to Mexican circumstances to solve its problems; the political group called the Científicos based their political struggle on positivism. The Científicos merely had the name, and their ultimate goal was to live off the public treasury. These differences must be taken into consideration. They all represent different interpretations of positivism. This study, which deals with positivism in Mexico, will present the different interpretations. Whether it was correctly interpreted or not, positivism produced different results in Mexican cultural life. None of them represented the authentic interpretation of positivism; each expressed the reality of Mexican circumstances. Mexican positivism was the philosophical interpretation of reality, apart from positivism as an ideal doctrine. Torres was right in this respect. Positivism in theory has nothing to do with positivism in practice. We are interested in the practical aspect of positivism, because it is in this aspect that we can find what is truly Mexican. The universal, the theoretical aspect of positivism has been studied by philosophers. On the other hand, the particular or circumstantial—and, in this case, the special, what is Mexican in this adaptation of positivism to Mexico—has not been studied. This work proposes to initiate such a study.

III. The Positivism of Auguste Comte

§ 9. *Comtism as the Expression of a Social Class*

The positivist philosophy of Auguste Comte, introduced into Mexico by Gabino Barreda, was the chief ideological instrument that Mexican positivists used to refute other doctrines. The way they used this philosophy will be explained later. I wish to emphasize the importance of Comtian positivism in Mexico. Mexican positivists borrowed their principal concepts from Comte and adapted them to Mexican circumstances. In turn, Mexican positivists refuted other doctrines.

The fact that Mexicans adopted Comte's positivism implies a certain affinity between Comte's ideas and theirs. Why did Mexicans adopt the doctrine of a foreigner who was unfamiliar with Mexican reality? If positivism was a doctrine that was valid anywhere at any time, then there is no problem. It would be valid for Mexico just as it was valid for France or any other country. But if one believes, as I have sustained here, that a philosophy is the conceptual expression of particular historical circumstances, it is necessary to seek the reason why Comte's positivism was adapted to Mexican circumstances.

The reasons why positivism was adopted in Mexico will be explained at length in this study, but now we must propose some ideas with respect to this problem. The social group for which Comte was the spokesman and the social group that adopted his ideas had something in common. Mexicans accepted Comte's ideas for the same reason that Europeans accepted them. Mexican desires may have differed from those of the Europeans, but not their philosophical formula. Otherwise, Comte's ideas would not have been accepted by the Mexicans. The ideal of the European positivists was the same as that of the Mexican positivists.

Karl Mannheim held the thesis to which I adhere, that is, that every ideology is the expression of a certain social class. This social class justified its interests on the basis of a doctrine, which Mannheim called an Ideology.[41] Thus, the priestly caste, the military caste, and the disinherited caste all had an ideology. The bourgeoisie and the proletariat had an ideology. Each group used ideas to justify its position or the right to its position. Max Scheler pointed out how a class in power tended toward a static philosophy, while a class without power tended toward a dynamic philosophy. The former justified its continuance in power and the latter justified its right to this power.[42]

Auguste Comte defended a certain social class. This was the bourgeoisie, which had reached its peak of development during his time after the political triumph of the French Revolution. This class made the revolution and acquired political power. But it discovered that the revolution was still going on. Other revolutionary groups were still active. They wanted the power that the bourgeoisie had acquired. They used the same ideas that the bourgeoisie had used against the aristocracy and the clergy, namely, the ideas of Liberty, Equality, and Fraternity. The bourgeoisie wanted to nullify a philosophy that, although it had helped them acquire power, now made that power unstable. A counterrevolutionary philosophy that emphasized order was needed to invalidate a revolutionary philosophy. But this had to be accomplished without going back to the old system. The European bourgeoisie was between the Scylla and Charybdis of the revolution and the old system. A new system that would avoid these dangers was

[41] Mannheim, *Ideología y utopía.*

[42] In addition to the works already cited, see Scheler, *Sociología del saber,* pp. 178 ff., concerning the relationship between ideologies and the different social classes.

necessary. It could not be static like the old one; neither could it be dynamic in the manner of the revolutionary bourgeoisie. It had to be based on the philosophy of Auguste Comte.

§ 10. *Order and Liberty*

Auguste Comte faced the problem of reconciling two apparently contradictory concepts—order and liberty. In its revolutionary phase, the bourgeoisie opposed its concept of freedom to the old regime, which emphasized order. The philosophers of the bourgeoisie predicated absolute freedom in spite of the old regime. They predicated a dynamic ideology, that is, progress. They opposed the ideology of static institutions that predicated permanent order.

The dynamic nature of the philosophy of the bourgeoisie justified their pretensions to seize power. Only an ideology that could see continuous progress in history could justify the struggle of the bourgeoisie to seize political and social power. Once they acquired power, this ideology opposed their interests. Unlimited progress limited the power of the bourgeoisie. It was necessary to submit this unlimited progress to a special system, which differed from the static system of the old regime. The philosophy of the bourgeoisie had supported progress; it had opposed the static order of Catholic-feudal institutions. It was necessary to continue to support progress but in a limited rather than an absolute way.

Comte tried to prove that "there is no order without progress, nor is there progress without order."[43] He tried to prove that they can be reconciled. According to the interests of his class, he tried to demonstrate that order and a revolutionary government could be reconciled. Today, said Comte, in referring to the European conditions of his time, the ideas of order and progress are incompatible. Order is presented as reactionary and progress is presented as anarchy. A half century passed before revolutionary social ideas developed their true meaning. One cannot deny that reaction sustains order and anarchy sustains progress.[44] Comte faced two great opposing forces: the old despotic governments that tried to recover power and the revolutionary governments that had seized power. The bourgeoisie stood between these two forces. The bourgeoisie made the revolution to acquire power. But once it ac-

[43] Auguste Comte, *Cours de philosophie positive*, vol. 4.
[44] Ibid.

quired power, it was no longer revolutionary. Both forms of politics were destructive. They attacked the order that the triumphant bourgeoisie desired. "Some are destructive in themselves," said Comte, "because they are clearly reactionary, and others because they are exclusively critical."[45]

Ideas concerning order, said Comte, belong to the theological-military political system, that is, the Catholic-feudal system. These ideas represent the theological phases of the social sciences. The doctrines of progress are derived from a purely negative philosophy—Protestantism and the Enlightenment—which constitutes the metaphysical phase of politics.[46] The social groups that held the former ideas proposed the return of the old system; those that supported the latter proposed the destruction of the old system. A political plan was created that no longer fulfilled its social mission, that is, a plan that consequently gave rise to a new and opposing political force. The existing order tried to maintain an already inadequate system. It was opposed by a revolutionary policy that denied all order and tried to direct society toward progress without order.[47]

The theological state, said Comte, cannot sustain itself in the face of natural intellectual and social progress. Thus, force necessarily had to disappear in the face of natural progress. But in resisting progress there was violence. Progress violently destroyed an incompatible regime. However, said Comte, the theological phase was less inconsistent and more appreciable than the metaphysical phase. There was "a perfect coherence of ideas compared to the frequent contradictions of the revolutionary school."[48]

On the other hand, the metaphysical phase, differing from the theological, was essentially critical and revolutionary. Therefore, it acquired the name progressive. But it became negative because it was critical. It destroyed rather than built. The mission of this school, said Comte, was transitory. It prepared society for positivism, "the real end of the revolutionary phase."[49] The destructive or negative work of the metaphysical phase was purely pro-

[45] Ibid.
[46] Ibid.
[47] Ibid.
[48] Ibid.
[49] Ibid.

visional; it ceased when the new phase arrived. In its metaphysical phase, progress was reduced to "the gradual demolition of the old system."[50] The necessary destruction of the theological phase and a more systematic concentration on revolutionary action during the metaphysical phase converted it into a doctrine of methodical negation opposed to all government regulation.

This, said Comte, was a useful and necessary way to destroy a system that had fulfilled its social function and was now an obstacle to the new system. Once the negative mission of the metaphysical doctrine was fulfilled, it should in turn be replaced by the positivist doctrine. But it refused to abandon the social field, and became an obstacle to progress. Thus, the metaphysical doctrine, an instrument to deny the theological order, was spontaneously transformed into a systematic denier of order.[51] It no longer distinguished between the theological and the positive order; it denied all order. Once its transitory mission was fulfilled, it changed into an instrument of anarchy and social disorder. This doctrine was more dangerous than the theological-feudal doctrine, whose only ambition was order. The metaphysical phase was more dangerous because it tried to change a purely exceptional and transitory situation into a permanent state.[52]

§ 11. *The New Order According to the Philosophy of Comte*

Comte, like the social group that he represented, was inclined toward theology when he had to choose between theology and metaphysics. But it was not necessary to choose: one could establish a new order, an order proper to this social group. At bottom it was an attempt to reestablish the old Catholic-feudal order, but this time it was to serve another class, which was neither the clergy nor the aristocracy. In the final analysis, Comte and his class were revolutionaries. They wanted to return to the system that was destroyed by the revolution, but they also wanted to conserve the privileges won by the revolution. Comte said that the structure of society, which was the same as it was in the theological phase, was unalterable. Therefore, he opposed the revolution that tried to alter it. For Comte, religion, property, family, and language were

[50] Ibid.
[51] Ibid.
[52] Ibid.

the unalterable elements of every society. They must remain identical in their three progressive stages. They improved in each stage. For Comte, progress meant a superior order. The dynamic aspect of the Comtian doctrine was subordinated to its static aspect; progress was subordinated to order. Comte opposed the Catholic church because the interests of his class could not be reconciled with it.[53] And since it was opposed to the interests of his class, it could not continue to control society. The revolution was fought because the Catholic church and the state supported by the church could not reconcile their interests with those of the new class. The French Revolution demonstrated that the old system could not continue. A new order that would consider the interests of the bourgeoisie was needed. Comte tried to replace the old system with a new one that represented the principles of the bourgeoisie once it had passed the theological phase.

Once modern man, or the bourgeois, lost his faith in Christianity, he placed his faith in the principles of science.[54] The philosophy of the revolution was combative. Its only objective was to destroy a system that could not be reconciled with the interests of the bourgeoisie. But this philosophy lacked the constructive elements to sustain the new edifice. It lacked principles in which one could put his faith. It was anarchic. It was opposed to everything. It destroyed but it did not construct. Comte called this philosophy the negative spirit. According to Comte, it culminated in Rousseau.

To support his social edifice, Comte based his philosophy on science. He tried to fabricate a new social edifice on the basis of science. The positive spirit, according to Comte, culminated in Newton. Comte's positivist philosophy was merely the basis for his politics. Every methodology and analysis of the different positive sciences were merely the foundations for his political doctrine.

§ 12. *The Ideal of Comtian Philosophy*

Comte established the ideal of a new social order whereby the interests of his class would be justified on the basis of the positivist

[53] Groethuysen, *El origen de la burguesía.* You can see the difference between the ideologies of the bourgeoisie and the Catholic church.

[54] José Ortega y Gasset shows, among other books in *Esquema de las crisis*, how different generations lost faith in some principles and put their faith in others.

sciences. Comte tried to substitute a new church for the Catholic church, the religion of humanity for the Christian religion, positivist saints for Catholic saints. He opposed the idea of ordered freedom, that is, freedom that would serve only order, to the revolutionary idea of unlimited freedom. He opposed the idea of a social hierarchy to the idea of equality. No man was equal to another; all men had a certain social position. That social position was not determined as it was under the old system, by the grace of God or by blood. It was determined by work. Work was a category that the old system, based on divinity and aristocracy of blood, refused to recognize.

In the new system, everyone would recognize the justice of his social position, because his position depended on his capacities. But this did not imply social disharmony. It simply implied the recognition that all classes were necessary and that all of them had special obligations to fulfill. Comte believed that some men are born to command and some to obey.[55] Superiors and inferiors must be subordinated to society. Society must be above the interests of the individual. Philosophers and the well-educated members of society should lead society toward progress, within the strictest order.

Comte's positivist philosophy and his religion of humanity were a utopia, that is, a dream of imaginary order that would serve the interests of a bourgeoisie tired of the disorder that threatened their conquests. This social doctrine was introduced into Mexico. What is interesting to know is why such a doctrine was so readily accepted by a group of Mexicans. Why did Mexicans attempt to apply a European philosophy to Mexican circumstances? These and other questions will be answered in this study.

[55] Auguste Comte, *Système de politique positive.*

IV. Mexican Positivism

§ 13. *Mexican Positivism as the Expression of a Social Group*

Just as Comtism could be explained as the ideology of a particular social group, so Mexican positivism—called this because of its practical application in Mexico—was the expression of a particular social group. This social group, although not the same as the one in Europe, had certain similarities to it. This study will show how this social group applied Comtian positivism to Mexican circumstances.

Justo Sierra, influenced by European culture, labeled this social group the bourgeoisie. He gave this group credit for the triumph of the Constitutional Reform. The liberals triumphed in the long war between conservatives and liberals. They led the Reform movement. They belonged to a certain social class, which Sierra called the bourgeoisie. "Those who deserve credit for the triumphant reform," said Justo Sierra, "were the middle class from the states, who went to the *colegios*, who had a head full of dreams, a heart full of ambitions, and a stomach full of appetites: the bourgeoisie supplied the new cause with officials, generals, journalists, tribunes, ministers, martyrs, and conquerors."[56] After a half cen-

[56] Justo Sierra, *Evolución política del pueblo mexicano*, p. 346.

tury of warfare this new group won out. It reached its peak during the period of Porfirismo.

The Mexican bourgeoisie, like the European, went through a combative phase. In this phase it confronted the groups hostile to it by means of a combative philosophy, the philosophy of the French encyclopedists. This phase of the Mexican bourgeoisie was called Jacobinism. The Jacobins, of whom one of the most important was Melchor Ocampo, were the principal leaders of the Reform movement. These men fought the Mexican privileged class with a combative philosophy. But when they triumphed, this philosophy became dangerous. It encouraged other social groups to demand rights from the conservative class. Here appeared a second phase of the Mexican bourgeoisie, that of order. Once the bourgeoisie acquired power, it was necessary to hold it. It needed a philosophy of order, which was that of positivism.

The Reform party, once it had acquired power, had to establish an order, but a permanent order. The roots of this order had to be deeply embedded in the Mexican mind. It was necessary to have what Mannheim called an ideology,[57] a special way of thinking that would serve as a basis for every real act—political and social. "[Juárez] understood," said Sierra, "that the bourgeoisie, which forcefully supplied the political and social leadership of the country, really needed an education that would prepare for the future, and entrusted the reform of the upper schools to two eminent men of science (one of them can be considered the founder). The secondary, or preparatory, school was the immortal creation of Gabino Barreda."[58]

Gabino Barreda was entrusted with the task of preparing the then young Mexican bourgeoisie to lead the destinies of the Mexican nation. His ideological instrument was positivism. Positivism gave Barreda the concepts to justify a particular political and social reality, that reality which the Mexican bourgeoisie established. Through the words of Justo Sierra, one can see how Barreda educated a particular social class and how positivism was nothing but the instrument to attain this education. Positivism in Mexico cannot be explained as a mere cultural or erudite curiosity, but as part of a plan of high national politics. The circumstances that

[57] Mannheim, *Ideología y utopía.*
[58] Sierra, *Evolución política del pueblo mexicano*, p. 423.

existed in Mexico were, therefore, different from those that existed in Europe when Comte created his system. Nevertheless, Barreda and the other Mexican positivists were able to find adequate concepts to adapt to Mexican reality. The application of positivist concepts to Mexican reality enables us to talk about a Mexican positivism.

§ 14. *Elements of Disorder in Mexican Society*

Gabino Barreda, like Auguste Comte, had to face disorder and social anarchy. The Mexican bourgeoisie, which Barreda represented, had to confront a privileged social class during the period that I call combative. We will give this class the generic name "conservative." It consisted of two groups: the clergy and the military. Not in its combative, but in its constructive, phase did the Mexican bourgeoisie face in its turn those elements—nourished in its own bosom—that refused to submit to order. Those elements were the so-called Jacobins.

Thus, there was a combative phase in which the Mexican bourgeoisie opposed the conservatives, which consisted of the clergy and the military. During this phase, the Mexican bourgeoisie used the combative ideology of the great philosophers of the French Revolution. During this phase the Mexican bourgeoisie used Jacobins to destroy the ideological basis of the Mexican conservative class. The Mexican bourgeoisie tried to demonstrate that the ideological premises of the conservative classes were false and that they could not justify their privileges. The Mexican bourgeoisie tried to point out that everyone had the same privileges and that neither divinity nor heroism were sufficient to deprive other men of their rights. God's representatives on earth and the heroes or military caudillos were merely servants of society. Society represented everyone. Everyone had the same rights. Certain men in society were charged with certain tasks, such as saving souls or defending the nation. But these were merely tasks, not privileges. These groups were to render an account to society; they were not to use society as an instrument or a mine to exploit.

But once the Mexican bourgeoisie had acquired power, once it had succeeded in dominating and using the aforementioned conservative class, it discovered that it faced a new enemy. This new enemy was the old liberals: those who had fought for social equality; those who saw the new dominating group as just another group with power. The Mexican bourgeoisie in its constructive phase had to face the Jacobin ideology, which it previously used to destroy the conservative ideology. The Jacobins now accused the Mexican bourgeoisie of what the bourgeoisie had previously accused the conservatives. The Mexican bourgeoisie, like the European bourgeoisie, wanted order. To acquire this order it had to wrangle with an ideology that had served it to destroy the previous system. The Mexican bourgeoisie also had to replace this combative ideology with an ideology of order. Positivism, although foreign to Mexican circumstances, was adapted to them and used to impose a new order.

§ 15. *The Law of the Three Phases of Mexican Positivism*

Mexican positivists, like Comte in Europe, identified the interests of the class that they represented with the interests of the Mexican nation. In this identification they used the concepts of Comtian positivism. According to the thesis of Comte, progress, and in this case the progress of the history of Mexico, was represented by three phases: theological, metaphysical, and positive.

The theological phase in Mexico, according to the positivist interpretation of the history of Mexico, was represented by the era when the clergy and the military held social and political power. This phase was followed by a combative phase in which the theological order was destroyed and replaced by the positive order. This was the metaphysical era. In Mexico it was identified with the period when the liberals fought against the conservatives. The battle culminated in the triumph of the former over the latter, the triumph of the Reform party. This phase was followed by the one whose initiation was entrusted to Barreda. It was necessary that Mexicans know that a new era had been initiated—an era that was no longer based on antiquated theological ideas, that is, the divine will or the military will of the caudillo. Neither was it based on metaphysical disorder. That era ended when the old order was destroyed. This phase was a new era, an era in which the positivist order replaced the theological order and the metaphysical disorder.

Mexican positivists continued to combat the ideas of the old establishment, which was supported by the conservatives. Positivism was now being attacked by another group besides the conservatives. It was the liberals, that is, the Jacobins, who refused to accept the new establishment. To combat these groups, the Mexican positivists used the same ideas that Comte had used to combat the old medieval order and the disorder provoked by the French Revolution.

As can be seen, there was a great similarity between the circumstances of the Mexican and those of the European bourgeoisie. This explains why this Mexican social group adopted the ideas of the European bourgeoisie, identified its development with that of the European bourgeoisie and its progress with that of Comtian positivism. Both bourgeoisies desired order. This order was the ideal pursued by both social groups in distinct, although similar, circumstances.

The ideals of the Mexican positivists, however, like those of Comte, went beyond their circumstances. Although at first the positivists identified the positivist phase of Mexican progress with Porfirismo, they soon discovered that the Porfirists diverged and began to follow their own paths, which were not those marked out by positivism. Mexican positivism, like Jacobinism, was the expression of a particular social class in its combative phase. By expression is meant that it was an instrument in the service of the Mexican bourgeoisie in specific circumstances. In these circumstances positivism was useful, but as these circumstances changed, the ideas that they had previously supported came to be impediments. The result was the hostility encountered by positivism within Porfirismo itself. On the one hand, there was the Mexican bourgeoisie with its interests and, on the other hand, there were the Mexican positivists and their ideals. The Mexican bourgeoisie used only that part of positivism that served its class interests. When positivism was contrary to its interests, the bourgeoisie did not accept it. Hence, the reason for the double interpretation of Mexican positivism: a positivism used by a social group identified with Porfirismo, which was the view of the generation of Athenaeum, and an ideal positivism that could not be realized because of the Mexican circumstances.

We are dealing here with a human experience that was valid not only in Mexico, but also wherever there were people. Circumstances, that which changes, move faster than man's ideals. Man wanted ideals that would transcend their circumstances and change. He wanted to conquer time with ideas that would be valuable for all time. But all that he created were ideas that were valuable for a specific time and place. And when this time, this place, and these circumstances changed, the ideals in which man placed all his faith turned into useless artifacts. Then man had to change, transform himself, and adapt those ideas to new circumstances. This is what happened to positivism in Mexico. It was introduced into Mexico to serve the interests of a new social class. But these interests changed, so it was necessary to adapt positivist ideals to new interests. This adaptation was opposed by the positivists who saw in positivism an ideal to be realized. These positivists were those like Torres who refused to recognize Porfirismo as the fruit of the positivist doctrine. The Mexican positivists had a constructive ideal, an ideal that was destroyed by Mexican circumstances. Many times this ideal was opposed to the interests of Porfirismo. The Mexican positivists had an ideal of order that did not always conform to the interests of the classes that participated in the Porfirist regime.

To acquire order, the Mexican bourgeoisie had to combine its interests with those of other classes. The established order had to accommodate the interests of different classes. Positivism tried to reconcile these interests. But the time came when the idea of order opposed the interests of those with whom the Mexican bourgeoisie tried to arrive at an understanding. The time came when the order based on positivism was not the order that reality demanded. The ideas of positivist order were converted into ideas of Jacobin disorder. Thus, positivism could no longer be justified as a doctrine of social order. Positivist ideas could not be reconciled with the circumstances. They were transformed into a utopia.

§ 16. *The Plan of This Work*

This study will justify the aforementioned ideas about positivism in Mexico. I will try to demonstrate by historical facts and the texts of the Mexican positivists what I have already mentioned in the Introduction.

This study will be presented in two parts. This book, as its title indicates, will deal with the origin and development of positivism in Mexico. The second part will deal with the apogee and fall of positivism. The first section of this book deals with the work of Gabino Barreda, and will search for the origins of positivist ideas in the work of José María Luis Mora. Mora's ideas anticipated the ideas of the Mexican positivists. In addition, Mora was the theoretician of the Mexican bourgeoisie in its combative phase. His ideas justified the adoption of positivism by the bourgeoisie.

In Gabino Barreda and his followers we will see the development of Mexican positivism before it was transformed into an instrument of active politics. In the second section of this first part we will take up Mexican positivism in its ideal aspect. We will see what the Mexican positivists wanted to do and the obstacles that they immediately encountered in their attempts to realize a utopia. For this part, we will use the brilliant exposition of Horacio Barreda, the son of Gabino, concerning positivist ideals in Mexico.

The second book will deal with positivism from a political point of view. It will examine the connection of positivism with the Porfirist regime, its application to the interests of this regime, and its decline as a doctrine to serve the Mexican circumstances.[59]

[59] See my book entitled *Apogeo y decadencia del positivismo en México.*

SECTION ONE:
THE BIRTH

I. The Positivist Interpretation of Mexican History

§ 17. *The Road Toward Emancipation*

On September 16, 1867, Gabino Barreda[1] delivered a speech, "Civic Oration," in the city of Guanajuato. Later that year Benito Juárez asked him to collaborate with a commission to write a new plan of education. Besides Dr. Gabino Barreda, this commission included Pedro Contreras Elizalde, Ignacio Alvarado, Fran-

---

[1] Gabino Barreda was born in Puebla on February 19, 1818, and died March 10, 1881. He studied to be a lawyer and later a doctor of medicine. In 1847 he fought in the Mexican-American War. A few months later he went to France and did not return until 1851. In Paris he met Pedro Contreras Elizalde, who brought him into contact with Auguste Comte. On March 11, 1849, Comte began a lecture entitled "A Course in Philosophy on the General History of Humanity." In 1851 when he received his diploma from the School of Medicine, Barreda returned to Mexico. From 1863 until 1867, the period of the French Intervention, Barreda lived in Guanajuato, where he practiced medicine and meditated on the philosophy of Comte. On September 16, 1867, he delivered the above-mentioned speech in Guanajuato. The following works on Barreda should be consulted: *Essai sur l'histoire du positivisme au Mexique*, by Agustín Aragón; "Gabino Barreda y sus discípulos," a speech by Aragón already mentioned; the works of Barreda that were annually published in the *Revista Positiva* to commemorate the death of the great teacher; and the prologue to *Estudios de Gabino Barreda*, by José Fuentes Mares.

cisco Díaz Covarrubias, and Eulalio M. Ortega.[2] Agustín Aragón said that Gabino Barreda was the driving force of this group. On December 2, 1867, the triumphant Republic, under the presidency of Benito Juárez, promulgated the law that oriented and regulated public instruction in Mexico, from the elementary to the professional level, including what was called preparatory education. The basis for this law of education was positivism, a doctrine that most Mexicans had never heard of.

What had Gabino Barreda said in his Guanajuato speech, if it is true, as Agustín Aragón believed, that it was this speech that decided President Juárez to name him to the commission?[3] Agustín Aragón mentioned many coincidental circumstances: the speech that Barreda made in Guanajuato; the friendship of Barreda with Dr. Pedro Contreras Elizalde, who introduced him to Comte and then to his friend, President Juárez;[4] the relationship of Barreda to the Díaz Covarrubias family through his marriage to Adelia Díaz Covarrubias. The members of this family were among the staunchest supporters of the Reform movement and its leader, President Juárez. Whatever influence these friendships and recommendations had on the appointment of Barreda to the educational commission, these were not the only reasons why Juárez selected a reformer as versatile as Barreda to draw up a new law of education. Juárez, as an intelligent statesman, had seen in positivism the ideology capable of carrying out the revolutionary reform by

[2] Aragón, *L'histoire du positivisme au Mexique*; Fuentes Mares, Prologue to *Estudios de Gabino Barreda*.

[3] Aragón, *L'histoire du positivisme au Mexique*, p. 16.

[4] Pedro Contreras Elizalde was considered the first Mexican positivist. His father was an ardent royalist who fought against the patriots in Venezuela. When that country was liberated by Bolívar, his father emigrated to Mexico. Then he returned to Cádiz, the place of his birth. Pedro Contreras Elizalde was born near León, Spain, in 1823 or 1824. He studied medicine in Paris. Through two of his teachers, Doctors Robin and Segond, both disciples of Comte, he was brought into contact with Comte and joined the Positivist Society. In 1855, when he returned to Mexico, his adopted country—his mother was from Yucatán—he became acquainted with the future president, Benito Juárez, with whom he became politically associated. He accompanied Juárez throughout the French Intervention. The esteem that Juárez had for Contreras Elizalde was perhaps one of the reasons why Juárez appointed Barreda to the commission on educational reform. See ibid., pp. 18 ff.

putting an end to the long period of anarchy that had existed in Mexico since its emancipation from Spain.

One of the enemies of the liberal party in Mexico was the Catholic clergy. The clergy opposed the Mexican liberal movement on several occasions, provoking revolts and foreign intervention. Gabino Barreda, a liberal, who had fought for the Reform party, spoke of the anticlerical aspect of positivism in his Guanajuato speech. He said that the positivist philosophy of Comte had as its final end the replacement of the Catholic church by a Positivist church; order based on the divine will by order based on the positive sciences. According to the thesis of Comte, the Catholic church, which had now fulfilled its mission and had no reason to exist, was only one stage in the evolution of human progress. In this speech Barreda presented the progressive evolution of Mexico toward complete political and mental emancipation. According to Barreda, the emancipation of humanity, of which Mexico represented a link, was threefold: scientific, religious, and political.[5] Mexico represented the emancipation of humanity.

§ 18. *Mexico as a Link in the Mental Emancipation of Humanity*

According to Comtian positivism, Gabino Barreda considered the history of Mexico as a link in the history of humanity. In the evolution of the mental emancipation of humanity, Mexico represented a high degree of progress. The internal struggles of Mexico were fought not only for Mexico, but also for future humanity. The last decisive battles of the positive spirit of progress against the negative spirit of reaction would be fought and won on Mexican soil.

Barreda, differing from Comte, saw in Mexican liberalism an expression of the positive spirit. It must be remembered that, for Comte, European liberalism, which culminated in Rousseau, represented a negative spirit. In his speech at Guanajuato, Barreda said that the liberals of the Reform represented the positive spirit of human progress. Barreda, unlike Comte, did not attack Catholicism because he felt that it had fulfilled its mission and needed to be replaced by another religion. But rather he attacked Catholicism

[5] Gabino Barreda, "Oración cívica," in *Opúsculos, discusiones y discursos*, p. 84 (reprinted in *La Revista Positiva* and in *Ensayos*).

because he saw in its social and material expression, that is, in the clergy, an obstacle to mental emancipation. He represented the clergy as the negative spirit that tried to obstruct the progress of the positive spirit. Here the revolution was presented as order and progress as a violent reaction provoked by the opposition to it. The goal of the Mexican Revolution was the mental emancipation of Mexico as well as of all humanity. Without the evolution of the positive spirit, one could not explain the history of Mexico. Neither, said Barreda, could one explain the independence of Mexico by the conquest of an unarmed people of a "clergy, predominate in universal education and armed with the glories of Heaven and the sufferings of the world."[6] This event had its explanation in "mental emancipation, characterized by the gradual decadence of old doctrines, and their progressive replacement by new ones."[7]

The Mexican Revolution was the struggle of the positive spirit against the enemies of progress. One of the enemy forces, the clergy, tried to hinder this progress; the result of its opposition was the accumulation of the progressive forces, which violently overcame the obstacles that opposed them. What should have been a natural evolution was transformed into a revolution. The Mexican Revolution that began in 1810 and ended in 1867 had its origin in a struggle between two forces that started out as positive but ended up as negative, because they opposed progress.

The clergy, said Barreda, was losing its positive strength. Its doctrines were no longer at the height of progress, because they could no longer explain the many problems of mankind. It was in the field of physics that the clergy first lost its capacity to explain satisfactorily the phenomena of nature. However, it did not recognize that its role in history had ended, because it continuously tried to dominate society politically without understanding that the same light that penetrated physics could also penetrate politics. "Why," asked Barreda, "prevent the light that emanates from the inferior sciences from penetrating the superior sciences? Just as the most surprising astronomical phenomena are explained as a law of nature, that is, with the enunciation of a general fact, which is no more than an inseparable property of matter, could one not

[6] Ibid., p. 83.
[7] Ibid., p. 84.

introduce this same spirit of positive explanations into the other sciences and consequently into politics?"[8]

The clergy, Barreda continued, did not understand this law of mental emancipation; if they had understood it, the clergy would not have supported it; or at least they would have begun to extinguish the light of mental emancipation in the field of physics so that it would not spread to other fields. Who denies the gods their lightning bolts also denies them dominion over man. Mexico was the country where the positive forces battled the negative forces for dominion over mankind, that is, for political dominion.

America, including Mexico, appeared in history at the very moment when the gods lost their lightning bolts; at the very moment when the Catholic church lost its capacity to explain satisfactorily the phenomena of nature. At this time physics was associated with theological explanations. America was discovered in the epoch in which mental emancipation was initiated in the field of physics. "In this period," said Barreda, "the principal ideas of the modern era were in full effervescence in the Old World and the conquistadors, already impregnated with them, unwittingly inoculated them into the new people who were the result of the mixture of the two races."[9] The clergy was unwittingly inoculated by the same ideas of progress that soon were to deny religion. Progress won them over "in spite of the fact that their own best interests advised them to reject it."[10] The clergy, against its will, cooperated in its own destruction. Positive science, which was passing from the most simple to the most complicated, was increasing. "Science, progressing and growing like a weak child, strengthened its forces in the open roads where there were no obstacles. As its strength increased, science entered into combat with prejudice and superstition and, in the end, science was triumphant after a bitter but decisive struggle."[11] The history of Mexico was the history of this decisive struggle, and the triumph of the revolution was the triumph of the mental emancipation of humanity. The triumph of the Reform party was the triumph of the positive spirit. It was in

[8] Ibid., p. 84.
[9] Ibid., p. 85.
[10] Ibid., p. 86.
[11] Ibid., p. 86.

Mexico that the lights of positivist science invaded the realm of politics and seized from theology the dominion over mankind.

§ 19. *The Struggle between the Negative and Positive Forces in Mexico*

The seeds of positivism came to Mexico with the Catholic religion. The clergy bore the elements that were to destroy it. "The chief disintegrating element," said Barreda, "came with its founders, and it could do no less than develop here as it developed everywhere, and finally it established an edifice whose foundations were already shaky."[12] Nevertheless, these forces refused to accept their natural displacement. They opposed progress. They tried to crush it by persecution, isolation, and other coercive measures; but it was already too late, and such measures "did no more than aggravate the explosion of one [the positive forces], and increase the destruction of the other [the negative forces] when the dikes yielded."[13] This combustion became fully effervescent after the independence of the United States and the French Revolution. "Only a spark was now necessary," said Barreda, "to start the fire."[14] This spark was lit on September 15, 1810; nothing, no one, could contain the fire. A group of men who had no arms, no power, and almost no forces, opposed the negative, and still vigorous, forces of a power that refused to recognize that its mission as a positive force in history had ended.

The positive forces were not immediately triumphant. They encountered anarchy, the disorder that remained in society as a result of violence. The enemy of the new order tried to oppose mental emancipation. It wanted to establish a regime similar to the one that was just overthrown. It wanted to establish an empire with a negative policy.[15] It conducted a long civil war. The positive spirit could not fall back; it continued its march in spite of the obstacles that it encountered. The men who headed the Constitutional Reform in Mexico represented the positive spirit. Through "a fatality, as lamentable as it was inevitable," said Barreda, "the party that was summoned to predominate by the laws of civiliza-

---

12 Ibid., p. 88.
13 Ibid., p. 90.
14 Ibid., p. 90.
15 He is referring to the empire of Agustín Iturbide.

tion was then the weakest; but with an ardent faith in the future, a faith inspired by a belief in real progress in human evolution, it felt strong enough to undertake and sustain a struggle that would be a fight to the death."[16]

Two types of order faced each other on the battlefields of Mexico: the static order, or negative forces; and the dynamic order, or the positive forces. The static order was opposed to all progress; that is, to mental emancipation in all its forms: scientific, religious, and political. The dynamic order defended the progress of mental emancipation. These two types of order were represented by "the clergy and the army as the remnants of the old regime; and by the emancipated and impatient intelligentsia who believed in future progress."[17] In this struggle those who were represented by the positive spirit, or the spirit of progress, triumphed. One of the first measures that the positive forces undertook was the separation of church and state and the disentailment of church property. In this way they wished to invalidate a power that was opposed to progress.

§ 20. *Mexico, Last Bastion of the Positive Spirit or of Progress*

The forces opposed to progress did not accept their defeat in Mexico. They had succeeded in stopping the march of progress in the rest of the world. Europe had stopped the progressive march and had fallen into an era of retrogression. These forces hastened to intervene in Mexico. The French Intervention in Mexico represented the negative spirit, which succeeded in hindering progress. Mexico represented, in the interpretation of Barreda, the last bastion of progress; it would be in Mexico that the future of humanity would be decided. The struggle against the troops of Napoleon III was not simply a struggle for the independence of Mexico, but the struggle for the independence of all humanity. May 5 was a victory that Mexico won in the name of the progress of humanity. "The soldiers of the Republic in Puebla," said Barreda, "saved, like the Greeks in Salamis, the future of the world by saving the republican principle, which is the modern standard of humanity."[18] Mexico, in this struggle, represented the positive

---

[16] G. Barreda, "Oración cívica," p. 92.
[17] Ibid., p. 92.
[18] Ibid., p. 96.

spirit of all humanity against the armies of Napoleon III, which represented the negative spirit. Europe entirely succumbed to those forces; only Mexico succeeded in opposing them; only Mexico won a decisive victory, the victory of the progressive spirit. "In this conflict between European reaction and American civilization," said Barreda, "in this battle of the monarchical principle against the republican, in this ultimate effort of fanaticism against emancipation, the republicans of Mexico stand alone against the entire world."[19]

Mexico, in its struggle, saved the whole world, including America. It rendered a great service to humanity and to American democracy. By stopping the invasion, said Barreda, Mexico saved American democracy from falling into the hands of the negative spirit, "which tried to enter the United States through Mexico."[20] The triumph of the republican party headed by Juárez was the triumph of progress against reaction.

19 Ibid., p. 96.
20 Ibid., p. 97.

II. Historical Circumstances in Mexico, 1867

§ 21. *The Triumph of the Mexican Liberal Party*

On June 19, 1867, the misguided Mexican emperor, Maximilian of Austria, was executed in Querétaro. Thus came to an end one of the bloodiest episodes in Mexican history. A war to gain political independence from Spain that was initiated in 1810 was converted into a civil war once political independence had been won. In this new struggle there were two opposing forces: the liberals and the conservatives. The liberals fought to make political independence a reality. They fought for independence from the conservatives—the clergy and the military—who were a legacy of colonial times. Although Mexico had won its political independence from Spain, it had not won its independence from the clergy, which continued to control the Mexican conscience. Neither had it won its independence from the military, which remained a powerful force in Mexico. It was these two forces that the liberal party opposed. In 1867 the liberal party triumphed.

When Maximilian of Austria was put to death, not only were the Mexican conservatives defeated, but also the dreams of conquest by a European despot were ended. The last conservative hopes vanished with the death of the emperor on the Cerro de las Campanas. The conservative leaders were either executed or forced into exile. Only the victors, the Mexican liberals, remained. Their situation, however, was not enviable. Although the Reform party was lord and master of the Mexican nation, Mexico was no more than a country in ruins. Ruin and desolation were found everywhere. Disorder and anarchy reigned in every corner of the Republic. The victors had to establish a new system out of more than half a century of anarchy. They had to lift the nation from the smoking ashes of the revolution.

The victorious, but ruined, victors were faced with the task of reconstruction. They encountered the same obstacles. Although they were victorious on the battlefield, they could not conquer the spiritual field, that is, the conscience of the Mexicans. In this field the clergy and the military were still the enemies. The clergy, although it no longer had property and political power, still had spiritual power, the power over conscience. The other enemy, the new military caudillos, who had won on the battlefields, refused to admit, like the caudillos whom they had defeated, that their mission had ended. The clergy and the military, from the altar and the battlefield, respectively, continuously provoked revolts and dissension against the new order.

The spiritual force of the clergy was great, in spite of the fact that it had lost its material strength. Catholicism had been, and continued to be, one of the spiritual ingredients of the Mexican people. Mexican independence had been political, not spiritual. Mexico continued to be as Catholic as it had been in colonial days. Those who initiated Mexican independence did not plan a religious independence. The clergy continued to enjoy its privileges and the liberals attacked these privileges. Educated in the doctrines of the French Revolution, they viewed the Catholic religion as an instrument in the service of a group of individuals; namely, the clergy. They saw that the clergy used its spiritual force to defend nonspiritual interests, that is, to defend the privileges that it had won in colonial times.

The liberals had to solve this problem once and for all if they were to establish order. Melchor Ocampo proposed a drastic measure. If the Catholic religion was an instrument in the service of a single faction, the only remedy would be to change the religion of the Mexicans. Ocampo wanted a religion that would not exploit the people. He felt that the most appropriate religion for

Mexico would be Protestantism. Justo Sierra quoted Juárez, who said, "It is hoped that Protestantism will become Mexicanized, conquering the Indians; they need a religion that will obligate them to read rather than to spend their savings on candles for saints."[21] In 1872 President Lerdo de Tejada tried to put these ideas into practice when he invited the first Protestant ministers into the country. But they failed because there was no understanding between them and the Mexican people. The Protestant ministers dealt with concepts completely foreign to the Mexican way of life. The North American model, which the liberals wanted to imitate in Mexico, failed completely in the spiritual field.[22]

On the other hand, there was the military, those who knew themselves to be conquerors. The triumph of the Republic had been won by force of arms. Military chiefs considered themselves due all kinds of privileges. But the military in Mexico was not conscious of its social responsibility. It did not consider itself as an instrument in the service of society; it would fight to the death in the name of its own ideals; but it did not feel that it owed a special service to a group called society. An army career originated on the battlefield, not in the academy. On the battlefield the ablest, fittest, and strongest triumphed. These eliminated one another and only the strongest, who were transformed into caudillos, survived. Mexico had spilled blood for many years in these wars.[23]

The liberal party was founded in the midst of this anarchy. It was triumphant through the military, but it was unable to make the military understand that it [the military] was only an instrument in the service of the Reform. The leaders of the liberal party knew that they were victorious for a great cause: the cause of liberty. But the instrument of this victory, the military, did not see it this way. The military fought for privileges. Instead of organizing the nation for whose independence it had fought, the military converted the nation into booty to be divided among its members. "All of them," said Justo Sierra, "longed for privileged

---

[21] Sierra, *Evolución política del pueblo mexicano*, p. 423.

[22] See José C. Valadés, *El porfirismo*, for information concerning the intention of Melchor Ocampo to introduce Protestantism into Mexico and of Lerdo de Tejada to put this idea into practice.

[23] See the chapter entitled "La fuerza de las armas" in ibid.; also see Sierra, *Evolución política del pueblo mexicano*.

positions, such as military autonomy with honors, with considerations, and with power, not only for themselves, but also for the war groups that they had formed to carry out their will."[24] It was necessary to end this state of anarchy, to organize and discipline the army, and to put it in the service of the nation. "The Republic," said Sierra, applying the Spencerian interpretation of history, "must pass from the military era to the industrial era, and it must do so rapidly, because the colossus growing at our side is drawing nearer and nearer to us. It will absorb and ruin us, if we are weak, through its great achievements in manufacturing and agriculture in its border states and the expansion of its railroads."[25]

§ 22. *The Basis for the Establishment of Order*

The liberal party, by virtue of having taken over the government, had to establish the basis for a durable social order. This responsibility could not be turned over to the groups that had been displaced: the clergy and the military. Nor could it be turned over to the new military, which continued to be as ambitious as that which was conquered. Hence, a social group that would guarantee order was selected. This class was the bourgeoisie. The Mexican bourgeoisie was the only class capable of guaranteeing social order. Sierra said that the leaders of the triumphant social movement came from this class. The Mexican bourgeoisie provided the banner and principles of the revolutionary movement against the conservative class. We will later take up the ideology of this class in its combative phase.

Since the leaders for the new social order were taken from this class, it was necessary to give them a special education. To establish the basis for this education, Dr. Gabino Barreda was called upon to collaborate with other members of a commission to write a new law of education. The new plan of education would be the instrument through which a new class of leaders, capable of establishing order, would be formed. This plan of education would also deprive the clergy of molding the Mexican mind. Up to this time, education had been in the hands of the conservative classes. Its

---

[24] Sierra, *Evolución política del pueblo mexicano*, p. 418.
[25] Ibid., p. 416.

structure justified and favored those classes. But since power had since passed into the hands of the Mexican liberal bourgeoisie, they would try to organize education in such a way as to benefit themselves.

One of the postulates of the Mexican liberal bourgeoisie was freedom of conscience. Without freedom of conscience the political independence of Mexico was no more than a myth. Hence, the leaders of the liberal party wanted to decatholicize Mexico. They believed that only by decatholicizing Mexico could the Mexicans be free from the influence of the clergy. To make this idea a reality, a non-Catholic education was necessary, an education through which the Mexicans could see the necessity of emancipating themselves from a religion that served the interests of a particular group instead of the interests of society in general.

Gabino Barreda in his speech entitled "Civic Oration" placed emphasis on the emancipation of conscience. He pointed out that according to the positivist interpretation of history, the Catholic religion and its clergy, which represented a negative force, refused to abandon a position whose mission had already been fulfilled. The order predicated by the clergy was not the order that corresponded to the era of the progress of humanity. Order was necessary, but this order had to be what the positivists called positive. The triumphant revolution represented this order. The republican, or liberal, party was charged with establishing the positive order, that is, of initiating the so-called positive phase. Finally, the liberal party had to establish the basis for the new and definitive stage to which humanity must arrive in its progression.

Positivism justified the Mexican Revolution and it furnished the basis for establishing an order according to the ideals of the revolution. It postulated liberty of conscience, which was summed up by Barreda as follows: "scientific emancipation, religious emancipation, political emancipation." These were possible only through mental emancipation, that is, through the decay of old doctrines and their replacement by others. The old doctrines were in this case those of the Catholic clergy; the new doctrines that would replace them would be the positivist doctrines. These would be the doctrines in which Mexicans would be educated. These positivist doctrines would eliminate the disorder that was provoked by a class that did not want to recognize the fact that its mission had ended.

The men educated in this doctrine would assume power and implant the new order in all fields.

§ 23. *Application of the Positivist Doctrine*
to the Historical Circumstances of 1867

Gabino Barreda intelligently adapted the positivist doctrine to the history of Mexico. He adapted it not only to the general circumstances, but also to the particular circumstances that existed in 1867. "Civic Oration" was delivered by Barreda in determined historical circumstances. We have already mentioned these circumstances: the triumph of the Mexican liberal revolution, which brought with it an urgent need for order. Barreda justified the triumphant revolution in his speech, but, in order to justify it, he had to alter in some ways the meaning Comte had given to his doctrine.

Remember that, in Comte's interpretation of history, the ideas of the French Revolution represented a negative spirit. This spirit culminated in Rousseau. These ideas became negative when they did not want to recognize their transitory character in the progress of humanity. The role of the ideas of the revolution was only transitory. The objective of such ideas was to destroy an order, the theological order, which could no longer keep up with progress.

In Gabino Barreda's speech, the revolutionary ideas, those that the Jacobin liberals had taken from the French Revolution, were presented as the positive spirit. On the other hand, the ideas of the Catholic clergy were represented as the negative spirit. They were the ideas that, according to Comte, corresponded to the theological period of history. According to the interpretation of Barreda, they were negative. They were the doctrines of those of the theological phase who refused to recognize that their positive mission had ended. These ideas were opposed to the progress of humanity. Progress was represented by the revolution, which Comte associated with the metaphysical, or negative, period.

In his speech, Barreda showed how the Catholic clergy hindered the march of progress and how the revolutionaries destroyed the obstacles to progress. The triumphant revolution represented the triumph of the positive spirit and the beginning of the period that corresponded to the positive spirit in history. Comparing this speech to Comte's doctrine of three stages, we find that in Mexico,

differing from Europe, the metaphysical spirit, which corresponded to the revolutionary stage, was a spirit conscious of its mission.
It destroyed the forces opposed to progress and, having destroyed
them, attempted to establish a new order. The revolution was
transformed into order. It was not, as Comte said, opposed to order.
It was opposed to the eternal enemies of progress in Mexico: the
clergy and the military. In this speech, Barreda did not attack the
liberals. Comte considered the liberals a negative spirit, but the
negative spirit of Mexico was represented by the clergy and the
military. The victorious liberals represented positivism.

In "Civic Oration" Barreda applied his interpretation of positivism to Mexican circumstances. He expressed the ideals of the triumphant liberal revolution and its zeal in destroying the forces
of conservative reaction. These same liberals were soon engaged in
a polemic with Barreda and his followers. But at the time of the
victory of the revolution there did not exist any discrepancy.
Barreda was called by those liberals to reorganize education.[26]
Later, when many of those liberals opposed Barreda, Barreda and
his disciples considered the liberals as representing the negative
spirit, as did Comte.

The triumphant liberals realized that it was necessary to establish a new order, a liberal order. It was necessary to establish a
republican order that respected the postulates of Mexican liberalism. Gabino Barreda expressed this liberal idea in the speech
he delivered in Guanajuato when he said "that in the future a
complete freedom of conscience, an absolute freedom of expression
and discussion that will admit all ideas and all inspirations, will
shed its light everywhere and will make every disturbance that is
not spiritual and every revolution that is not intellectual unnecessary and impossible. The material order preserved at all costs by
the government and respected by the governed should be a sure
guarantee and a safe way by which to continue ever on the happy
road to progress and civilization."[27] The order that was wanted was
simply material, an order that did not invade the spiritual, or in-

[26] Valadés, in *El porfirismo*, said: "Barreda had given the formula for Mexican liberals to construct their philosophical and social basis. Barreda said: 'scientific emancipation, religious emancipation, political emancipation' to flatter
Jacobin vices and to make their past look agreeable."

[27] Barreda, "Oración cívica," p. 105.

'tellectual, field. It was an order that would respect the Mexican liberals' principle of the freedom of conscience, and not attack it as the conservatives did.

The liberals, that is, the Jacobins and the backers of the Reform movement, once they were triumphant, wanted to establish a new order to transform Mexico into a strong and respected nation. An ideology to establish such an order was needed. The positivism of Barreda offered this ideology. Such a revolutionary ideology as that of the Mexican liberals tried to transform itself into an ideology of order. To accomplish this, the conservative ideology of Comte was used. Discrepancies between liberal and positive ideas soon became apparent. But, for the time being, positivism was presented as an adequate doctrine to establish the liberal order. Gabino Barreda altered the Comtian motto: love, order, and progress, or simply order and progress, to "liberty, order and progress, liberty as a means, order as a base, and progress as an end."[28] By changing love to liberty, Barreda expressed the liberal ideal. The ideology of the Mexican liberals was summarized in the motto adopted by Barreda. Both liberals and positivists soon became engaged in polemics. In order to be consistent in their ideology, the positivists had to give the concept of liberty a meaning that it did not have for the liberals. The Mexican Jacobins tenaciously defended their liberal concept against the positivist interpretation.[29]

§ 24. *The Adaptation of the Positivist Doctrine to the Religious Policy of the Juárez Government*

To combat the clergy, the liberals tried to decatholicize Mexico; however, they were aware of the fact that such a task was almost impossible. They knew that the great masses of the Mexican people were Catholic. The Jacobins themselves, although violently anticlerical, did not completely give up their Catholicism. A statesman of the status of Benito Juárez knew that to decatholicize the country by force would incite revolts and merely continue the anarchy in Mexico. The new government needed to establish order,

[28] Ibid., p. 105.

[29] Later, note the polemic of the positivists against the liberals and Catholics concerning the concept of "liberty." Horacio Barreda gave an excellent summary of this polemic in "La enseñanza preparatoria ante el tribunal formado por el Bonete Negro y el Bonete Rojo," *Revista Positiva* 9 (1909).

and this order would not be attained by continuing a war of religion. Justo Sierra said that "no one wanted the continuation of the war except those who lived on disorder, those despicable in any normal situation. Everything was sacrificed to Peace: the Constitution, political ambitions. Everything. Peace above all things."[30] Any ideal that led to extremes had to be sacrificed for peace. The liberals considered Catholicism dangerous because the clergy used it as a political weapon. The only thing that the liberals wanted to do was to invalidate it as a political weapon, and to do this they came up with the idea of a clergy resembling the Protestant.[31] At least the political arm of Catholicism had to be invalidated, since it was impossible to decatholicize Mexico. Hence, the Reform Laws separated church and state, that is, spiritual power from material power.

The Mexican liberals did not deny the clergy their spiritual power. The only thing that they wanted was material or political power, for only in possession of this power could they guarantee freedom of conscience. The Catholic clergy, with material power in their hands, did not guarantee this freedom. Gabino Barreda expressed this idea in "Civic Oration" when he said that the spiritual arm of the clergy had not been touched by the Reform Laws; on the contrary, it had been strengthened:

Because by entirely separating the church from the state, thereby liberating spiritual power from the degrading pressure of temporal power, Mexico took a step more advanced than that of any other nation along the road of true civilization and moral progress. It exalted the present clergy as much as possible, and only after its betrayal and when Maximilian wanted to disgrace it as the French clergy had been disgraced, did the clergy understand the moral importance of the separation of church and state established by the Reform Laws. And it protested, although too late, against the tutelage to which it had been subjected. It longed for the same thing that it had attacked.[32]

---

[30] *Evolución política del pueblo mexicano*, p. 442.

[31] Valadés said that they wanted to put the church under the tutelage of the state "according to the political interpretation of Luther, who gave the princes a divine mandate. He considered them the only ones called upon to rule over priests and bishops."

[32] Barreda, "Oración cívica," p. 94.

The liberal government of Juárez wanted to respect Catholicism. Knowing that it was not easy to repudiate Catholicism, the Juárez government was content to keep religion out of politics. Mexican positivism tried to adapt itself to this idea of government. Positivism was adopted by the Mexican liberals as a political weapon. The liberals wished, said Barreda, that positive science would seize political power from the clergy just as it had seized the lightning bolt from religion. The clergy should be left with spiritual power in exchange for its nonintervention in political affairs. Positivism was transformed into a doctrine of political order, but, unlike Comtian positivism, it was not a doctrine of the spiritual order, at least in Mexico. Gabino Barreda had to suppress the teaching of religion.[33]

In Mexico, in contrast to other American countries, such as Chile and Brazil, the ecclesiastical rites that Comte added to his philosophy were not implanted. There was no attempt to establish a new church, which would have caused new upheavals and new disorders. What was wanted was order, and positivism was used to bring about this order. It was transformed into a neutral doctrine of the social order but, at the same time, it did not attack any idea, be it Catholic or liberal. Positivism, as we will see later in more detail, was presented as a doctrine at the service of the material order. At least, the men in the government attempted to use it as such. It did not want to invade the spiritual field of the Catholic church. It attempted to be a doctrine of the social and not of the individual order. The individual was free to believe what he wanted; what he was not free to do was to impose his ideas on society.

This effort of Mexican positivism to be the only valid ideology for society, as opposed to other doctrines, which were valid only for the individual, resulted in multiple disputes. It was impossible to distinguish exactly what field belonged to society and what field belonged to the individual. An ideology created to oppose both Catholicism and Jacobinism could not accommodate these ideologies, saying that they belonged to the individual order. From the

---

[33] Antonio Caso, in *Filósofos y doctrinas morales*, said that Barreda had to suppress the teaching of the religion of humanity. Pedro Henríquez Ureña said that "the positivists did not implant here, as they did in Brazil, the ecclesiastical rites of the religion that Comte added to his philosophy" (*Horas de estudio*).

neutral ideology that Juárez and the other liberals intended it to be, positivism was transformed into an ideology that, like all ideologies, attempted to include everything, to be valid in all fields, in the material, or political, as well as in the individual. This ideology could not accept the fact, as did the Reform Laws, that spiritual power should continue to be in the hands of the Catholic church, nor could it accept being subordinate to the state as an instrument of order. The transformation of Mexican positivism into an ideology that would satisfy everyone, one that would be at the service of the positivist ideal, could be seen in this attempt. One ideal of the Mexican positivists was to make their doctrine a spiritual power that would orient and guide material and political power.

This ideal remained a utopia. It was opposed by the clergy as well as by the Jacobins and even by the members of the Juárez government. Both groups, the clerical and the Jacobin, will see in positivism not a social doctrine in the service of order, but a sectarian doctrine in the service of a certain social group.[34]

[34] See note 29, Section One.

SECTION TWO:
THE ORIGINS

I. The Forces of Progress and Reaction

§ 25. *The Liberal Antecedent of Mexican Positivism*

In the foregoing chapter we have seen how the introduction of positivism into Mexico was not the result of curiosity or caprice. We have seen the historical circumstances that prevailed in Mexico when Barreda introduced the doctrine, which he learned directly from Auguste Comte. Without these circumstances, Barreda's knowledge of the positivist doctrine would have been useless. Positivism would have been no more than an armchair philosophy discussed by a few people; it would never have been a philosophy adopted by a nation. One of the reasons for the success of positivism as a national doctrine was the anarchy that existed in Mexico. The new liberal government needed a new order, an order based on principles that differed from those of the defeated conservative party. It needed an order that would satisfy the interests of the triumphant liberals. Also, positivism was successful as a doctrine for the liberals, because they were ideologically predisposed toward it. Had the liberals not been ideologically predisposed toward positivism, it would have been no more than the exclusive doctrine of a gentleman named Gabino Barreda.

Positivism, as we have already seen, furthered the interests of the triumphant liberals. It supported the ideals of those who up-

held the Reform Laws. Before Gabino Barreda introduced positivism into Mexico, the Mexican liberals held an ideology that fit
easily into the ideas brought by the first Mexican positivist. It was
a combative ideology similar to the one that was to serve as their
instrument to establish peace.

The writings of Dr. José María Luis Mora, considered as the
theoretician of the Mexican liberals, present the best exposition of
the Mexican liberal ideology.[1] He formulated the ideology for the
class that Justo Sierra labeled the bourgeoisie. Mora was the best
exponent of the ideal of the class that adopted positivism as an instrument of order. He expressed the ideals of his class in their
combative stage. In him we can find the ideological reasons, the
class reasons, why positivism was later adopted as an instrument of
order. The ideology of Mora was combative, but he anticipated the
ideal of his class in respect to a new system that was opposed to
that of the conservatives.

I do not wish to say that Mora was a positivist, a philosophical
forerunner of positivism in Mexico. I only wish to say that Mora
anticipated the ideas that were introduced by positivism. Mora
had discussed such concepts as *progress* and the *positive*; however,
this would not be sufficient to consider him a positivist like Gabino
Barreda and his followers. We could consider him a positivist if the
positivism of Barreda and his followers were exclusively a Mexican doctrine that merely used European positivist ideas as instruments. What I wish to say is that we can talk of a Mexican
positivism in connection with Mora if we judge it by its content
or meaning and not simply by its form. Mora, like Gabino Barreda
in his speech at Guanajuato, interpreted the history of Mexico
as the struggle between two great forces: the progressive and the
reactionary.

Dr. Mora defined these two opposing forces in the following
way: "by political progress that should be carried out more or less
rapidly, I mean state seizure of clerical property; the abolition
of clerical and military privileges; the extension of public education, absolutely independent of the clergy, among the lower
classes; the suppression of monastic orders; the absolute freedom

[1] For information concerning José María Luis Mora, see the excellent prologue written by Arturo Arnáiz y Freg to the works of Mora, which were published under the title of *Ensayos, ideas y retratos*.

of opinion; the equality of foreigners with natives in civil law; and the establishment of a jury in criminal cases. . . . By reaction," Mora continued, "I mean that which tries to abolish the little bit that has been done in the aforementioned branches."[2] In 1837 Mora gave the same interpretation to Mexican history as Barreda did in 1867. Mora identified progress with the ideals of Mexican liberalism, and reaction with clerical and military opposition to these ideals.

The forces of progress were represented by those who saw in public power an instrument of civil service, that is, service to the citizens or, as Mora called them, the Civiles. The Civiles were not members of the clergy or of the military; they believed in work and industry, and they longed for an order that protected the interests derived from such work and industry. This class, for which Mora—and, later, Barreda—was the spokesman, was the class that Sierra labeled the bourgeoisie.

It was a class that loved order. It saw the revolution as an inevitable means to attain the order that would protect its interests. This class viewed the Mexican Independence movement with a certain repugnance because it brought about much chaos and it brought into existence a class that was an enemy to all order: the military. "You can be sure," said Mora, "that no one moderately well-off, as much as he desired independence, cared to have Hidalgo enter Mexico."[3] And elsewhere Mora said: "The revolution that broke out in September 1810 was as necessary for the winning of independence as it was pernicious and destructive for the country."[4]

§ 26. *The Forces of Reaction*

We have already seen what Mora meant by progress and reaction. He felt that the war for independence merely gained independence from Spain, the Mother Country. On the other hand, it brought into existence the military, enemy of progress. It did not touch the other reactionary forces, such as the clergy. The clergy and the military were the enemies of progress. They were the same forces that Gabino Barreda attacked in 1867. The war for

---

[2] José María Luis Mora, "Revista política de las diversas administraciones que la República Mexicana ha tenido hasta 1837," in *Obras sueltas*.

[3] Mora, *Ensayos, ideas y retratos*.

[4] Ibid.

independence, instead of gaining that independence, gave birth to the power of the clergy and the military, who, in turn, transformed civil power into an instrument to serve their own particular interests.

"The revolution for independence," said Mora, "was a universal and effective disintegrating force that ended not only caste distinctions, but also old family ties, privileges of nobility, and opprobrious notes." But, he continued, "the independence proclaimed by the priesthood increased the power of the clergy; and independence, whose most visible manifestations were fought for and won by material force, made the military predominate. Brutal force and priestly aspirations were soon considered as the only powers."[5] The revolution for independence destroyed one order, one power, but it created a new power perhaps more tyrannical than the one that it destroyed. It was this new power that was opposed by the forces of progress. It was a power that was interested only in increasing and defending its own privileges. It was not a power in the service of the nation.

With the winning of independence, the clergy and the military won many privileges that they refused to surrender. Thus, independence was converted into a force to protect these privileges. The forces of progress viewed the military and the clergy as obstacles. This does not mean that Mora and the group that he represented were opposed to the existence of the clergy and the military. They knew that these forces were necessary in every country. The clergy was necessary to help man and to direct his moral life. What was not tolerated was the fact that the clergy used its moral influence in the service of its own interests rather than in the service of society. Hence, it was necessary to divest the clergy of all civil power. The clergy should have only spiritual power. Its mission was to help save souls, not to intervene in man's civil life.

The military too was necessary to keep order and to defend the nation. But, instead of keeping national order and defending the nation, it provoked disorder and tyrannized over the nation. "The Mexican republic," said Mora, "spends fourteen million pesos to support soldiers that tyrannize over it instead of defending it."[6]

5 Ibid.
6 Ibid.

The military, like the clergy, had been transformed into a power that served interests foreign to the nation.

The clergy and the military exist to serve the nation, that is, the people. The people do not exist to serve them. "Each Mexican," said Mora, "should ask himself daily if the people exist for the clergy or if the clergy was created to satisfy the needs of the people."[7] And what is said of the clergy should also be said of the military. The forces of progress struggle to subdue the forces of reaction and to convert them into what they should be: forces in the service of progress.

§ 27. Clerical and Military Interests

The clergy and the military were interested only in defending and increasing their own privileges, which Mora called corporate interests. The interests of society were sacrificed to satisfy the corporate interests of these two groups, which, instead of helping society, were merely a heavy burden. The clergy and the military shared the task of tyrannizing over society in both the spiritual and the material fields. "The two great agents of man are *thought,* which organizes, and *action,* which executes: the clergy was charged with directing the former, and the military with regulating the latter. But since they followed a reactionary course, they felt it necessary to keep others from working toward progress. The clergy identified those who were capable of thinking well and the military persecuted them."[8]

The clergy and the military, which were supposed to be instruments in the service of society, used society to serve their own ends. Civil power, that is, the government, which was supposed to serve society, was used to serve the church and the military. In civilized nations the clergy and the army served the government; in Mexico these two powers used the government for their own purposes. Thus, the government, instead of being an instrument in the service of society, became an instrument in the service of a class, a corps.

The governors could not serve society, because the interests of society were subordinated to ecclesiastical and military interests. The governors identified the interests of the government with the

[7] Ibid.
[8] Mora, *Obras sueltas.*

interests of the corps to which they belonged rather than with the interests of society. "The men in these *corps*," said Mora, "are identified with their peculiar interests and the dogmas of their creed . . . in their position, if circumstances should force them to embrace a resolution, they could not pledge themselves against the *corps* to which they belong; if they did, they would provoke the indignation of the *corps* and become targets of its persecution. In other words, the *corps* tyrannize over their members; this makes *civil liberty and personal independence*, to which their members as citizens are entitled, an illusion.[9] . . . They," Mora continued, think little of "conserving and securing common rights; their principal effort is to advance the *corps*, to establish their exclusive jurisdiction, and to diminish civil authority."[10]

These groups not only diminish civil authority, but also incite anarchy and disorder by trying to subdue every other corps, that is, the interests of others, to their own interests. "What is agreeable for one," said Mora, "is harmful for the other; while one urgently requests, the other energetically refuses."[11] The order based on the interests of the corps fostered dissension in society. In fact, it was complete disorder rather than order. Here order meant the use of force against any opposition to the interests of the corps. In the minds of the privileged classes, order was merely a gag for those who were concerned about the interests of society. It was an order opposed to those who did not belong to the privileged classes.

Thus, order established by a government headed by a particular corps meant anarchy, because a government "without laws, composed of people who organized *corps*," said Mora, "could not progress. A constitution with declarations and principles favoring the masses was placed in the hands of their members, public functionaries and organized powers to achieve these objectives were provided, but they were ordered to observe laws that are in opposition to these objectives, and to respect tendencies that would destroy them. What has been the result of this? Further disgust and bloody revolutions incited, sustained, and protected by the *corps*."[12] A government that served the interests of these corps fostered dis-

9 Ibid.
10 Ibid.
11 Ibid.
12 Ibid.

putes, arguments, and revolutions; it could not fully satisfy the interests of all the privileged corps. Mora and his class saw this happen in Mexico.

§ 28. *Civic Interests*

As can be seen, a government serving the interests of a corps could not be a government. What actually existed was a coalition of factions that tried to satisfy those whom they represented. Such a government merely sustained the privileges of the corps that supported it. It was impossible for such a government to have a constitution because the laws that justified the privilege of the corps predominated. José María Luis Mora and those who thought as he did were opposed to a government based on disorder. They wanted a constitutional government, a government at the service of society and not at the service of a particular corps.

Opposed to the order that favored a particular social corps was the ideal of an order in the service of all society. The corps, said Mora, were concerned with serving *persons*; their interests were *personal*. Opposed to them were the *civicos*, which placed emphasis on *things* rather than on individuals. By stressing *things* Mora meant that they were not concerned with the interests of *individuals*, but with the interests of society. A true government should stress things and not persons, that is, society and not a corps.

Thus, two forces were opposed to each other: the forces of reaction and the forces of progress. The former consisted of corps, called the clergy and the military, that were interested in upholding the privileges of certain people. The latter consisted of a group that was interested in society as a whole. It wanted the government to protect not certain privileged classes, but society *as a whole*. It was concerned with the *things* of society and not with certain *individuals*.

Was Mora's disinterest in a particular social group and his interest in society as a whole sincere? Could it not be that Mora and his class were defending personal interests, namely, the interests of the group to which they belonged? If they were defending the interests of society as a whole, were they not actually defending their own interests? By opposing the clergy and the military, were they not opposing the interests of a class to which they did not belong?

II. Mexican Liberalism's Ideals of Education and Government

§ 29. *Education as a Class Instrument*

We have seen how Dr. Mora attacked the privileges that the clergy and the military granted themselves, but this does not mean that he was opposed to the existence of such groups. What he was opposed to was their obtaining privileges at the expense of other social groups, classes, and bodies. He gave these social groups the generic name society.

The clergy and the military were necessary, provided that they served society. But, what society were these two groups supposed to serve? It consisted of only a certain social class, the class to which Mora belonged, which was neither that of the clergy nor that of the military. It referred to the class that Sierra called the bourgeoisie. Mora and those who viewed society as he did were defending the neglected interests of their class, that is, the interests of a nonprivileged class, the interests of the middle, or bourgeois, class.

Now the first thing that this class should have done to reclaim its rights as a member of society was to develop what the Marxists called class consciousness. It was necessary that the Mexican bourgeoisie be conscious of its obligations and rights as a social class and that it know its ideals and interests. This was necessary because the members of this class, since they were not yet conscious of themselves as a class, would join any cause or group and protect any faction or social body to which they did not belong. Mora gave us various examples of this situation, including the coup d'état of General Santa Anna who received the support of this class in spite of the fact that his only concern was to satisfy and gain privileges for the military faction that he represented.

Hence the necessity of an education, said Mora, to prepare the elements of "a middle class, which should be formed in the next generation, and which is so lacking in the present."[13] Mora anticipated the education that would be put into effect by the positivists. In 1833, said Mora, "the positive men were called to execute reforms, especially educational," because the old education "falsified and destroyed at the roots all the convictions that constituted a positive man."[14] This education could not be put into effect in the era of Mora, because the men affiliated with reaction assumed importance and persecuted the positive men. A long civil war was necessary, and victory against the French, before those representing a positive spirit triumphed and carried out Mora's ideal. It was the positivists who, after having triumphed, elaborated a system of education that embodied the ideals of the Mexican bourgeoisie. This system was created by Gabino Barreda.

Mora expressed an educational ideal that was not dogmatic but based on experience. He criticized the old education, which he said separated theory from practice. "Theory," said Mora, "consists of certain knowledge capable only of adorning the mind, and not susceptible to practical results. . . . It [the old education] consisted of doing things the way they were done centuries ago in specific cases and circumstances, without examining them or believing that they were susceptible to betterment and progress."[15] As can be seen, the old education was opposed to progress; it promoted reaction. Thus, education served the interests of a certain class. Mora was conscious of this fact when he proposed a type of education

---

[13] Ibid.
[14] Ibid.
[15] Ibid.; Auguste Comte points out, in *Primeros ensayos*, that the separation of theory and practice was a sign of decadence in the old order.

that would serve the interests of the middle class, that is, a dynamic, and therefore progressive, education.

In another paragraph Mora said, with reference to the old education, that, "instead of creating the *spirit of investigation* and *doubt*, which more or less fosters the understanding of truth, it inspired dogmatism and argumentation in the young, qualities which are distant from truth in purely human learning."[16] Note the words *spirit of investigation* and *doubt* because they referred to the ideal methodology adopted by positivist education. Positivism rested on this spirit of investigation and doubt. It did not rest on any dogmatic affirmation; every affirmation was to be proven by facts.

§ 30. *Relations between the State and the Citizens*

Dr. Mora sustained the thesis, which the Mexican positivists later held, that the state should not defend any doctrine. The individual should believe in whatever doctrine or ideas that he wished, but he could not force society to believe in a particular doctrine. In other words, he could not force society to believe as he did. "Man," said Mora, "has a right to make laws or to demand that one work in a certain way, but he has no right to change doctrines into dogmas or to force others to believe as he does. This absurd right would presuppose a doctrine that contained all truths, or the existence of an infallible authority."[17] This, Mora continued, was the reason why "everyone should think as he pleased.[18] . . . Therefore, the government should not proscribe or defend any doctrine; it should merely see that its subjects observed the laws."[19]

According to the liberal conception of Mora, the state was a simple guardian of order. The state could not be a person or a protagonist; it was simply an instrument in the service of the individuals who made up society. Neither should the state intervene in the personal life of its citizens. This is what happens when the state defends a particular doctrine. Every doctrine is an exponent of a particular social group, which Mora called a corps. If the state defends a doctrine, it defends the corps that expounded the

[16] Mora, *Obras sueltas.*

[17] Mora, *Ensayos, ideas y retratos.* See Barreda on the idea of "a common fund of truths," §§ 38 and 44.

[18] Mora, *Ensayos, ideas y retratos.*

[19] Ibid.

doctrine. Thus, the state is converted into a person, namely, into part of the corps, and it becomes an instrument of that group. As such, it intervenes in favor of certain elements, disputing like an individual with other individuals. By protecting a doctrine or a group of ideas, it becomes a member of a group that sustains this doctrine or group of ideas. In this case the state does not exist; it is merely one more individual in a dispute with other individuals. It is one doctrine held by a group of individuals, fighting other doctrines sustained by another group of individuals. A state transformed into an individual opposed to other individuals creates anarchy; and, the function of every state is to keep order.

Mora's interpretation of the state, that is, that it ought to maintain order and serve all citizens, was the thesis sustained by all Mexican liberals. This thesis served as the banner of the movement for the Reform Laws: freedom of conscience, and separation of church and state. By separating the material power of the state from the spiritual power of the Catholic church, the state was able to fulfill its mission: to serve society as a whole. The relationship between state and citizens should deal strictly with maintaining order. "A government," said Mora, "is more liberal the less influence it has over the person of the individual citizen, and the citizen is freer the less relationship he has with the agents of governmental power."[20] Thus, the relationship between the state and the citizens should be minimal. Even though the state is a necessary instrument, it should be resorted to as little as possible.

§ 31. *The State as an Instrument of a Faction and as an Instrument of Society*

The evil of office seeking, which today is called bureaucracy, was one reason, according to Mora, why the state was converted into an instrument of a single faction or corps. The public employee, instead of serving society, tried to protect his own interests as an individual. He considered his job not a social responsibility, but an instrument to care for his own daily necessities. Whether for fear of losing his position or for better remuneration, he unconditionally served the dominant faction or corps, forgetting that he had a social mission to fulfill. "The evil of office seeking created

20 Ibid.

by the employees," said Mora, "places at the disposal of power, enemy of liberty, a great mass of force to suppress liberty, and, at the same time, it degrades, debases and demoralizes its citizens."[21]

To avoid this it was necessary to separate the mission of the state from the interests of individual citizens, who must not use the state for their own personal concerns. The state must be used to serve society as a whole. It must be the guardian of the interests of society and thus of each individual citizen. But it should never be an active instrument in the defense of special interests. The state becomes evil when it is used to protect its own well-being. It then is no more than a mine from which privileges are extracted by its dominant factions. Public employees have also used the state as a measure of subsistence. The public employee feels like a servant of the faction that exploits society rather than like a necessary servant of society.

Mora said that it was necessary to separate individual from state interests. Only in this way could one avoid *retrocession*, because "the custom of living from stipends," said Mora, "destroys initiative and perfectability."[22] Those who used the state for their own interests were enemies of change and progress, because progress would alter the position that they occupied. Thus, the struggle between the forces of reaction and the forces of progress was the struggle between two conceptions of the state: one, which held that the state was to serve a particular faction; and the other, which held that the state was to serve society. The former conception led to a static situation, because it knew that progress would alter its privileged position; the latter conception, on the other hand, led to progress, because it knew that progress would alter its own non-privileged position. The important thing was to see what happened when the social class that believed in progress rose to a privileged position.

To avoid the evils of the state, Mexicans should look for sources of wealth outside the state. These sources included industry. Mora believed that the evils that existed within a state could be avoided if Mexicans would obtain their wealth from industry and work. "Work, industry, and wealth make men truly and solidly virtuous," said Mora; "they will make Mexicans absolutely independ-

21 Ibid.
22 Ibid.

ent and they will help them form a firm and noble character to resist the oppressor and to discourage every attempt at abuse. One
accustomed to live and support himself without having to humble
himself before power, or beg the state for subsistence, will never
further its corruption, projects of disorganization, and tyranny.
Hence, these three sources of personal independence and social
virtues were necessarily choked by the evil of office seeking."[23]
Individual interests should be satisfied in other ways to prevent
the state from being the granter of privileges. This is the only possible way for a state to keep order and to serve society as a whole
rather than a particular faction.

The state should protect the interests of every individual in society. To do this, it would have to discontinue being a mine of
privileges for certain groups of individuals. Privileges should be
sought in other areas, namely, in personal work, which the individual can do through his own strength. Nothing would better
prove this strength than industry. He who makes industry his
source of wealth needs no privileges from the state; he can gain
these privileges from industry itself. The state should be a source
of protection so that an individual's efforts are not invalidated by
those who do nothing. If privileges, wealth, and social well-being
were sought outside the state, then the state would be what it
should be: a guardian of public order.

§ 32. *The State as the Guardian of Public Order*

"We should cast aside," said Mora, "the erroneous idea that
government has a magical character that perpetuates the prosperity of empires. We should replace this false idea with the truth,
that is, with the idea that the status of man can be improved
through morality and industry."[24] The prosperity of a nation and
of its nationals should not be associated with the idea that the state
obtains or can obtain this prosperity. The only way that one can
gain this prosperity is through individual industry separate from
any mission of the state. The idea that the state had a magical
character that could put any idea into practice also endangers public order, because such an idea diverts the state from its real mis-

---

[23] Ibid.
[24] Ibid.

sion. It makes the state an instrument of chimeras and utopias, and it ignores the social reality that it should serve. Its social function is sacrificed for a mere idea.[25] Mora said: "it is important not only that the rebels be restrained, but also that an intelligent doctrine erase impossible projects and extravagant fallacies from the mind and that it destroy confused human desires that pursue imaginary improvements."[26] Reality was being sacrificed for an idea. The idea that the state possessed the magical character to effectuate chimeras made order impossible. When every individual group wants the state to fulfill its ideas, ideas are bound to clash and, consequently, bring about disorder. The state should not effectuate ideas. The state should sever its relations with both individuals and chimeras. It should serve neither a social *body* nor social ideals and chimeras.

Dr. Mora said that the ideals of Mexican independence were used by certain factions once independence was won. Because of the ignorance of the people, said Mora, they saw their new governors as heroes and saviors, and not as what they actually should have been, namely, civil servants at their orders. The people, forgetting that their own interests were the interests of society, handed them over to the caudillos who won their independence. The caudillos knew how to use the ideas of the people to their own advantage.

A government created to carry out certain ideas is necessarily revolutionary, since it tries to alter the existing reality to make it conform with its own ideas. Violence is necessary for such a government to subjugate reality, but in turn, this violence creates caudillos. Government thus forgets social reality and, instead, carries out its own ideas. These ideas are effectuated by men of action, namely, caudillos. Once triumphant, caudillos and ideals are confused. The people feel the same admiration for caudillos as they felt for ideas; they see in the caudillos the embodiment of such ideas. They unconditionally serve these caudillos, thus creating tyranny, that is, a government of factions.

Hence the necessity to evade what Mora called the revolution

[25] In our period many notorious examples of this concept of the state are presented.

[26] Mora, *Ensayos, ideas y retratos.*

of men and to aid the revolution of time. The state should not be an instrument at the service of the revolution of men, but it should not obstruct the revolution of time; it should cooperate with it. "The ability of those who lead the state," said Mora, "consists principally in knowing the necessities of the degree of civilization to which man has arrived. One could conjecture that the people will arrive, sooner or later, at political freedom. National leaders should crave liberty for their subjects as soon as possible rather than be terrified by such a thought."[27] Thus, there is a revolution of men, which leads only to disorder and, consequently, reaction; and there is a revolution of time, which is the true revolution that leads to progress. Compare this thesis with the one sustained by Barreda in his Guanajuato speech and you will note how they resemble each other in considering the revolution that they represent as the revolution of time obstructed by the forces of reaction. Note that Mora, like Barreda, spoke of the revolution of time as the arrival of political freedom, which Barreda called "political emancipation."

Mora said that ideas imposed by force fail; therefore, he was opposed to the state's imposing such ideas. The individual should think as he pleases. No one should force him to think otherwise. One cannot impose an idea through force. Ideas that should be effectuated will be effectuated without imposition, despite obstacles. This, for Mora, represented the revolution of time as opposed to the revolution of men. The former will be carried out in spite of opposition; no one can detain progress. The latter will not. "Opinions concerning doctrines," said Mora, "should be completely free."[28] The only mission of the government is to protect order. "Governments," said Mora, "have been established to preserve public order and to guarantee the rights and properties of everyone as prescribed by the law."[29] If the state assumed any other mission, such as that of defending certain ideas, the result would be disorder. When a state becomes an instrument of one ideological doctrine to the detriment of others, the other doctrines would acquire an unsuspected value, making their adherents attack the opposition

[27] Ibid.
[28] Ibid.
[29] Ibid.

to them. "If," said Mora, "one wishes to approve a doctrine, all he needs to do is to proscribe it."[30]

The state should not defend any doctrine. However, in spite of his affirmations, Mora recognized the necessity for a doctrine of order when he said, "It is necessary not only to curb the rebels but also to have an *intelligent doctrine* to erase chimerical projects from the mind."[31] It was necessary to have a doctrine void of the chimeras that cause disorder. In other words, a doctrine of order was necessary. This seems like a theoretical contradiction because, on the one hand, it was affirmed that no doctrine should be imposed and, on the other hand, the necessity of establishing a doctrine of order was affirmed. Elsewhere Mora said that the state had no right to "change a doctrine into a dogma, or to force others to believe as the state wanted them to. This absurdity would presuppose the necessity for a doctrine that would include all truths . . ."[32] And elsewhere he spoke of the necessity of a doctrine of order, a doctrine that took account of reality, one that was devoid of every kind of imaginary thing and chimera. Was this a contradiction?

No, it wasn't. It is a matter only of something created by circumstances. Mora was talking about the ideology of a class that was trying to acquire certain privileges but was obstructed by the social groups that possessed power. He was opposed to those groups using their power to impose an ideology that justified themselves. But, at the same time, Mora's class was sustaining an ideology that claimed to be valid for all society. The Mexican bourgeoisie wanted order, but it did not want the old order. It considered the old order a source of disorder, because it opposed the order that it wanted. To establish this order, it was necessary to have an ideology that would justify the order that it wanted to establish as if it were the order of all society, at the service of all citizens; in reality it was the order of a specific social class: the Mexican bourgeoisie.

This doctrine of order was positivism. Positivism represented what Mora called "a symbol or body of doctrine comprehensive of all truths" and what Gabino Barreda called "a common fund of

---

[30] Ibid.

[31] Ibid.

[32] Ibid. Positivism, too, intended to include all truths. See "Gabino Barreda's Plan of Education" in Section Three of this study.

truths."[33] The Mexican bourgeoisie, once triumphant, tried to establish an order, claiming that that was the order of all society. It sustained the *intelligent doctrine* that was to banish "all chimeras." This doctrine claimed to differ from its competing doctrines. It was not to be a dogma that one was forced to believe without proof: its dogmatism rested on evidence. It claimed to base its doctrine on truths that were evident and therefore incontrovertible. Therefore, it differed from competing doctrines, which were based on faith, such as Catholicism, or on a feeling of admiration for heroes, as happened with those who believed in caudillos. Positivism was to be the intelligent doctrine that was to erase every kind of chimera. It was to be supported by what was called evident reality. Therefore, there was nothing inconsistent about Mora's theory: it was merely the class expression of the Mexican bourgeoisie in its combative phase. It was trying to reconcile its opposition to the existing order with the ideal of a new order.

[33] Gabino Barreda, "De la educación moral," in *Opúsculos, discusiones y discursos,* and "Carta a D. Mariano Riva Palacio," where he says: "In order that practical conduct be sufficiently harmonious with the real necessities of society, it is necessary that there be a common fund of truths from which we all must depart" (*Opúsculos, discusiones y discursos,* p. 28).

III. The Ideology of the Mexican Bourgeoisie in Its Combative Phase

§ 33. *"Liberty," a Concept in the Service of a Social Class*

Mora, as we have already seen, expressed the feelings of a particular social group called the Mexican bourgeoisie. He anticipated the middle-class ideology of the Porfirian era. The Mexican bourgeoisie should not be confused with the European bourgeoisie, although there were many similarities.[34] The middle class for which Mora was the spokesman, like the European middle class, supported industrialism. However, the Mexican bourgeoisie did not gain its strength from this field, despite the fact that great strides were made to form a strong Mexican industrial bourgeoisie during the Porfirian era.[35] In spite of this effort, big industry remained in the hands of foreigners. It was the Europeans who supported and encouraged such industry in Mexico. The Mexican bourgeoisie consisted of landowners and speculators, who, instead of encouraging Mexican industry, allowed European capitalists to develop it.

[34] See Bernhard Groethuysen, who has already been mentioned, concerning the European bourgeoisie (*El origen de la burguesía*). Concerning the Mexican bourgeoisie, see the interpretation of Samuel Ramos in his book, *El perfil del hombre y la cultura en México*.

[35] José C. Valadés, in *El porfirismo*, has dedicated a chapter entitled "La locura de riqueza" to this topic.

The bourgeoisie of the Porfirian era was a comfortable, selfish man who did not want to be disturbed. He wanted to get rich with the least possible effort. He loved peace and order, the peace and order of Porfirismo. He felt that everything should serve his interests. However, we saw through Mora, who was the embodiment of that class, that the ideological suppositions of this class affirmed just the opposite. He did not want the state to be the tool of a particular class, of a particular social corps. He wanted the state to serve society as a whole. But we have also seen that this idea originated in the nonprivileged circumstances of the Mexican bourgeoisie. And when it said that the state should serve society as a whole, it included the bourgeoisie in this whole. The Mexican bourgeoisie wanted the state to serve society as a whole, because the state served only a class that did not include the bourgeoisie. When the bourgeoisie demanded the rights of society, it demanded its own rights. Once this class triumphed, it forgot that other classes in society also had rights.

Dr. Mora expressed this ideology when he said, "If love of country is subjected to an exact analysis, in the final result it is no more than the desire for one's own convenience."[36] The phrase, "one's own convenience," used in the last sentence, is the end to which this class reduced love of country and the ideals for which it fought. It was a class that fought for its own interests, which it gave national importance. The nation appears here to be tied to the interests of the Mexican bourgeoisie. And this was nothing scandalous. The nation was the expression of man, not a separate entity. The interests of the nation are always the interests of a certain number of men, and cannot be the interests of everyone. Sometimes the nation represented the interests of the blood aristocracy, sometimes those of the aristocracy chosen by divine right, and sometimes the money aristocracy. Sometimes the nation was tied to the interests of the nobility, other times to the interests of the proletariat. But it has always, in every era, been tied to the interests of a certain group.

In this specific case, the country, that is, the nation and everything that it represented, was tied to the middle-class desire for comfort. Perhaps this desire was pursued by every social class, but

[36] Mora, *Ensayos, ideas y retratos.*

nowhere was it so evident, so flagrant, and so open as in the bourgeoisie. For the Mexican bourgeoisie progress meant the fulfilling
of their aspirations. But once the bourgeoisie reached its goal, or
was thought to have reached it, then progress would be detained. It
became a word without a meaning. The ideal of this class was
summed up by Mora: "Life and the means to sustain it and live
it agreeably; I mean here each man, I mean here everything that
he asks for and only that which interests him."[37]

In pursuing its interests, the Mexican bourgeoisie had to face
an enemy: the clergy and the military. The bourgeoisie maintained an idea to which the clergy and the military were opposed,
the idea of freedom. But the military caudillos whom the bourgeoisie opposed also upheld this idea. "The word *freedom*, which
has often served to destroy its own meaning," said Mora, "has
been the usual pretext for all political revolutions throughout the
world; its leaders have banished it like a vision when it was no
longer necessary for the attainment and success of their ambitions."[38] These words could be applied to those who started out
with the ideal of freedom and, once triumphant, became enemies
of freedom. They interpreted freedom according to the meaning
that was given to it by the Mexican bourgeoisie in its combative
phase. The word *freedom* in this phase had a different meaning
from that it had once the bourgeoisie acquired power. One will be
the interpretation of freedom by the so-called Mexican liberals,
and the other will be the interpretation of freedom during the
Porfirismo era. I have already mentioned that the liberals and
the positivists did not have the same interpretation of freedom.
Barreda did not interpret the word *freedom* in his Guanajuato
speech as he did when he discussed it with the liberals. The concept of freedom will be, in fact, tied to the interests of the class
that sustains it.

§ 34. *Persuasion as an Ideological Tool*
of the Mexican Bourgeoisie

"It is necessary," said Mora, "for a stable reform to be gradual
and characterized by *mental revolutions* that extend to society and
modify not merely the opinions of certain people, but those of the

37 Ibid.
38 Ibid.

whole population."[39] In these words Mora anticipated the idea that the Mexican bourgeoisie adopted by making positivism a tool of its ideology and interests. Positivism was intended to carry out the *mental revolution* that Mora spoke of: uniformity of all opinions so that all Mexicans would think according to what Barreda called a "common fund of truths." But this mental revolution, this uniformity of all opinions of the Mexicans, could not be accomplished through violence—we have seen how Mora was against all violence. Uniformity was to be achieved through persuasion.

The Mexican bourgeoisie, lover of order and enemy of disorder, could not be a partisan of violence, which only provoked disorder. Everyone had to be taught to think alike, without the use of corporal violence. There would have to be another type of violence, namely, mental violence, through education to which all students should be submitted. Hence the necessity of making education uniform. "The effects of force are rapid," said Mora, "but transitory; those of persuasion are slow, but sure." Education was the weapon used by the Mexican bourgeoisie to persuade other classes that it had a right to the privileges that it had gained. Thus, it was necessary for this class to have a doctrine to persuade all Mexicans that the order of the Mexican bourgeoisie was the order of society.

But these men, partisans of order and enemies of force, were obligated to use violence against violence. They were aware of the fact, however, that violence was not the weapon that would definitively give the bourgeoisie the power that was previously held by its enemies. They knew this because they, who were lovers of order, had had to use violence to defend themselves from violence. On various occasions Mora complained about the violence committed against the men of progress. Violence sowed violence. Violence was necessary to conquer groups that used it; but, once those groups had been conquered by violence, they should be convinced that their overthrow was necessary. They should be convinced that the position that they wanted was not the position that they should have had, and that their actions were mistaken and unjustifiable, and contrary to nothing less than the progress of humanity. The clergy and the military had to be convinced of this. The Mexican

---

[39] Ibid.

liberals did not feel like enemies of the clergy and the military. Mora said, "No civilized or religious nation can exist without the clergy or the military."[40] The liberals were not the enemies of the clergy and the military except when these groups were enemies of society, that is, insofar as they acquired their privileges at the expense of the privileges and rights of society. The bourgeoisie merely wanted the clergy and the military to fulfill the social function that was assigned to them. They were opposed neither to their ideas, nor to the way that they used them. They were, however, opposed to the fact that these ideas were used to exploit society.

The insistence of the clergy and the military upon sustaining privileges to which they had no rights forced the Mexican bourgeoisie to use violence. Also, the clergy and the military did not show a willingness to fully accept the new social order. As long as there was a possibility that they would attack this order, it would be necessary to use violence against violence. Later the bourgeoisie would have to convince the clergy and the army of their error through nonviolent methods. Violence had a necessary transitory character.

Revolutions and upheavals [said Mora] are going to exist by the sheer force of the events themselves, until one of the political ideologies that are in conflict decisively overcomes the other. In order to achieve this, it is necessary that the defeated ideology lose even the hope of recovering the power that has slipped through its fingers, and, since triumphs and defeats have also been—through the very momentum of events— frequent, alternating, and of short duration, this hope will not be easily destroyed, except through a regime vigorous and energetic enough to repress the factions and enlightened enough to satisfy these social needs that will not be easy to refuse without endangering the regime.[41]

As can be seen, Mora and his class wanted to make a revolution from below. An armed revolution would not suffice; it would merely provoke a counterrevolution. A more profound revolution, whose force would differ from physical force, was necessary. It should be the force of *enlightenment*, that is, the capacity to know when a reform was necessary and the capacity to foresee all possible danger. It would be necessary, as Comte said, *to foresee in*

40 Ibid.
41 Mora, *Obras sueltas.*

order to act. The revolution of the Mexican bourgeoisie had a socio-political character. The desired reform was not only political but also social. Politics was understood as a social tool and not vice versa. Thus, an educational system was necessary that would educate Mexicans to a new way of viewing society. Education would be the most adequate tool to carry out a revolution that desired more than a simple political change.

During the Porfirian era, what Mora wanted was attained: a strong regime capable of suppressing all factionalism. The clergy and the military, once overthrown by the Mexican bourgeoisie, became a tool of the Porfirian government. They were bureaucratized.[42] The bourgeoisie, once it became a government force strong enough to prevent the clergy and the military from hoping to recover power, would convert them into what they wanted them to be: tools in the service of the bourgeoisie. However, the bourgeoisie did not consider the condition imposed by Mora's doctrine, that of gradually making the concessions that society demanded. It did not consider the interests of the social classes that appeared later, and were to turn the revolution of time into a revolution of men.

§ 35. *Respect for Ideas*

The liberal ideal of persuasion carried with it the ideal of respect for the ideas of others. Nonviolence implied nonintervention in the ideas of others. However, this desire not to interfere in the ideas of others was not realized, because others felt that their ideas were being attacked. The Mexican bourgeoisie, against its own wishes, supported a partial ideology that necessarily clashed with other ideologies. It was necessary to convince other Mexicans that the bourgeois ideology was the one that they ought to accept, that this ideology was valid not only for a corps, but also for society as a whole. But it had to convince them through nonviolent means. Mora said in this respect: "What is the obligation of the good citizen? To continue to form opinions gradually and to pave the way for reforms that will one day be attained, not through the shedding of blood, but spontaneously and easily, and meanwhile to abstain from conspiring, from forming or adhering to sub-

---

[42] Valadés, *El porfirismo*, describes how the clergy and the army were assimilated and bureaucratized during the Porfirismo era.

versive plans. Prudence dictates this, and the laws of honor and public order demand this from every citizen."[43]

As can be seen, we are dealing with an ideology of prudence, one that was opposed to violence and disorder. To change society, it was necessary, above all, to form public opinion gradually and not through violence. This is what the bourgeoisie tried to accomplish through an education based on the positivist doctrine.

The Mexican bourgeoisie tried to acquire power smoothly through persuasion; in other words, *rationally*. However, this was impossible because the classes that possessed power would use violence to defend it. Violence against violence was necessary. In this battle there were two contradictory ideas: one that made the state a source of wealth and another that made the state a guardian of wealth. At the beginning, the Mexican bourgeoisie did not want the state to continue to be an instrument of privileges; its only mission was that of guardian. Privileges would have to be sought from other sources. Privileges, as we have already seen, should have their base in industrial work. However, the Mexican bourgeoisie felt obliged to use force of arms to contend for power. Conspiracy, subversive plans, and an armed movement were necessary.

Once the Mexican bourgeoisie had triumphed, it tried to justify its victory through persuasion. It claimed that the state was a servant of society. It offered to respect all ideas and not just certain ones. It indicated this by sustaining the thesis of the secular school. However, reality demonstrated that these claims would remain claims and nothing more. The state had to be something other than a tool of society. It had to be a tool of the Mexican bourgeoisie. In the new distribution of privileges, the Mexican bourgeoisie got the lion's share; the rest was divided between its former enemies: the clergy and the military. During the Porfirian regime all these classes united. A single body was formed to hold on to the privileges that had been gained. It defended them in every possible way. Furthermore, industry, as an instrument of wealth, was left in the hands of the active European bourgeoisie; the Mexican state once again became a source of wealth and privileges.

However, the Mexican bourgeoisie continued to justify its privi-

[43] Mora, *Ensayos, ideas y retratos.*

leges on the basis of a necessarily rational plan. The Mexican bourgeoisie identified its own interests with the interests of society.
The privileges that it won were not the privileges of a class but
those of all citizens, who had rights as members of Mexican society. Mora gave almost Machiavellian advice about this identification of interests when he said, "To influence others, what is
necessary is knowledge of the human heart, an invariable con-
stancy in the projects that are to be realized, a *total dexterity
in identifying common interests with your own,* and, above all,
great precaution to avoid anything that might offend the ideas of
those who by circumstances considerably influence the masses."[44]
This is what the Mexican bourgeoisie did. It identified its own
interests with the interests of others, and it was careful not to
offend those ideas that still influenced the masses. The bourgeois
ideology was a *cautious* one.

Positivist education was careful, as we will see later, not to
offend other ideologies. It claimed to respect all of them. It said
that it was not opposed to any idea or to any religious doctrine. It
said that it merely desired that these ideas stay in their proper
place and not claim to be the only ideas, because this claim would
cause disorder. The Mexican positivists said that they were not opposed to the spiritual doctrines of the Catholic church. They were
opposed only to the political or material pretensions of the Catholic church. The Mexicans could be Catholic or Jacobin, whatsoever
pleased them; but, above all, they should be good citizens. Their
ideas must not serve as tools to gain political advantages.

In accord with the Mexican positivists, the state did not
care who possessed the true religion or the better doctrine. The
only thing that mattered was that these doctrines not change the
system. Mexican citizens could profess whatever ideas they wanted, provided these ideas were not used as a tool to improve their
own material situation at the expense of others. There should be a
reason for every privilege besides its being a gift of God or an inheritance from heroes or caudillos. Individuals had only those
rights that they obtained through their own initiative. No idea or
doctrine should limit those rights. The worth of a man must be
based on what he was capable of accomplishing and not on the

---

[44] Ibid.

doctrines or ideas that he professed. He who accomplished more should have more rights than he who accomplished less. Hence, the positivist doctrine defended the rights of the stronger. It justified itself on the basis of biological doctrines, including the doctrine of Darwin and others. Vasconcelos attacked positivism in Mexico on the basis of this thesis. Each man should have what he merits, and this no one should touch. Mora said, "We should reform abuses without intervening in the lives of individuals except when necessary."[45] The individual should be disturbed only when he uses his rights as a tool against the rights of others, basing his actions on unacceptable ideas: ideas that hold that privileges have sources other than those of the individual's own capacity. Why did the Mexican bourgeoisie sustain these ideas? They were actually contradicting themselves. Their ideas justified their right to the power and privileges that they desired. When they said that the privileges obtained through one's own capacity were legitimate, they upheld the right of the bourgeoisie to gain certain privileges. This thesis contradicted the one held by those groups that obtained privileges on the basis of other justifications. It was a thesis that held that each individual had the right to that which he was capable of gaining through his own efforts. It contradicted the thesis that held that man's privileges were a divine gift. Furthermore, it contradicted the thesis that held that all privileges should be conceded to caudillos or national heroes. Man was considered the heir of his work and not the heir of God or of caudillos.

§ 36. *The Thesis concerning the Rights of Others*

"A reformer should be cold in his passions and invariable in his goals,"[46] said Mora, when he spoke of social reformers. This was his ideal. Neither sentiment nor passions should influence the aims of the new reformers. This was the ideal of the Mexican positivists *who placed more importance on method and doctrine than on passion and sentiment.* Everything that could not be reconciled with the positivist method must be renounced. This type of reformer, Mora continued, "should vigorously attack institutions and preserve the rights of individuals."[47] Reforms should attack insti-

[45] Ibid.
[46] Ibid.
[47] Ibid.

tutions rather than individuals. Individuals, according to this criterion, must be respected. Only those institutions that failed to fulfill their social mission, such as the mission to safeguard the rights of the individual, must be changed. One could alter the institution that served as a tool of a *corps*, without implying that he wanted to attack the individuals who made up that *corps*.

Mora, like the later Mexican positivists, wished to distinguish between the *rights of the individual and those of society*. The latter guaranteed the former, provided that the individual did not use the rights of society for his own benefit. Mora wished to preserve the equilibrium between the personal and the social. But it was impossible to reconcile the ideology of the Mexican bourgeoisie with the conflicting social corps, because each corps wanted to use society as its own tool.

By sustaining this thesis the Mexican bourgeoisie defended its own rights on the basis that they could be reconciled with the rights of the conflicting corps. The Mexican bourgeoisie did not deny the fact that individuals, such as the clergy and the military, who belonged to corps, had certain rights that belonged to them as individuals. But, it was opposed to the corps as a social institution that conflicted with the personal interests of others who belonged to the same society. When it attacked the clergy and the military, it did not attack their personal rights. It attacked them because they were acting as tools for a particular group at the expense of others instead of serving society. The clergy and the military were necessary for society, but they had to fulfill their social function. Hence, said Mora, the reason why each Mexican should ask himself if the people exist for the clergy or if the clergy exists for the people. Each citizen should fulfill his own social function, which can be reduced to Juárez's formula: Respect for the rights of others is peace. Obligations to society are obligations to others.

Would the Mexican bourgeoisie fulfill the postulates of this thesis? The Mexican bourgeoisie wanted all Mexicans to be indoctrinated into its ideology through a positivist education. The Mexican positivists wanted their doctrine to be a social doctrine based on peace and respect for the rights of others. In view of the fact that positivism was a social doctrine, it was imposed on all Mexicans through education. The Mexican bourgeoisie found in the positivist philosophy the theoretical expression of its view of the world and life. That is why positivism was adopted. But by adopting positivism the bourgeoisie used it not only for what it was, namely, a doctrine for its class, but also as a doctrine for Mexican society. By conceding their ideology a social character, the bourgeoisie claimed to respect personal ideologies. Arbitrarily dividing the conscience of man into two categories, the Mexican bourgeoisie attempted to make positivism the valid doctrine for one of those categories, the social category. As social beings, everyone should assimilate the positivist doctrine as a social doctrine. On the other hand, there was another category, the individual, in which one could do as he pleased. The Mexican positivists said that their doctrine in its concern for the social field did not invade the personal field.

The Mexican positivists wanted to regulate the ideas of the Mexicans in the social field, but their attempt had the opposite result, as Mora himself saw when he said, "If the faculty to regulate [ideas] is conceded to any authority, this authority would soon abuse this same power."[48] So it was. The Mexican bourgeoisie, which, like all bourgeoisie, was an enemy of physical violence, created spiritual violence by the use of positivism. Mexican positivism tried to educate all Mexicans in the ideology of the Mexican bourgeoisie. The Mexican bourgeoisie justified its own privileges and defended them on the basis of the positivist philosophy. Positivism tried to *demonstrate positively* the *scientific* origin of its privileges. And when these scientific demonstrations were inadequate, the bourgeoisie used its former adversaries, the clergy and the military, to convince by their own methods those who were not convinced by positivist methods. In other words, when doctrinal persuasion proved to be inadequate, the Mexican bourgeoisie, once it acquired power, used the method that it had previously repudiated: physical violence. In regard to the party of reaction, Dr. Mora said something that can also apply to the Mexican bourgeoisie once it had attained its desired goal: "No one has screamed louder against this imperfect and temporal dictatorship than those who wanted it to be eternal, complete, and absolute . . . because they are the victims when they aspire to the honor of executioners. In other words, they wanted a dictatorship,

---

[48] Ibid. This was attempted through positivism. (We will refer to this later.)

not for themselves but for others."[49] The Mexican bourgeoisie, once it had triumphed, would try to impose its own ideas on society. It would try to use society as a tool by convincing the Mexicans that whatever was done was done in the name of "social necessity." The class that fought the dictatorship of the clergy and the military would have to impose another dictatorship no less oppressive: Porfirismo.

[49] Mora, *Obras sueltas.*

SECTION THREE:
THE DEVELOPMENT,
"GABINO BARREDA"

I. Gabino Barreda and the Problem of Freedom

§ 37. *Freedom as an Individual Right*

We saw how Benito Juárez commissioned Gabino Barreda to reorganize education according to the principles of the triumphant liberals. Barreda's mission was to organize education to serve as the basis of a new social order in Mexico. The Mexican nation, exhausted by civil wars and the French invasion under Napoleon III, needed order. To make this order permanent, Mexicans had to be conscious of its necessity. Material order, or order maintained by force of arms, was not enough. What was needed was an order based on the conscience of the individual, that is, a spiritual order.

To implant this order, the spiritual order of the clergy, supported by the military, had to be destroyed.[1] But this was not the only enemy. The Reform created a new enemy of order. This enemy was what the positivists called Jacobinism. The Jacobins were those liberals who did not accept the order supported by the Mexican positivists. They were Mexican liberals who believed in the full meaning of freedom. They understood freedom as the right

---

[1] Barreda, like Aragón, Sierra, and other positivists, spoke of the clergy and the military as causes of social disorder in Mexico. Years later, however, liberal ideas were also accused of causing disorder. (This topic will be discussed later.)

to think and act as one wished. Opposed to those two enemies, the conservatives and the liberals, the positivists considered the latter more dangerous because they were triumphant. Having won the revolution, they were unwilling to accept a new order. The clergy and its ally, the military, were temporarily conquered, and would be slow to regain strength.

Barreda had before him a difficult task, to reorient the minds of those who had destroyed the old theological-type order. He became engaged in a polemic with the Mexican liberals. In his writings he complained about the hostile reception that his ideas received in government circles. He would have to create an ideological bond to bridge the gap between liberalism and positivism if his ideas were to be accepted. This bond, as we have already seen, was established in his Guanajuato speech.

In "Civic Oration," Barreda adapted the Comtian doctrine to the interpretation of the history of Mexico from a liberal point of view. According to this interpretation, the positive spirit was represented by the revolution and the negative spirit was represented by the clergy and the military. The motto of Comtian positivism—love, order, and progress—was changed to liberty, order, and progress. This change and the anticlerical character of his speech at first attracted the interest and approval of the liberals. The Mexican liberals supported his educational reform because Barreda presented the positivist doctrine as liberal and anticlerical. The engineer, Agustín Aragón, said that among the reasons Gabino Barreda was called to collaborate in the educational reforms was that President Juárez read this speech: "Il n'est pas téméraire d'affirmer que la lecture du discours du Dr. Barreda décida le président Juárez à l'appeler auprès de lui en qualité de collaborateur."[2]

In "Civic Oration," Barreda said that the desired civil order did not contradict individual freedom. On the contrary, it promoted individual and spiritual freedom. In the same speech Barreda said "that in the future a complete liberty of conscience, an absolute freedom of expression and discussion, which will admit all ideas and all inspirations, will shed its light everywhere and will make every disturbance that is not spiritual and every revolution that is

---

[2] "It is not rash to say that the speech delivered by Dr. Barreda made President Juárez decide to ask him to be one of his collaborators" (Agustín Aragón, *Essai sur l'histoire du positivisme au Mexique*, p. 16).

not intellectual unnecessary and impossible. I hope that the material order, preserved at all costs by those who govern and respected by the governed, will be a sure guarantee and a safe way by which to continue ever on the happy road to progress and civilization."[3] He proposed an order or a civil dictatorship that would promote freedom. Mexicans would be freer in this way; they would be freed from the obligation imposed on them by the material order. The material order represented that which was least noble, that toward which Mexican ambitions should least tend. The material order should be entrusted to the state. But the state should merely be the guardian of the material order, so that complete spiritual freedom would be possible.

He wanted to convince both the conservatives and the liberals that the state's power was material and not spiritual. The state's only mission was to guide the material order. The spiritual order, on the other hand, should remain in the hands of the free individual. The Mexican was free to direct his conscience. The new education did not try to interfere in the personal life of the Mexican. It tried only to make him conscious of the need for a material order to facilitate the work of the state. Thus, the reason for the secular school thesis, which held that the state did not want to impose any ideology on the Mexicans. Each Mexican was free to choose his own ideology. The state promised not to interfere with the individual's spiritual freedom. Each family was completely free to indoctrinate its members as it pleased. The mission of the state was to make the members of the family good citizens so that they could better serve society and respect the state as the guardian of order, because this was the only possible way to maintain material order. By respecting material order there would be peace, and with peace there would be freedom of thought and discussion.

Every Mexican was free to think as he pleased; he could be Catholic or Jacobin. The only thing that he was not free to do was to use his belief to alter the material order. Consequently, the state could not sustain any ideology, be it Catholic or Jacobin. Its only ideal was peace and order. Ideologies should be for individuals and not for the state. Individuals were the only ones that could hold specific ideologies, provided they did not threaten the material

[3] Gabino Barreda, "Oración cívica," in *Opúsculos, discusiones y discursos*, p. 105.

or social order. On the other hand, society's only ideal was progress
for the benefit of all its members. Therefore, the state based its
educational ideal on the scientific, or positive, order, because this
ideal did not attack individual ideologies. It merely demonstrated
self-evident truths that were within the reach of every individual.
Besides, these truths belonged to the material field in which progress represented the progress of all individuals, that is, the progress
of society. Positivism, according to this thesis, was considered the
best way to teach Mexicans how to protect and defend the social
order; it was considered as a tool of the material order. The material order was still compatible with the spiritual order. Upholding the civil order did not imply the necessity of interfering in the
life of the individual. On the contrary, the individual order would
be guaranteed in this way. The idea of freedom, as the liberals
interpreted it, was not irreconcilable with the idea of the positive
social order. However, positivism implied an idea of freedom that
could not be reconciled with Mexican liberalism. This idea was
soon to lead the positivists to dispute with the Mexican liberals.

§ 38. *Freedom within the Positivist Order*

In 1863, four years before he delivered his famous Guanajuato
speech, Barreda published in Number 839 of *El Siglo XIX* an article entitled "De la educación moral."[4] In this article he defended
the right of the state to administer the moral education of its citizens when he said: "In addition to political duties, the citizen has
other duties that are even more important: the duties of the moral
order. And this, as much as or more than anything else, is the
obligation of the state."[5] Barreda felt that the state had the obligation, among other things, to train morally good citizens. This could
be accomplished through education.

It is necessary to understand that Barreda did not associate
morality with religion and metaphysics. According to Barreda,
man was good or bad regardless of the religious or metaphysical

---

[4] This and other articles were published in *Opúsculos, discusiones y discursos*.
This article was also published in *La Revista Positiva* and in a collection of Barreda's works edited by José Fuentes Mares, entitled *Estudios de Gabino Barreda*,
published by the University of Mexico.

[5] Gabino Barreda, "De la educación moral," in *Opúsculos, discusiones y discursos*, p. 107.

ideas that he professed. Quoting Condorcet, Barreda said that one should "look into the person himself and not into religious dogmas for the cause and basis of morality."[6] History, he said, has demonstrated the existence of atheists who, from a moral point of view, were at least equal to the best believers. By nature men possessed good and bad inclinations that originated in their respective faculties. Hence, for the individual, as well as the species, to attain moral perfection, he must develop the faculties wherein the good inclinations reside and "diminish as much as possible those wherein bad inclinations reside."[7] If the faculties in which the bad inclinations reside did not function, they would atrophy. Barreda drew his conclusion from the positive laws tested in the biological and physical sciences.

Barreda felt that just as physical faculties developed through gymnastics, and those that were not exercised weakened, in the same way, through education, one could elicit "the sympathetic, or *altruistic*, acts, as Comte called them, and, at the same time, could avoid the destructive and selfish ones whenever possible."[8] This thesis facilitated the establishment of order with roots deeper than those that were simply material. Moreover, for Barreda, morality, like any material thing, was a practicable object of reform. Morality, according to Barreda, was independent of the spiritual field. It belonged to the social field, and therefore was possible through education. It could not be left to the individual because it was part of the social field. Therefore, it must be the object of the interest of a social organism. Provisionally, the state, through public education, was responsible for training morally good citizens. But Barreda did not mean that this task belonged to the state. In fact, he felt that it belonged to a social corps, independent of the state. He wanted a social corps to be entrusted with spiritual matters as the state was entrusted with civil matters. It is obvious that Barreda and the most important Mexican positivists tried to invade the terrain that it had seemed to leave free according to the liberal concept.

Freedom, taken in the laissez faire sense of liberalism, became impossible in the degree to which the positivist order was to be

6 Ibid., p. 108.
7 Ibid., p. 111.
8 Ibid., p. 112.

established. Absolute freedom contradicted the idea of order that
Barreda wanted to establish. We have seen how Barreda altered
Comtian positivism by introducing the concept of liberty. He introduced this concept to justify positivism to the liberals. The idea of
liberty, however, had to change, because it was irreconcilable with
positivism. Four years earlier when the liberals triumphed and,
in turn, collaborated with the government, Barreda gave freedom
a meaning that was compatible with positivism. It was expressed
in Barreda's article concerning moral education. It later became
the touchstone in the fight between Barreda and the Mexican
Jacobins, and in the struggle of Barreda's followers against the same
Jacobins and the clergy. The clergy adopted the liberal thesis to defend their own interests.

Barreda opposed the laissez faire idea of freedom held by the
Mexican liberals. "Freedom," he said, "is commonly thought of
as the right to do anything or to want anything without any regard for the law or the force that might limit it. If such freedom
did exist, it would be as immoral as it would be absurd, for it
would make any discipline, and, consequently, all order, impossible."[9] In these words Barreda showed the contradiction that existed between freedom in the liberal sense and order in the positivist
sense. Barreda believed that liberty and order were not irreconcilable, but he had given the concept of liberty another meaning, that
is, a positivist meaning. Barreda said, "Liberty, far from being
irreconcilable with order, consists, in all phenomena, both organic
and inorganic, in submitting fully to the laws that determine
those phenomena."[10] Something was free when it followed its
natural course, that is, when it encountered no obstacles; law,
order, is inherent in nature. Barreda gave physics as an example.
He explained that when one said that a body falls freely, one
meant, according to the law of gravity, that if "it falls directly
toward the center of the earth with a velocity proportionate to the
time, that is, subject to the law of gravity . . . then we say that it
falls *freely*."[11] The same held true for the moral field. In this field
man acted freely if he followed his moral impulses, which led him
either toward good or toward evil. The state's role was to use educa-

[9] Ibid., p. 113.
[10] Ibid., p. 113.
[11] Ibid., p. 113.

tion to fortify good impulses and hinder evil impulses. The free development of the altruistic impulses was achieved in this way.

Barreda did not believe that the individual was free to do what he wished. Freedom ought to be subordinate to the interests of society, namely, to the interests of the Mexican nation. The individual was not free to do what he wished, because this freedom might become an obstacle to the free development of altruistic sentiments. If one were to understand freedom in the laissez faire sense, disorder would follow. Disorder was an obstacle to the development of freedom in the positive sense, because it was a check on the free and natural development of the altruistic, or positive, feelings that led toward the progress of humanity. Freedom in the liberal sense meant the stimulation of egoistic sentiments, and therefore it was an obstacle to the development of altruistic sentiments. Freedom of the individual, that is, an egoistic freedom, must be subject to the laws of the free development or progress of society. The freedom of the individual must subordinate itself to the social order.

Thus, the state should intervene, as an instrument of society, in the moral education of Mexicans. It must prepare Mexicans to be good civil servants by stimulating their altruistic sentiments. Mexicans, as individuals, could be liberals or conservatives, Catholics or Jacobins. This meant nothing to the state. What was important was that all Mexicans should be good citizens. The individual could think as he wished, but he had to work for the interests of society. One could believe whatever he wished, but he could not obstruct the free movement of society with his beliefs.

Morality, which, according to Barreda, must not be associated with religion, stimulated or impeded the impulses, actions, and good or bad acts of man. Acts of social character were important because they were susceptible to regulation by a social organism. That is why Barreda believed that morality belonged to the social field. Morality could be divided like any other physical force. It was susceptible to development or to atrophy just like any other physiological organ. Regarding the separation that Barreda established between facts and ideas, a separation that could also be established between positive science and theological and metaphysical ideas, morality belonged to the former, to facts and, therefore, could be an object of positive science. For Barreda, morality was a fact independent of all religious or metaphysical ideas. "Religions," said Barreda, "have changed in the different phases of humanity and only in those places that remain stationary, as in India and in China, do they not change. But the basis of morality remains the same, although the practical results continue to improve from day to day, especially where there is progress in civilization."[12] Religions change, that is, they are transformed in accordance with the people and the era. That is why religion—and what Barreda said of religion should also be applied to what the positivists called metaphysics—cannot be the mover of altruistic sentiments. Sentiments are a part of man, and therefore they should be developed by positive methods, that is, by a gymnastics similar to physical gymnastics. The roots of morality, unlike those of religion, do not change. These roots are found in man himself and should be stimulated.

Summing up, we can say that Barreda saw freedom as a progressive and ordered march of society, free of all obstacles. Freedom should neither disturb nor place obstacles in the way of order. This concept of liberty was opposed by both the Jacobins and the Catholics. Each group sustained that the positivist interpretation of freedom was irreconcilable with true freedom, that is, the freedom of conscience guaranteed by the constitution.

[12] Ibid., p. 108.

II. Barreda's Defense of the Interests of the Mexican Bourgeoisie

§ 39. *The Defense of Catholicism against Jacobinism*

In 1868, scarcely a year after Barreda had been called to collaborate with the Juárez government, he directly attacked the Mexican Jacobins when he was asked to approve or disapprove a book entitled *Catecismo moral*, by Nicolás Pizarro. The book was proposed by the author as an official ethics textbook, because he felt that it fulfilled the requisites of secular education.

Separation of church and state demanded that the state prepare good citizens. Thus, the author felt that this book would fulfill a moral need. A catechism on morality, which would respect the ideas inculcated by the family, was necessary to prepare the student to be a good citizen. In order not to attack individual beliefs, those learned in the bosom of the family, it was necessary that this catechism, or moral treatise, contain no dogma—theological or metaphysical. Its objective was to train students to be good citizens without interfering in their specific beliefs. Hence, the need for a book of morals based on purely human and scientific concepts that would be "entirely independent of theology, as well as of man's transcendental social, domestic, and personal problems."[13] What

[13] Gabino Barreda, "Informe presentado a la Junta Directiva de Estudios," in *Opúsculos, discusiones y discursos*, p. 120.

was needed, said Barreda, was a moral education that did not conflict with the laws and interests of society, the family, or the individual, but one that would conciliate them so that they would cooperate in the "consummation of the same and constant end: the unceasing moral, intellectual, and material improvement of humanity in general and the individual in particular."[14]

Thus, in spite of the claims of the author of *Catecismo moral*, Barreda did not feel that this book fulfilled the above-mentioned requirements. The author, instead of being free of dogmas and beliefs, put forward ideas that contradicted Catholicism. Pizarro was not neutral. He became the standard-bearer of one ideology that was opposed to another. Barreda felt that to accept the book as an official text would contradict both the laws of the Reform and those of justice and equity. It was like admitting a preference for a certain doctrine that, no matter how acceptable, did not represent the interests of society as a whole.

Barreda recognized the fact that the majority of the Mexican people were Catholic, the religion that the author of *Catecismo moral* attacked. If the Junta de Estudios, which was instructed to establish the ideological basis for a social order, voted in favor of the book, it would be like showing preference for a particular ideology. And in this case, the ideology would be one opposed by the majority of society. To choose this book would be to oppose society's goal, order. The state and every social organism in the service of society must renounce every ideology, theology, and metaphysics to maintain order. Their only concern should be to protect the social order and to care for the ideal well-being of society. Their concern should not be to defend or contradict the beliefs of any member of society. The author of *Catecismo moral*, as an individual, was free to think as he wished. But he could not force the state to accept ideas that contradicted the ideas of other members of society. This would merely lead to disorder.

Gabino Barreda defended the Catholic religion against the Jacobinism professed by Nicolás Pizarro. Barreda stated that the author of *Catecismo moral* had no right to consider "the existence of all the clergy as worthless and harmful."[15] In defending re-

14 Ibid., p. 120.
15 Ibid., p. 122.

ligion and the Catholic clergy from Pizarro's claim that they were fraudulent, Barreda said that Pizarro was "unaware of the relevant virtues and the ardent and sincere faith of thousands of churchmen who have given the most irrefutable proofs, and who have sacrificed their lives in defense of the doctrine that they preached."[16] Barreda asked, what right has one to call Saint Vincent de Paul, Fénelon and Bousset, Bishop Quiroga, Saint Francis Xavier, Saint John Nepomuceno, and others abusers and impostors. The fact that the ideas of these men cannot be reconciled with the ideas of our time, said Barreda, does not mean that they were fraudulent. On the contrary, "the state of intellectual evolution was manifested in them."[17] If one did not consider intellectual evolution, it would be impossible to understand the history of humanity. Barreda justified the existence of the Catholic religion as a doctrine that corresponded to a certain era in the evolution of humanity. On the basis of this idea, he defended the church against the attacks of Pizarro.

The main reason why Pizarro's book was not adequate as an official text was that its ideology contradicted social interests and would therefore incite conflicts that would bring about disorder. In this book Pizarro upheld certain ideas inappropriate "to the immense majority of the nation because they were Catholic and because they upheld the belief in hell, the necessity and efficacy of oral confession, and many things that the author qualified as frauds meant to deceive the people."[18] To accept this book, said Barreda, would contradict not only "the laws of the Reform, but also those of justice and equity."[19]

The desire for order prevented the religion of humanity from being established in Mexico. The insistence upon positivism as a religion would contradict the religious ideas of the majority, and it would provoke new disorders, that is, another civil war. Gabino Barreda, conscious of Mexican reality, took from positivism only those ideas that would provoke no controversy that could be carried to the battlefield. Positivism was to be merely an ideological basis

---

[16] Ibid., p. 122.
[17] Ibid., p. 123.
[18] Ibid., p. 129.
[19] Ibid., p. 121.

for peace. He adopted positivism's abstention from examining or interpreting any theological and metaphysical theory. In this way, he wanted to avoid controversy and discussion and, consequently, any motive for disorder that could degenerate into armed battle. By abstaining from accepting any ideology not based on facts, he wanted to avoid all discussion and disorder. The only idea that he wanted to support was that of order. It was up to the individual to adopt the theological and metaphysical ideology that he wanted, provided it did not alter the social order.

The state as a social organism in the service of all society abstained from adopting a prescribed ideology. In this way it could respect all beliefs and see that all of them were respected without exception. It left the spiritual field up to the free will of the individual. The state remained within the material field, that is, the field of the social order. But the fact that the positivists in principle supported this thesis does not mean that they would not aspire to spiritual power as the Catholic church had done. However, the Constitution of 1857, which upheld freedom of conscience, hindered them in this ambition in spite of the fact that they tried to get around it by giving positivism a special interpretation.

§ 40. *The Defense of Private Property*

In his critique of *Catecismo moral*, Gabino Barreda defended private property against the attacks of the author, Pizarro. Pizarro cited a phrase from Renan's book *La Vie de Jésus*, which said, "If you want to be perfect, sell what you have and give it to the poor."[20] Barreda attacked this thesis. He said that it contradicted the spirit of the times and the interests of society. This principle, he said, did not belong to our times, which are different from those in which this principle was pronounced, the Judeo-Roman era. In that era, wealth was the result of "conquest and exploitation, which, not yet having any social end, could not be sanctioned by public opinion."[21] Wealth in that era was the result of egotism, that is, injurious to society. All the wealth was in the possession of Rome, taken from the oppressed peoples, including the Jews. Barreda said that this was why the phrase that Renan attributed to Jesus was so successful.

[20] Ibid., p. 125.
[21] Ibid., p. 125.

But this principle cannot be upheld "after almost two thousand years when the military civilization has been replaced by a civilization in which capital, that is, wealth, which was useless and harmful in the previous era, is the principal and indispensable instrument of progress in the modern era."[22] Barreda said that if these ideas should be put into practice today, in a short time the conquests that were the pride of humanity would be finished. What would become of commerce, industry, agriculture, and manufacturing, asked Barreda, if the merchants, industrialists, and landholders had "to sell their holdings and their factories to throw their capital out the window to be caught by the first idler who happened to pass by?"[23]

The distribution of wealth was considered by Barreda as an ideal for the theological period of history, but in no way did it fit into the positivist period. Only by looking at private property from a theological point of view was it possible to disapprove of it as an obstacle to the attainment of eternal life. This negative idea of private property was unacceptable in a positivist period in which wealth was the principal instrument of progress. In the positivist period the odious character assigned to wealth in the theological stage would disappear. To uphold this thesis would be contrary to the social interests of the period. "The proprietors and the rich," said Barreda, "would perhaps go to heaven, but the others would remain in a true inferno."[24] Also, this thesis was opposed to the social order because the poor could see how the rich held wealth that morally should have been divided. "To regulate property and not to destroy it," said Barreda, "to humanize the rich and not to transform them into paupers, should be the aim of modern philosophers and moralists. This is . . . a great and transcendental problem, an eminently progressive problem that metaphysics with all its wordiness and entities can neither understand nor avoid; that theology, more prudent and more systematic, can very well cast aside by holding it in disdain as essentially worldly; but that only positive science can resolve."[25]

22 Ibid., p. 125.
23 Ibid., p. 125.
24 Ibid., p. 126.
25 Ibid., p. 128.

§ 41. *Noninterference of the State in Private Property*

Although Gabino Barreda considered it one of the state's obligations to intervene in the moral life of Mexicans through an education that would stimulate their good sentiments, he was opposed
to state intervention in the regulation of private property. He was
opposed to the ideas of Pizarro in *Catecismo moral*, which held that
the state should impose a series of civil sanctions against abuses
committed by usurers. Barreda considered this thesis regressive;
that is, it was opposed to social interests. He said that "the results
would be as reactionary as they would be perturbing if the government should regulate interest rates on money."[26] And elsewhere
he said, "I do not censure the Catechism because it wants to correct a fundamental abuse, which is usury, but I am opposed to
civil coercion, which not only is an intolerable tyranny and the
motive for new immoralities, but also is insufficient to pursue the
objective that it seeks."[27]

The state should in no way tell the individual how to administer
his property. What it should do is to make the possessors of wealth
see, through moral education, that "the rich, although they are
morally authorized to take from their capital, which the social
order has made it possible for them to increase and to conserve,
what is necessary for their real needs and also for the maintenance
of their rank and dignity, should seek to cultivate and use the
excess, under pain of moral responsibility, as a public power that
society has put in their hands for the common good and common
progress."[28] It is not necessary to regulate wealth; what should be
done is "to humanize the wealthy." Wealth is a social necessity
and, therefore, so are the possessors of wealth. The wealthy class
is necessary for society once society has reached the positive stage.
Hence, the reason why we should consider "property as a basis of
society and not as a source of personal enjoyment, as the theologians view it."[29]

Here, as opposed to the way his doctrine had been previously
expressed, Barreda defended private property. Barreda, who was

----

[26] Ibid., p. 126.

[27] Gabino Barreda, "Carta al editor del 'Semanario Ilustrado,'" in *Opúsculos,
discusiones y discursos*, p. 138.

[28] G. Barreda, "Informe presentado," p. 127.

[29] Ibid., p. 127.

opposed to the laissez faire meaning of freedom in reference to ideologies with ambitions of social predominance, supported the full liberal meaning of freedom with reference to private property. The rich could do anything they pleased with their money except divide it up. If everyone divided his wealth, it would dislocate society. Barreda did not deny that the rich were responsible to society as to how they used their money, but this was no more than a moral responsibility. Although the rich were considered as trustees of society, society could not intervene and regulate this trust. Barreda considered this intervention as intolerable, that is, as an attack on freedom. It is clear here that he is using the concept of liberty in a different sense from that he had given it to conform to positivism. Society could intervene in education, but it could not intervene in the regulation of property except through persuasion. The rich must be convinced that they had social duties, but they could not be forced to fulfill these duties.

The character of the state in regard to private property and individual ideas was mixed, unclear. The state could not meddle, because to meddle would provoke disorder. It would mean favoring the interests of a certain group, which opposed the interests of others. Therefore, when one supported ideas regarding private property, such as those Pizarro upheld in his *Catecismo moral,* it meant favoring a certain social class. In this case it would not be the rich, because they would be forced to divide their wealth. The nation had poor and rich. To favor the poor would provoke disorder. The only position to adopt was to respect the state of affairs and abstain from judging the situation. Wealth was an instrument of social progress, and it was in the hands of a certain group of individuals called the rich. One must leave it where it is. The only thing that should interest society was that this wealth should serve the ends of social progress. Wealth, as an instrument of progress, should be protected by the state. In spite of all the abuses that were committed and the inequality provoked through wealth, the most that one could do was to appeal to the moral responsibility of the rich. One could not attack wealth, because that would stifle initiative and therefore progress.

§ 42. *The Justification of Barreda's Ideas within the Mexican Reality of His Time*

We have seen how positivism was adopted in Mexico to justify the interests of a certain social class that Sierra called the Mexican bourgeoisie. Barreda was asked to establish the ideological basis for a permanent order, the order of the new class, which now possessed power. Wealth was a stimulant for this new class. To attack wealth was to attack the class that established the government now at its service. The mission of the state was to see that this wealth, which was considered as private property, was respected. It could not intervene to find out if such wealth originated in personal work or in the profit and exploitation of the poor.

When Mexico was freed from Spain, it received only political independence from the Mother Country. Economically, it was at the mercy of the same trustees of economic power as in colonial days. The origin of this economic power was essentially agricultural. The great landholders throughout the Mexican Republic were the masters of the Mexican economy. This situation did not change with independence. Political power passed into the hands of the old insurgents, who then fought among themselves; economic power remained in the same hands. Independence was accomplished through a revolution that was only political and was not fully consummated until the liberals triumphed in 1867. But there was no land reform. In fact, the rights of the landholders were strengthened.

Neither did the Reform movement accomplish anything in this respect. It was essentially against clerical intervention in politics. It was merely another stage in the political independence that was initiated in 1810. The revolution of 1810 was against the political intervention of Spain. The Reform was against the political intervention of the clergy. The Reform's only aim was to liberate the Mexican state politically from clerical intervention. It stripped the clergy of its wealth because the clergy used its wealth to interfere with Mexican politics. The clergy used wealth to buy men and arms to defend the rights in Mexican politics that it had held since colonial days. To uproot their wealth was a political measure, not an economic measure. This wealth passed into the hands of new proprietors, who later formed the nucleus of the supporters of the Porfirist regime. This class continued to exploit the workers. The liberals, who gained control of the government, did not intervene in the economic field. Their only interest was to preserve order. The distribution of clerical wealth increased the number of individual landholders within the Mexican economy. The later agrarian revolution brought about the disorder that the Mexican bourgeoisie did not foresee. The bourgeoisie was complacent in its ideas of peace and progress; it considered progress the progressive increase of its wealth.

Thus, it is obvious why Barreda could not approve a textbook on morality that attacked private property. The revolution for which he supplied the ideological basis was not economic; it was political. Barreda was commissioned to regulate the moral life of Mexicans through education in order to obtain a permanent order. The regulation of private property could not be reconciled with this order. To obtain political order one could meddle neither with the individual's personal ideas nor with the individual's personal property. Each Mexican could think what he wanted and he could manage his wealth as he pleased. The only thing that he could not do was to use these ideas or this wealth to provoke social disorder. The laissez faire meaning of liberalism was valid in the ideological as well as in the economic sphere, provided it did not interfere with the political sphere.

Political power should intervene neither in the field of ideas nor in the field of private property. These were concerns of the individual. Every Mexican was free to exploit or be exploited. But he was not free to take advantage of this exploitation to favor certain political interests. The state had neither a transcendental mission like the one of the theological and metaphysical periods, nor an economic mission, such as the distribution of wealth. Its mission was to preserve social order. In the name of social order, the state could regulate education to make Mexicans orderly. The state, as a tool of society, should be concerned neither about an individual's personal ideas nor about his economic status. It should be concerned only with the preservation of order. Let Mexicans think as they pleased. Let them exploit or be exploited. The only thing that concerned society was order. Behind the neutrality of the state in the area of personal ideologies and private property, which were defended by Barreda, are the interests of the Mexican bourgeoisie. This class attempted to justify its social situation by a philosophy which prohibited any change of the established order.

III. Gabino Barreda's Plan of Education

§ 43. *The Plan of Education Proposed by Barreda*

In a letter of October 10, 1870, to Mariano Riva Palacio, the governor of the state of México, Barreda explained how the National Preparatory School was reorganized and the reasons why he made this reform.[30] According to Barreda's plan, education should include all the positive sciences. However, he had to change his plan because of pressure from the liberals and the Catholics, who opposed the plan from the beginning. Education should include all the positive sciences, beginning with mathematics. After mathematics, the natural sciences should be studied in the following order: cosmography, physics, geography, chemistry, botany, and zoology. Logic was to be studied last. Between these courses, Barreda inserted modern languages: French, English, and German. He said that Latin should be studied the last two years rather than at the beginning as was customary. In former times Latin was a useful language to begin with because scientific and other works of universal importance were written in that language. Therefore, it was necessary to learn Latin at the beginning of the course

[30] Gabino Barreda, "Carta dirigida al C. Mariano Riva Palacio," in *Opúsculos, discusiones y discursos.*

of studies. But now, said Barreda, every scholar writes in his own language, so it is necessary to know that language. He said that French was probably the most important language because it replaced Latin. Besides, said Barreda, modern languages had another function: to improve relations with citizens of foreign countries. Latin, Barreda continued, now has a different function: to facilitate the study and cultivation of jurisprudence and medicine, that is, it is useful in the study of careers undertaken after the preparatory course. Therefore, if Latin were studied in the beginning of the preparatory course as was customary, the students would have forgotten it before entering professional school.

He said that Spanish should not be studied until the third year of preparatory school. By that time the student has a more mature mind and he will be conscious of the importance and usefulness of such a course. Logic should be taken at the end of the preparatory course because it cannot be understood before its workability is demonstrated. This is done by studying the positive sciences in a certain order. Once the workability of the sciences is understood, then one may study their theoretical bases. Hence, Barreda was opposed to studying logic prior to the positive sciences. He was opposed to a theoretical education. He felt that theory should be adapted to reality. Logic cannot be taught in the abstract, that is, without examples, and examples are obtained through the scientific disciplines. Logic cannot be studied in the abstract; it must be made practical through the support of the positive sciences.

This idea originated from the positivist thesis, which held that knowledge should be based, not on authority, but on experience. To make logic abstract was to uphold the principle of authority. The student who studied the positive sciences would be disappointed when he discovered that logic would not resolve the problems posed by the sciences. This disappointment would result in scepticism and dismay. According to Barreda, knowledge based either on pure theory or on pure practice would produce two types of persons: one, who refused to admit that there was anything new, believing that everything that could be explained on the basis of theory had been said and done; and the other, who was always looking for something new and practical, and was never satisfied. With reference to these two types, Barreda said that "the customary incomplete and vicious education has produced, according

to public opinion, theoreticians, while only in exceptional cases
have practical men been produced by the *colegios*."³¹

Separation of theory and practice merely produced disorder because an incomplete education created prejudices and false ideas,
which caused dissension. Incomplete persons, both theoreticians
and practical men, are those who are opposed to progress. Some
think that there can be nothing new under the sun; others think
that everything is new and that everything changes. The former
support a decrepit order; the latter support disorder instead of
order. In both can be detected the two social groups that opposed
Barreda and positivism: the conservatives and the Jacobins. According to Barreda, both conservatives and Jacobins were the result of an incomplete education.

§ 44. *Uniformity of Thought as a Basis*
for the Protection of the Social Order

Barreda said that every man has certain prejudices that cannot
be destroyed except through a well-rounded education, that is, an
education that includes all knowledge. This education should touch
every possible area of one's consciousness where there might be
some prejudice. The lack of a well-rounded education, said Barreda,
caused many people to fear the dead, although they knew that the
dead cannot move. The same can be said with respect to certain
religious prejudices. "What will happen," said Barreda, "if one
professes ideas that, because they are most susceptible to discussion or because they are less frequently discussed, are definitely
rooted in the mind regardless of how false and inadmissible they
may be? In this way, because of improper preparation, errors will
be embedded in the mind and these errors will form the real basis
of a great many, if not all, of one's acts, even though at times this
basis will be unknown or concealed."³² These prejudices, hidden
in the consciousness of man, will produce prejudiced results. Lack
of unity in education, and lack of enlightenment of prejudices, said
Barreda, meant that "persons of equal intelligence and capable of
reasoning with equal precision arrive at conclusions diametrically
opposed, and likewise they engage in opposite forms of conduct.
Thus, one can explain the diverse religious and political beliefs.

³¹ Ibid., p. 40.
³² Ibid., p. 27.

One can explain, finally, the complete anarchy that currently reigns in minds and in ideas and that is being incessantly felt in the practical conduct of everyone."[33]

Thus, social and political disorder had its roots in the disorder of conscience. Social order depended on uniformity of opinion. Thus, it would be possible to avoid social anarchy through the uniformity of opinion. If all members of society thought alike, every source of dispute and therefore social anarchy would end. Thus, it was necessary that all Mexicans have what Barreda called "a common fund of truths."[34] This basis should be as complete as possible so that not even a crack would be open for error. Barreda attempted to realize these ideas in the National Preparatory School through a plan of studies that would achieve such unification. Gabino Barreda, speaking of education, said, "It must be the same for all regardless of what profession a man chooses, for no matter how much the professions differ, they must all work together, since they have a common objective—social well-being."[35]

Gabino Barreda believed in the complete planning or ordering of the student's mind, so that as little as possible be left to his own interpretation. "A single road that lends itself to error," said Barreda, "a single source of ideas that abandons itself to arbitrariness and to individual whim, is enough to ruin an entire educational program regardless of how well put together the rest of it may seem."[36] Barreda said that the plan of the Society of Jesus, which was the most perfect example of an educational plan, failed because it left to individual interpretation a series of facts that the Society could not accept because they contradicted the dogmas of the church, or, rather, because of the Society's backwardness in scientific knowledge. If the Society continues to be influential in our time, said Barreda, it is because it has had to broaden its educational program.

Barreda said that education should be the product of the destruction of prejudices; it should not impose certain ideas and dogmas. It should try not to uphold specific ideas but to demonstrate truth

[33] Ibid., p. 27.
[34] Ibid., p. 28.
[35] Ibid., p. 28.
[36] Ibid., p. 29.

in all its aspects. This, said Barreda, was "the surest prelude to peace and social order, for it will place all citizens in a position to appraise all the facts in a similar manner, and therefore it will make all opinions uniform as far as possible."[37] Thus, education has an almost exhaustive purpose: to offer the maximum truth on which an individual can base his criteria. Every individual should begin with this principle. One should not begin with preconceived ideas, because they are merely prejudiced truths that agitate the consciousness of the individual and cause disunity. Opinions should rest on theories that can be demonstrated by the positive sciences.

The thesis expounded by Barreda, that is, that everyone should be taught to think alike, can only produce selfish, incredulous, and materialistic men who have no ideals. Everything that was not useful, that is, everything that did not have an immediate or *positive* end, had to be renounced. Man could disagree as far as his ideals were concerned, but he had to agree with everyone else when it came to anything considered useful. Positivism, one of whose slogans was progress, could not live up to this slogan, because progress, like it or not, was disorder. And the group of Mexicans who professed positivism wanted order. They sacrificed, in the name of peace and order, every idea that was not useful. Ideas were considered the main cause of disorder. Without ideas, the only field that remained was the material: the increase of wealth. Here we can understand why the positivists opposed state intervention in the organization of private property. Progress could be realized only in the material field, the field of wealth, not in the spiritual or cultural field. Progress could be conceived of only as the progressive increase of wealth.

§ 45. *Compulsory Education*

Barreda's plan of education to orient the Mexican mind so that all Mexicans thought alike and would agree would not be entirely successful if it was going to be limited to the National Preparatory School. It was necessary to introduce this plan of education into the primary schools where it would be more effective. It was necessary that all Mexicans, without exception, be educated exactly alike. In 1875 Barreda proposed that primary education be com-

[37] Ibid., p. 30.

pulsory for all Mexicans. This idea was opposed by the liberals, who considered it an attack on the rights of man, that is, the right to act and think freely. Barreda, in referring to the attacks of the liberals, said: "The perfect sincerity of this belief—that of compulsory education—has finally overcome everywhere the scruples of certain metaphysical consciences. These consciences, believing that compulsory education is an attack on individual freedom, are resigned to seeing us die of inactivity before supporting a measure that our social state urgently demands, just because they feel that it violates one of the rights of man."[38]

For Barreda, the rights of man could be reduced to the right held by everyone "to live and to pursue his development and well-being."[39] In opposing the thesis of the liberals, which held that man as an individual had the right to do as he pleased, Barreda said that "the rights of society are more important than the rights of man."[40] The rights of society were reduced to the well-being of all its members. The common well-being, that well-being to which all men are entitled, said Barreda, was a right to which every man should and can aspire. The rights of man, as individual rights, are opposed to the right possessed by the members of society as a whole—the right to well-being.

Gabino Barreda later attacked the liberal thesis concerning freedom. He said that freedom should not be understood in a laissez faire sense, but as something limited by the necessities of society. He openly opposed liberalism, which eight years earlier he had tried to cajole in his "Civic Oration," when he said that "many members of the liberal party in good faith still believe that the law that decreed compulsory primary education is irreconcilable with the principles that they profess,"[41] and therefore they have attacked it. Freedom, Barreda said, is a very useful principle. Respect for individual freedom was a tenet of the liberal creed. It assumed that the government should not intervene in the private life of the individual and the family. "But it is universally acknowledged that there are many exceptions to this rule. Nobody believes that

[38] Gabino Barreda, "Algunas ideas respecto a instrucción pública," in *Opúsculos, discusiones y discursos*, p. 160.
[39] Ibid., p. 160. Remember Mora; see § 33, note 37, of Section Two.
[40] G. Barreda, "Algunas ideas respecto a instrucción pública," p. 160.
[41] Ibid., p. 161.

public authority is transgressing the law of individual freedom when it prevents an individual from violating the life or property of another, or when it inflicts a punishment on anyone who has committed such offenses. No one admits that to punish someone for fraud or for neglecting to fulfill a contract is an attack on freedom."[42] If these evils were not prevented, freedom would be a calamity rather than a good.

Barreda explained freedom on the basis of social *statics*. Through social statics one can find out whether an institution is essential for society and its evolution, "and it will depend on the conclusions arrived at," said Barreda, "as to whether the corresponding institution will be considered justifiable and moral."[43] There have been areas in which freedom was socially possible in some periods of history and impossible in others, for example, the area of slavery. The right to have slaves was indispensable in a period like that of ancient Greece. But nowadays, said Barreda, it is a crime whose price one pays for with one's life. The same can be said of compulsory education. It is a question of convenience and social stability. "If we admit that it is useful and advantageous, we should not be concerned as to whether that obligation is opposed to the principles of freedom. If we can prove that in the present state of civilization primary education is not purely a condition of improvement, but is necessary for existence and the progress of society, the question will definitely be solved not only in favor of primary education, but also in favor of an authority to impose that obligation on all citizens."[44] Freedom, therefore, depended on progress. Individual freedom was increasingly limited as social obligations became more numerous.

Barreda was also opposed to the liberal thesis that held that freedom was an unchangeable natural right of man. For Barreda such a natural right did not exist. The only right that existed was one that originated in society, that is, one that evolved historically. What was a social good yesterday may today be evil. Hence, the freedom in education that the individual used to have was a social good yesterday; but now this freedom represents backwardness and social evil. The freedom of the individual should be subordinated to

42 Ibid., p. 161.
43 Ibid., p. 166.
44 Ibid., p. 167.

the good of society. Compulsory education was a social necessity, said Barreda, "because we are convinced that this is the only road, slow but sure, that avoids the evils that afflict society, especially ours."[45]

§ 46. *Education as a Means to Avoid Social Anarchy*

Anarchy was the social evil that Barreda wished to avoid through a plan of education for all Mexicans. Anarchy sprouts from the absence of firm beliefs. In the evolution of society a series of beliefs disappeared. Either they were not replaced by other beliefs or they were replaced by fantasies. The absence of firm beliefs makes individuals take refuge in scepticism, which leads to anarchy. Or they blindly, through the use of violence, take refuge in dogmas that are opposed to reason and demonstration. "This same lack of faith in our so-called principles," said Barreda, "can be seen in the violent means to which we resort to support them, means that reveal the depths of our souls, in which instead of conviction there is inconstancy, and instead of enthusiasm, there are tyranny and puerile inanity."[46]

Mexico had fallen into anarchy and violence through the absence of beliefs. Barreda proposed to end this anarchy and violence by offering the Mexicans new beliefs. These beliefs were to be supported by positivist demonstration. To attain a new social order, it was necessary that the individual abandon every interpretation based on scepticism and intolerance and subordinate these interpretations to demonstrated truths. The purpose of schooling was to offer Mexicans demonstrated truths and to eliminate ideas based on fantasy or scepticism. The new beliefs were to be based on scientific demonstration. No belief could be imposed except by demonstration. Through this education, said Barreda, "terror and the inquisition will never arise again, not because of the objections of philosophers and moralists, but because the point of view has changed. The methods used in solving problems are different. Observation and experimentation have replaced authority, and science has replaced ontology."[47]

Education based on a positive philosophy would make Jacobin

[45] Ibid., p. 170.
[46] Ibid., p. 170.
[47] Ibid., p. 174.

and conservative violence impossible. Forceful imposition of ideas had passed into history; now every belief or idea was to be demonstrated. The school was the laboratory where all ideas and beliefs were demonstrated and proven. In school one would find out the real truths. In school every individual would learn a body of truths that were demonstrated and not imposed. The school would make tyranny impossible. All violence and disorder would disappear, because tyranny was merely imposed anarchy. "The permanent perspective of being able to transform mere belief into conviction, faith into demonstration," said Barreda, "is not only the best and most incessant stimulant for learning, but it is also the best defense against the intolerance of tyranny. He who is certain of being able to convince will never be tempted to impose a belief by force; he will be able to sympathize with him who does not have the aptitude to understand demonstration, but he will never persecute him; he will be more or less inclined to instruct him, but not to exterminate him."[48]

Barreda wanted to establish a new type of belief through which social order would be possible; he wanted to convince Mexicans, through demonstrated truths, of the necessity of order. He wanted to convince rather than impose. These new truths, demonstrated by positive science, were considered not to contradict other beliefs or ideas; for this it was necessary to abstain from interpreting these other beliefs, because they could not be demonstrated. Positive science was certain of its truths. Therefore it did not have to impose them. It did not have to use violence on those who did not accept them. It knew that its truths could be demonstrated to the incredulous when they were ready for them. Therefore, "positivist philosophy does not abhor theologians or theology," said Barreda. "It considers the former retarded in the march of humanity and it tries to pave and illuminate for them the way to progress and emancipation. . . . Of all the emancipating philosophies, positivism is the only one that recognizes the great services of theology to humanity."[49] If positivism opposed theologists and metaphysicians, if Barreda opposed clerical and Jacobin ideas, it was because their supporters tried to impose their doctrines. Barreda held up Robes-

[48] Ibid., p. 183.

[49] Gabino Barreda, "Rectificaciones históricas," in *Opúsculos, discusiones y discursos*, p. 205.

pierre as an example of Jacobin or metaphysical intolerance. This revolutionary was the symbol of those who used force as an instrument to convince, justifying this procedure by the supposed existence of a metaphysical entity called a Supreme Being, which gave freedom to man. According to this idea, said Barreda, "the Republic was decreed by the Supreme Being from all eternity; then everything that is not republican infringes on divine laws and merits death."[50] "Anyone who did not believe in the sovereignty of the people, in equality, and in the political dogmas of the revolution was an enemy and deserved to die."[51]

§ 47. Jacobinism Considered by Barreda as the Chief Enemy of His Plan of Education

We have already seen how Barreda considered the extreme liberals, the Jacobins, as the most dangerous enemies of his plan of education. In 1877, ten years after praising the liberals as the embodiment of the positive spirit, he spoke of those same liberals as the incarnation of the negative spirit, that is, of anarchy, when he said: "We do not want to attack anybody; we do not come to occupy a place that is now deserted; we have come to set up the banner of science where the others have fallen either by their own weight or by the corrosive action of negativism; we have come to set up the unshakeable standard of truth and the full concordance of the objective and the subjective, to replace the desolate discord that the eighteenth century has left us as an inheritance; we have not come to injure beliefs, but to awaken them in those who have none. Anarchy in every form—intellectual, political, moral, personal, domestic and civil—is the only monarch that we wish to dethrone, the only banner that we want to overthrow; the others have already been demolished. Our responsibility is no greater than that an astronomer observing an eclipse has for the lack of light. If having anticipated the lack ahead of time, he orders that other light be supplied, this does not justify to sensible people the accusation that he is the author of this phenomenon."[52]

---

[50] Gabino Barreda, "Mahoma y Robespierre," published in *Revista Positiva* and in *Opúsculos, discusiones y discursos*, p. 247.

[51] G. Barreda, "Rectificaciones históricas," p. 220.

[52] Gabino Barreda, "Discurso leído en la distribución de recompensas escolares," in *Estudios* and *Opúsculos, discusiones y discursos*, p. 221.

Barreda's mission was to reestablish order. Nothing was more violently opposed to this mission than the liberal doctrine, which originated in the eighteenth century. The ideas that originated in this century, according to Barreda, made social order impossible. Barreda said that the positivists were not opposed to any idea; they respected all beliefs. All that they were opposed to was anarchy in all its forms. They were not opposed to any banner, because there were no longer any banners; but they wanted to set up a new one. They did not wish to be polemical, because there was nothing to argue about. They wanted only order. To secure this order they would have to confront every ideology that continued to support disorder. They did not come to injure beliefs, because beliefs did not exist; they only came to awaken them. Instead of coming to destroy by force, the positivists insisted that they came to construct. The Mexican bourgeoisie had entered into its constructive phase. It now opposed the ideologies that previously had served them as instruments to destroy an order that was not theirs. The doctrine of the Mexican bourgeoisie was now constructive; it wanted to bring about order, no longer having reason to fight. The bourgeoisie, once it had destroyed the old beliefs, would try to establish new ones. In this constructive work, the Mexican bourgeoisie knew that it would have to be careful not to destroy what had already been constructed. In its combative phase, it saw how some ideas destroyed others and how the struggle could provoke anarchy. Thus, it was careful not to oppose those ideas that it would try to construct to the ideas that still remained. Thus, it also adopted a doctrine of abstaining from judging ideas that could not be demonstrated.

To favor any one idea or group of ideas is to provoke disorder. Hence, through Barreda, the bourgeoisie insisted that it did not oppose any idea or belief. The social order should be separated from the personal beliefs of each Mexican. The banner that he wished to set up was a social banner; therefore, it should be in the service of everyone. It did not contradict the ideas of the individual. The ideas that the Mexican individual professed were not dangerous so long as they did not oppose order; if they opposed order, then they were dangerous. This was the case of the Jacobins, who were not content to maintain their ideas as individuals, but who defended them and opposed them to the social order. For

Barreda, Jacobinism represented a doctrine of disorder and violence. In a polemic concerning Robespierre, which Barreda sustained with Justo Sierra,[53] he attacked Jacobinism as representing a doctrine of violence and disorder. Opposed to this doctrine was positivism, which was incapable of affirming and much less of imposing anything that had not yet been demonstrated. Positivism was the only philosophy that could make order possible. Its theories could not provoke disorder, because they were available to anyone who wished to prove the truth, that is, to all Mexicans. It was the only philosophy in a position to offer a common fund of truth for the order and well-being of all Mexicans.

[53] G. Barreda, "Mahoma y Robespierre."

IV. Barreda's Defense of His Plan of Education

§ 48. *Attacks on Barreda's Plan of Education*

Gabino Barreda's plan of education suffered a series of attacks by both the conservatives and the liberals. In the foregoing chapter we noted the allusions that Barreda made to some of these attacks, which were gradually mutilating his original plan. Barreda's plan was first reformed in 1868 and in 1869. In 1873 his plan was bitterly attacked. His opponents considered some of the courses in medicine and jurisprudence, namely, analytical and infinitesimal calculus, as unnecessary; hence, they were eliminated. In 1877 the minister of education, Ignacio Ramírez, arranged that future architects no longer had to study Castilian grammar, literature, and logic.[54]

In 1880, when don Ezequiel Montes was secretary of public education, a law attacking positivist education was passed. It decreed that the logic texts of John Stuart Mill and Alexander Bain, which were used in the preparatory school, be replaced by the

---

[54] Concerning the reforms made in Barreda's plan of education, refer to the excellent exposition of his son, Horacio Barreda, entitled, "La Escuela Nacional Preparatoria: Lo que se quería que fuese este plantel de educación y lo que hoy se quiere que sea," *Revista Positiva* 8 (1908). A résumé of these reforms is found in the prologue by José Fuentes Mares, *Estudios de Gabino Barreda.*

logic text of Gilleraume Tiberghien. This Belgian Krausist intellectual became known in Mexico in the *colegio* of lawyers through the lawyer Juan José de la Garza. Montes supported this law for the same reasons that the Catholics and the liberals opposed positivism: positivism gave no sure answer to questions regarding the moral order, the existence of God, the existence of the soul, and the destiny of man. On the other hand, the logic of Tiberghien, although written by a liberal, contained a spiritualist philosophy. This same decree stated that positivism attacked freedom of conscience because it denied the spiritual education imparted by the parents to their children. The government, said the decree, was not concerned about the fact that positivism was the only philosophy. It was concerned about the fact that it was a philosophy that attacked the rights of respectable citizens. Positivism was a doctrine that attacked the individual's dominion over home and conscience. The government should be neutral, that is, it should protect all cults. It should not permit this type of instruction.

"In vain," stated the decree, "is it said that positivist logic does not contradict religion, because it claims to neither affirm nor deny anything. This is not true; it affirms that you cannot know anything, that is, that it is impossible to be certain about anything."[55] Such a thesis necessarily led to religious scepticism. The decree considered the text of Tiberghien less hostile toward religion. Another accusation against the positivist philosophy was that it caused social corruption: "suicide, disturbances, lack of obedience, vice, and libertinism are observed in youth," which are caused by positivist instruction, said the decree. Furthermore, because of positivist education, hostility toward democratic institutions has increased and the enemies of such institutions have been strengthened. The Catholic church, said the decree, had gained in strength as parents tried to rescue their children from an education opposed to morals. There has been an increase in the number of seminaries and Catholic schools in which "there is taught a hatred for democratic institutions and for those who defend these institutions." The dilemma described in this decree was as follows: Either it eliminate an education that, through its scepticism, was opposed

[55] The text of the decree can be found in Emeterio Valverde Téllez, *Bibliografía filosófica mexicana*, vol. 2.

to religion and morality, or let it be, while religious instruction that was opposed to the government increased.[56]

Behind these attacks, which came from members of the Mexican government itself, one could perceive the desire for order that characterized the Mexican bourgeoisie. Positivism claimed to be the ideal instrument to make Mexicans think in terms of order. However, this original idea had been refuted because positivism clashed with other ideas. It did not remain neutral. It has already been seen in the afore-mentioned decree how the scepticism caused by the positivist philosophy attacked religious dogmas. Positivism was useful, provided it did not try to impose a doctrine on society. That would be dangerous because the enemies of the bourgeoisie would join to condemn it. Barreda's plan of education was gradually sacrificed by order of the Mexican bourgeoisie. Positivism was an instrument in the service of the Mexican bourgeoisie. Therefore, the bourgeoisie could accept only those ideas that were useful; it had to exclude everything that endangered the order that it had established. The Mexican bourgeoisie's ideal of order came to supersede the positivist ideal of order.

§ 49. *The New Plan of Public Education and Its Criticisms*

In spite of the attacks against positivism by those who saw it as endangering order, the Mexican positivists defended the thesis that the positivist order was the one needed by Mexican society. They did not concede to their enemies the right to say that their plan of education was against the constitution or the interests of society. If order was the objective of positivist education, then one could not say that this education was opposed to order. Gabino Barreda wrote and published an article entitled "Instrucción pública."[57] In this article he criticized the plan of educational reform of those who wished to destroy his own plan. The new plan was formulated by a group of liberal ideological deputies, one of whom was the lawyer Guillermo Prieto. Gabino Barreda analyzed the proposed educational reform and demolished it paragraph by paragraph.

Barreda defended his own plan on the grounds that it accomplished the aim for which it was intended. The best way to establish a permanent social order, said Barreda, was through education.

[56] Ibid.
[57] Gabino Barreda, "Instrucción pública," *Revista Positiva* 1 (1901).

Education should be an instrument in the service of order. Order in the mind and spirit produces order in society. Social or material order depends on spiritual order. Citizens with ordered minds are citizens with an ordered society. The educational reform of Barreda proposed to order the mind. This order was indispensable after more than half a century of disorder in which the Mexicans destroyed themselves because of the absence of a doctrine to unite them. Once the material order was obtained by the military weapons of the conquerors, a spiritual order was necessary to make the material order permanent. Order imposed by weapons was not enough. The material order would merely be ephemeral if Mexican minds continued to be disordered. A durable material order was not possible except through a spiritual order. The school of Barreda tried to produce this type of order. Hence, every new attempt at educational reform had to be careful not to alter the order that the present law of education sustained. When he analyzed the reform project proposed by the liberals, Barreda said, "I am persuaded that the resolution concerning such a grave matter, taken at a time when everything leads us to believe that peace is definitely consolidated in our country, and the plan to be adopted, could contribute very powerfully, if they are successful, to perpetuate this peace and to cement order, the only basis and guarantee of real progress."[58] On the basis of this consideration, Barreda criticized the new plan. He tried to determine if the liberal plan was capable of protecting the social order. Every point proposed in the projected reform was a criticism of Barreda's plan of education. Barreda in turn defended his own plan and criticized the new one.

The first point advocated absolute freedom of instruction. It said that no requisite should be demanded of the students other than that of instruction. This point attacked the reform of Barreda as being sectarian. Implicitly, it manifested that the instruction in force in the preparatory schools was doctrinaire. It said that a doctrine was being taught in spite of the fact that the constitution had declared that education should be secular. The authors of the new project felt that the only mission of public education was to instruct, that is, to teach the students a series of subjects that would

[58] Ibid., p. 259.

be useful for them in an instrumental sense; for instance, lawyers should be taught law, doctors medicine, and engineers mathematics. But it should try not to make all of them think in a certain and uniform way. The way a person thinks should be up to him. The authors of the project were opposed to Barreda's thesis of making all students accept "a common fund of truths." The truth was something that each individual should seek for himself through his own reason.

The thesis sustained by the authors of the project was, according to Barreda, a thesis that was opposed to the social order and to public peace. An individual should think and believe as he pleases, provided that his thoughts and beliefs do not alter the social order. The mission of public education was not merely to teach; it was to make public order possible. Besides, said Barreda, this point was invalid, because preparatory education was already free. Of course, we already know what Barreda meant by freedom. When he said that preparatory instruction was free, he meant that all the sciences taught in the preparatory schools could be demonstrated. Everything taught in the preparatory schools was demonstrable, which meant that it could be accepted freely by everyone. Everything that could be demonstrated must be accepted by all; here there was no room for freedom in a negative sense; no one could deny that which could be demonstrated beyond any doubt. This was what was accomplished in the preparatory schools: to teach the positive, that is, the demonstrable, which meant that one was free only to affirm, not to deny. With reference to what the project said about useful education, Barreda said: what greater utility and what better education can there be than to teach the students to live as good citizens?

The second point that opposed the educational reform of Barreda proposed that professional students not be overloaded with sciences that were not used in their field. This second point was opposed to the encyclopedic character of education, which was established to give the students a common fund of positive truths. It was opposed to Barreda's thesis in favor of an organic education, whereby he wanted every student to know the positive sciences, no matter what career he chose. We have seen how Barreda considered this kind of education to be indispensable for establishing the social order. If all students studied the same scientific courses, there would be uniformity of opinion, regardless of the individual's profession or occupation. The student would then be in a better position to understand his fellowman.

Barreda said that if this second point was approved, which, in fact, it would be, the existence of the preparatory school would be unnecessary. The student would then pass directly to the professional school. According to Barreda, the preparatory school had a greater mission than to prepare professionals. That mission was to prepare Mexicans to live together as good citizens. Only this living together would make national order possible. Social order was possible through the unity of criteria obtained through an encyclopedic and organic education. If this type of education was attacked, the preparatory school would lose its reason for existing.

The third point recommended an increase of specialized schools. Such an increase, said Barreda, would be an attack on order. To establish schools of specialization was to foment discord among Mexicans, because each individual would understand only his field of specialization. The fourth point stated that there should be no more special students. This point, said Barreda, was no reform because in fact no student in the preparatory school could pass from one grade to the other without having finished the corresponding studies.

The fifth point of the reform project stated that "primary education should be free and compulsory throughout the Republic."[59] Barreda agreed wholeheartedly with this point. We have already seen how Barreda defended free and compulsory primary education. However, he adopted a position of extreme realism when he said that, although excellent, such a desire is impracticable at this time except if one understands by "the whole Republic" the Federal District. If it meant the whole Mexican Republic, the government was financially unable to realize this project. Barreda's criticism on this point was not significant, because he agreed with it. His criticism amounted to pointing out the impracticality of the project. He criticized the education that the authors of the project had received, and went on to criticize the former system of education to which, he said, the authors of the new project wished to return. At the same time he tried to point out the advantages of his own reform.

[59] Ibid., p. 265.

The former education developed dreamers, men who were unrealistic and who wished to adapt reality to their fantasies. "The replacement of those five years badly spent in that purely Scholastic and empty education by another five years employed fruitfully in studying nature as it is and not as we want it to be, in seeing the facts themselves and not what we imagine them to be, and, finally, in making of ourselves practical men in the true meaning of the word and not political dreamers or any other class of dreamer, has been, as I propose to demonstrate later, one of the principal advantages in favor of the plan that is now in effect."[60] Those who attacked Barreda's plan, then, were unrealistic, that is, they had had an impractical education. Their education had made them impractical idealists and dreamers. On the other hand, those educated in the positive sciences were genuine realists. They were practical men who did not waste time on dreams. They wanted only what facts demonstrated to be possible. Those educated in the positivist doctrine were practical. They did not dream. But, was not the positivist ideal also a dream? Weren't the positivists also idealists and dreamers in spite of themselves? In fact, these realists tried to produce an ideal person.

§ 50. *The Defense of Spiritual Power against Civil Power*

The final points of the project and Barreda's criticisms against them were most important because they brought to light an ideal that had hitherto been hidden by the positivists. This ideal would be clarified many years later by the followers of Barreda, including his son, Horacio Barreda. This ideal was that the positivists would take over the spiritual vacuum left by the Catholic church. Although this ideal was not made explicit by Barreda, it still became apparent, as will be pointed out later.

The sixth point of the project against Barreda's reform stated that the Junta Directiva de Educación should not be constituted of professors who taught in the public schools. This, said Barreda, meant the loss of most of the members from the Junta Directiva, because all of them were practicing professors. "Do they wish to declare," asked Barreda, "that anybody on the street is better qualified [Barreda referred to texts, a task assigned to the Junta] than those who have dedicated their lives to the honorable teach-

---

[60] Ibid., p. 266.

ing profession and to the study and continuous meditation that it demands?"[61] If so, Barreda continued, then "most of the functions of the Junta would disappear and, consequently, the usefulness of the Junta would also disappear, because its members would not have an intimate, immediate, and continuous knowledge of the public schools."[62] Furthermore, "to ask that the consultative body of public education not be composed of professors, because they have personal and corporate interests, would be like saying that the Mexican secretaries of state should not be Mexicans, because they would be partial."[63]

In this way Gabino Barreda defended the group that was entrusted with the task of ordering the minds of the Mexican people. This was the same group, said Horacio Barreda, that they wanted to divest of the spiritual power of the nation. We have seen that the mission of public education was to establish spiritual order through which material and social order would be possible. Educators had the task of guiding and ordering the minds of the Mexicans; the state had the task of preserving material order. Educators and governments were two forces that had a mission of order: one the spiritual order and the other the material. They needed each other but they should not interfere with each other's particular functions. Each should fulfill his own mission without disturbing the other. Hence, the material power should not interfere in the functions of the spiritual power, which should be given full freedom to fulfill its functions efficaciously. To prohibit the members of the Junta Directiva de Educación, the only ones capable of the task, from directing the spiritual field is to destroy spiritual power. To substitute people foreign to educational occupations for the professors of the Junta is to destroy spiritual power, which was left as a vacuum in Mexico after the spiritual power of the church collapsed. The partiality of which the members of the Junta were accused was characteristic of any body. Those who represented the spiritual power of Mexico had to be partial in regard to its problems, just as every Mexican official had to be partial in regard to the problems of Mexico. The purpose of the reform program of the liberals was to destroy a power that was discrimina-

61 Ibid., p. 269.
62 Ibid., p. 272.
63 Ibid., p. 273.

tory. They knew that by taking the professors out of the Junta Directiva de Educación they could destroy the basis of a possible spiritual power with which they disagreed.

The Mexican liberals wanted to destroy the basis of a new spiritual order, hence their hostility to a homogeneous education called "a common fund of truths" for everyone, regardless of what profession one pursued. In fact, it was this type of education that was meant to be the basis of a new spiritual power. Remember that Barreda intended to accomplish with the Mexican mind what the Jesuits failed to do; namely, he did not want to leave a crack open to the individual, lest he make an error. The individual was not to interpret anything according to his own criterion. Barreda proposed a plan of education that would make all Mexicans think alike. But, who would be in charge of this task? Who would have the power to mold the minds of the Mexicans? This power would be in the hands of a new social group, that is, a new caste, which we can generally call the positivists. The Mexican liberals would unite with the Catholics against this power, this new corps. The developing struggle was a struggle for spiritual power.

Barreda defended the ideal of a new spiritual order, which would be directed by those educated in the positivist philosophy, when he defended his plan of education from the attacks that were launched against it. In defending an organic and encyclopedic education, he said: ". . . they desire [he refers to the authors of the educational reform] that preparatory studies be planned in such a way that the student would acquire only knowledge needed in his profession."[64] They merely wanted, said Barreda, to return to an education of castes. Barreda said that education should have a social end and not one of castes. And this end should be the same for all citizens. To attain this result, professions could not be shrouded in secrecy and made to serve only certain individual goals. It was necessary to show how all the professions were linked together in the pursuance of a social goal. The mission of the preparatory school was to establish a bond of union among all the professions. This mission would be realized through showing the relationship between the positive sciences, which would create a feeling of cooperation among all the students.

[64] Ibid., p. 284.

Barreda said that an incomplete education was one worthy only of a theological age and not of a positive age, such as we now live in. An education that tried to form only professionals was an education that was similar to the one of castes. In a society of castes, said Barreda, each social class had a certain mission that could not be transferred. The individual was predestined to dedicate himself to a certain profession. The class to which he belonged determined what kind of education he would receive. Every man was educated to be either a doctor, priest, or king. Since the education for these professions was secret, it could not be transferred to those who did not belong to the castes. According to this type of education, discoveries were kept secret. "Anyone who made a discovery that led to the founding of an art or a profession," said Barreda, "had to keep it, as well as its development, a secret. He would make it his own patrimony and later that of his family. . . . This obligation to keep a seal on every type of knowledge made an education that was not entirely specialized impossible."[65] It was impossible, said Barreda, for this system of education to be any more than antisocial and selfish.

Now, said Barreda, this system of education has been replaced by Catholic education. Upon taking over education, the Catholic church established a homogeneous type of education, one that was the same for everyone. The Jesuits were most associated with this type of education. "With this institution, and with the objective of the clergy to abolish the hereditary character of its functions and priestly dignities, every vestige of caste education completely disappeared."[66] And, said Barreda, "to attempt today to revive in a republic this inadequate and narrow education called specialties . . . is to go back three thousand years, that is, to an age in which the most evident necessities of our era were unknown."[67]

This is the way that Barreda defended the idea that everyone should be educated alike. He accused those who tried to change this principle of being reactionary and selfish. It was necessary to have a positive education to fulfill the needs of a positive society. Nothing, except the ignorance of the authors of the project, could explain their opposition to this idea. "With positive satisfaction,

65 Ibid., p. 285.
66 Ibid., p. 285.
67 Ibid., p. 286.

I recognize and proclaim that my friend Mr. D. Guillermo Prieto is, in my judgment, the best lyric poet in my country and, perhaps, in America. No one surpasses him in expressing his emotions and personal affections, but I cannot give him credit for subjects that he is not familiar with, subjects that he has never studied."[68]

Barreda was saying that only those educated in the sciences were qualified to talk about education. He defended the rights of those who were to form the new spiritual power against outsiders who he said were not competent to make judgments. No one had the right to talk about education except educators themselves.

Barreda went on to defend the present plan of preparatory studies. He explained how each subject was useful in forming capable citizens who would benefit society and themselves. In his defense of his plan of preparatory studies, it is interesting to note his reference to literature. Literature seemed to be incompatible with a positive type of education, which generally included the natural sciences. But Barreda included literature and he defended it as a useful subject in his overall plan, that is, to form useful citizens in society. Barreda considered literature useful because it balanced the heart and the head, the sentiments and the reasoning faculties. He said that an education concerned only with the positive sciences would form an individual without sentiments. Such a person could feel no love for his fellowman; his heart would wither. "As a branch of education it is impossible to fail to cultivate one of the fine arts most apt to inspire in us the sentiments of beauty, harmony, the just, and the great. The abstract study of the pure sciences tends to wither our hearts; it is best to use poetry as an antidote before the evil becomes incurable. Poetry, I say, will prevent pure science from withering up the heart."[69]

These men, such as Barreda and his followers, who subordinated sentiments to positive reality, were looking for an escape for these sentiments. This escape, they believed, would be found in the fine arts. Order at all costs would make the development of the sentiments impossible. Thus, it was necessary to look for a substitute where these sentiments could be sublimated. They could not accept anything that the positive sciences did not demonstrate. They wanted to work only with demonstrated realities. They did not

[68] Ibid., p. 293, note at the end.
[69] Ibid., p. 320.

want to idealize. Everything that upset order and social well-being was fantasy. However, fantasy, the faculty of idealizing, sentiments, could not be destroyed, considering that they were a part of human nature. The positivists, as much as they tried, could not ignore the fact that they were human. Hence, they looked for a substitute that would give an outlet to their sentiments. That substitute was sentimental poetry, fantastic legends, and imagination. This was an era in which those educated in positivism were not concerned about their companions of flesh and blood. On the other hand, moved by poetical fiction, they suffered with the protagonists of the novel and applied their imaginations to common events, making them seem extraordinary.[70] They were the same men who, like one of the followers of Barreda, supported harsh theses against the dispossessed classes while at the same time they talked of a great love for a fictitious entity called humanity. Not included in that humanity were those who needed the cooperation said to be due humanity. In the name of this entity the positivists wanted a particular order in which they would enjoy the best position.

The liberals attacked this order. Barreda called them sectarian and blind because they could not see that the order that he supported was that of the new era. Barreda said that they were blind to the progress of humanity, which had arrived at its positive stage. Furthermore, he accused them of wanting to establish a new sect and new infallible authorities that had no basis of support. "The substitution of the natural sciences for the syllogism, of inductive reasoning for the interpretation of texts and authorities, and of the interpretation of nature and experimentation for argumentation should little by little change that state of things. But this change was not so easy as one would believe at first sight. We have already noted that the present-day intellectuals, those who are not too familiar with the natural sciences, would oppose it just like the theologians who condemned Galileo. The only difference was that, instead of using a text from the Bible or a canon as a major premise for their syllogism, they started with a principle of Rousseau, Hobbes, Adam Smith, or Chevalier."[71]

[70] Concerning the imaginative feeling of the Mexicans in this period, refer to José C. Valadés's chapter entitled "La poética de la sociedad," in *El porfirismo*.
[71] G. Barreda, "Instrucción pública," p. 320.

A dispute over spiritual power was behind all this discussion. The liberals would accuse the positivists of being sectarians and vice versa. Actually, both liberals and positivists were sectarians; both were fighting for spiritual power. The clergy also entered the dispute to regain its power. Later it will be seen how the clergy, which lost its spiritual power, and the liberals, who also aspired for a certain order, would unite to attack the common enemy: Mexican positivism. Furthermore, the state would intervene in this battle, alleging the same reason as the liberals and the Catholics who opposed positivism. This reason was: it was a sectarian philosophy. They were correct. The state, exponent of the interests of the Mexican bourgeoisie, which held material power, would discover that positivism did not offer the desired basis for order. It would realize that positivism was merely an instrument in the service of a group that wanted to control spiritual power. And it was opposed to the original desire of the Mexican bourgeoisie, that for peace and order. To entrust spiritual power to another group implied the return to anarchy, for it was taken for granted that the liberals and the Catholics would fight for this power. For the Mexican bourgeoisie, positivism was merely an instrument in the service of the material order. For such an order, it was necessary that various beliefs exist together in society and that no particular belief represent the spiritual power. Positivism was one of these beliefs. It was necessary to have a society in which Catholics, Jacobins, and positivists could live together. This idea would be carried out during the period of Porfirismo. To fulfill this idea it was necessary to destroy the power that threatened to be dominant. Hence, the reform of Barreda's original plan of education. Social equilibrium was sought in these reforms. Those points concerning social interests were changed without any concern for the positivists, who claimed to possess the true philosophy, that of a common fund of truths valid for all society.

Gabino Barreda, according to Agustín Aragón, foresaw "the progressive and complete independence of education from public, civil or political power, through the Junta Directiva de Instrucción Pública of the Federal District."[72] Through the Junta, which the liberals wished to divest of its professors, as we have seen, Gabino Barreda tried to establish a spiritual power independent of the ma-

[72] Agustín Aragón, "Gabino Barreda y sus discípulos."

terial power, which would fill the vacuum left by the Catholic church. Horacio Barreda will express this idea more explicitly. However, the idea would not be successful, because it was opposed to the interests of the class that possessed the material power, the Mexican bourgeoisie. The positivists who would be successful within this class were those who would sacrifice their ideology to the material interests of the class to which they belonged. The positivists who had the better posts in the Porfirian government were those who used positivism as a tool of material power. They used positivism as a political weapon in a purely material sense.

SECTION FOUR:
THE DEVELOPMENT,
"THE DISCIPLES"

I. The Positivists and the Construction of the New Order

§ 51. *The Foundation of the Asociación Metodófila*

On February 4, 1877, ten years after the triumph of the revolution called the Reform and Gabino Barreda's entry into the Juárez government to reorganize public education, the bases that were to regulate the Asociación Metodófila "Gabino Barreda" were approved under the presidency of Barreda himself. The approved regulations provided for the following:

1. A treatise, whose subject would be announced one month in advance, will be read at each session.

2. The members will carefully select the author of the treatise.

3. All the members can propose subjects.

4. The member who formulates a subject is to make clear the idea behind it.

5. The sessions will be held on Sundays. They will last two hours, beginning at 10:00 A.M.

6. In case no one asks to speak, the president may recognize any member.

7. Every three months, instead of a scientific dissertation, the biography of one of the benefactors of humanity is to be presented.

8. The society is not opposed to anyone speaking about any problem as he desires.[1]

Most of the members in this society came from the medical school. Also, there were two from jurisprudence, one from engineering, and one from pharmacy. Later, some of the students from this group became outstanding second-generation positivist teachers. They included Porfirio Parra, Miguel S. Macedo, Luis F. Ruiz, and Manuel Flores. The engineer Agustín Aragón was also important. He joined the positivists because he read two of the papers published by the Asociación. Aragón said the following: ". . . le travail du Dr. Parra sur *les causes premières*, l'essai sur *les devoirs réciproques des supérieurs et des inférieurs* par l'avocat Miguel S. Macedo: ces deux dernières études, dont les auteurs devraient devenir mes maîtres, dénotent une acceptation franche et complète des idées d'Auguste Comte. Ma conversion au Positivisme date de cette époque."[2] The work of Gabino Barreda in this society was that of teacher. He saw that the exposition and reply of the papers presented by his followers did not deviate from the method that he taught them. This method, which everyone considered the firmest and surest, was the positivist method. Barreda carefully interpreted every idea and question that was proposed according to the positivist method. Every idea that could not endure such a test was eliminated.

One of the chief purposes of the Asociación Metodófila was to show how a group of men in different fields of specialization could understand each other and unite by means of certain basic principles, and by means of a method of interpretation that could be applied uniformly to diverse problems. Various studies on different problems were presented by the Asociación Metodófila. They dealt with astronomy, physics, chemistry, biology, medicine, mathematics, sociology, and the lives of such great men as Dante and Galileo. The Asociación followed Barreda's ideal of supplying

---

[1] *Anales de la Asociación Metodófila "Gabino Barreda."*

[2] "*Las causas primeras*, by Dr. Parra, and *Ensayo sobre los deberes recíprocos de los superiores y de los inferiores*, by the lawyer Miguel S. Macedo: these two studies, whose authors were to become my masters, denote a frank and complete acceptance of the ideas of Auguste Comte. My conversion to positivism dates back to this period" (Agustín Aragón, *Essai sur l'histoire du positivisme au Mexique*, p. 44).

a "common fund of truths." There was only one method applied to the different questions that were presented to the Asociación: the positivist method. The members of the society subjected their ideas to the method that they had learned in the Preparatory School.

The young men who met every Sunday under the direction of Gabino Barreda were for the most part students educated at the National Preparatory School. They represented the first fruits of the reform carried out by Barreda in the preparatory school. By meeting with their teacher they were to prove the results of his work. In the Asociación Metodófila the ideas resulting from the ideological foundation that these students had received were tested. The success of the social mission entrusted to Barreda, who supplied its ideological basis, depended on this test. The followers of Barreda would prove whether they were men of orderly mind and capable of protecting the order that Mexican society so badly needed.

Porfirio Parra, in expounding the motives of the founders of the Asociación Metodófila, said, "We consider it a sacred duty to collaborate with our contemporaries to develop the great work of the future; hence, the obligation of explaining the nature of the subjects to which we are dedicated, in exposing the grain of sand that we intend to contribute toward raising the great edifice of reconstruction, of explaining to the public the reasons why we are asking for its attention."[3] The ideal of the followers of Barreda, expressed by one of their most outstanding members, was to reconstruct a great edifice, which was the Mexican nation. They said through their expounder that they wanted to collaborate with a grain of sand in the work of raising the destroyed edifice. It was this grain of sand, converted into a hard block, which would impose the sense of order that would inspire the great period known as Porfirismo. These young men entered public life conscious of the fact that they possessed a method of incalculable value. Parra said in a humble tone, ". . . however much we are convinced of our personal inadequacy, however little we signify in the solemn current of progress in our century, we consider ourselves active although imperceptible members of the great body of societies."[4] As

[3] Porfirio Parra, Introduction to *Anales de la Asociación Metodófila*, p. 6.
[4] Ibid., p. 6.

members of this body of societies, they were obligated to cooperate in the great task of constructing the building that secured and organized them. And, although conscious of possible personal inadequacy, they were also conscious of the fact that they possessed a method of reconstruction considered as infallible. They knew that they possessed an instrument capable of fully carrying out the work of social reconstruction. Porfirio Parra spoke of the marvelous method that would be used in reconstruction: "Initiated in the scientific method, thanks to a systematic and eminently philosophic education that we apply to every class of phenomena and in every case draw definite conclusions capable of inspiring the most intimate convictions, we are convinced of its excellence and ability. Today we look upon it as the only way to arrive at unequivocal and guaranteed results. It is like an infallible touchstone of truth, which, like a magic word in the Arabian Nights, unfolds before us the marvels of the phenomenal world in its effective link and indicates to us the points of support for which human activity, like Archimedes, seeks in order to fix in place the lever that changes the face of the world."[5]

The method learned from Barreda was considered by his followers to be the best and most perfect instrument to reconstruct an almost annihilated society. Barreda fulfilled the mission that was entrusted to him. He established the basis for a new faith and set up the banner of a new creed where, as he himself said, none remained. He made it possible for a group of men to feel capable of carrying out a reconstruction project after a terrible epoch of destruction and social anarchy. He made possible the return of a sense of security. His followers felt capable of changing the world. They felt supported by a lever as powerful as the one that Archimedes sought to place. With such minds it would be possible to establish a permanent order.

§ 52. *A Feeling of Crisis in Barreda's Followers*

In this their first phase, the disciples of Barreda considered themselves to be a group of wavering individuals in a period of transition. They still had visions of an anarchical Mexico, that is, of Mexicans fighting each other. This vision disheartened them. They

5 Ibid., p. 6.

were disillusioned in a past that they could not understand. They did not see the disillusioning past as Barreda saw it, that is, as the struggle of the positive spirit against the negative forces that opposed it. The disillusionment in the past was complete and was expressed by Parra as he observed contemporary society. Society "oscillates between a past that it abhors and a future that is indefinite, it presents hostile characters proper to a period of crisis, it is the scene of violent mental upheaval that threatens to destroy the tender blossom of morality."[6] These men felt uprooted; they could not conform to their surroundings. For them this was pure anarchy. They lacked a past of which they could be proud and a future that was secure. They looked outside their circumstances for a basis of support. The only thing of which they could be sure was a method that they would use to construct the new social edifice.

Disillusioned in their past, they looked to their own history in a negative way. Of their Spanish heritage they saw only the Spanish conquerors and the clergy. They tried to forget Spain, turning toward other countries, such as France. They renounced a culture to which they were legitimate heirs and imitated French culture in all its aspects, often to the point of being ridiculous. In social circles they did not talk about the new and uprooted class; they talked about the latest French novelties. They cast aside the authentic values of Mexico[7] and turned their attention to foreign things. Little did they care to know about Mexican reality. They tried to make Mexico and its society conform to European models. They possessed an imported method that they considered infallible and the new society would be constructed in accordance with this method. The important thing in this method was order, the only thing that one could desire after a disordered past. Order at all costs was what they wanted. They accepted order at the expense of their own positivist doctrine, should this doctrine be transformed into an instrument of disorder. This was the ideal of the Mexican bourgeoisie whose ideological formation was entrusted to Barreda. The fruits of his teachings began to be felt. Future teachers of the bourgeoisie expounded their ideas concerning the multiple problems that arose within their circumstances.

[6] Ibid., p. 7.
[7] See Samuel Ramos, *El perfil del hombre y la cultura en México*.

Those without roots in the past and without a guaranteed future, who felt that they were undergoing a crisis, found support in the positivist method. Porfirio Parra, continuing the description of how he felt about his era, said that "in a period whose shades of twilight inspire illusions of survival in the last representatives of philosophy in its death throes, and the Voltairian laughter of a sceptical misanthropy, we believe that only the scientific method, frankly and explicitly applied to the study of social phenomena, will be the real cure for the present evils. It will be the rainbow of serene peace, which is a sign that the storm is over, and only the vivid rays of the sun of science can extinguish the last vestiges of ontological phantoms that still shade the most elevated regions of human wisdom."[8] The dying philosophy and the ontological phantoms of which Parra spoke were the ideas imparted by the Catholic church. The Voltairian laughter and sceptical misanthropy were allusions to liberal ideology. Neither religious beliefs nor the scepticism of the liberals could bring light to the darkness in which these men existed. Light, support, the instrument needed to cure all these evils could be found only in the positivist method. They did not want to know anything about ideas or beliefs that were not based on this method. The only thing that could offer them their desired security was "conviction, the child of unimpeachable demonstration."[9] Opposed to blind faith and scepticism was the rigorous and therefore incontrovertible demonstration of its truth offered by the positivist method.

§ 53. *The Rigor of the Positivist Method and What the Followers of Barreda Expected from Such Rigor*

The young followers of Barreda did not deny their origin, but rather emphasized the fact that the force that made them feel so certain was a result of the education that they had received from their teacher. When Porfirio Parra talked about the reasons why Barreda should preside over and direct the Asociación Metodófila, he said, "He, who for ten years kept up a titanic struggle to establish among us a system of general and uniform education, whatever the student's final field of specialization, a system that establishes an intimate and spiritual union between those who are

8 Parra, Introduction, p. 7.
9 Ibid., p. 7.

submitted to it, replacing blind faith with conviction based on demonstration; he who guided our first steps along such a fertile way, was the only one to whom we should turn to direct our subsequent steps."[10]

The followers of Barreda considered themselves a united group, bound by the certainty of a fund of truths common to all, regardless of the profession one pursued. They were united through a plan of education that provided a uniform criterion. Unified by a common criterion, they tried to unite to solve their diverse problems, those that they confronted as individuals, as subjects of a particular form of life, through their profession. Grouped together in a society, these individuals demonstrated how their method could be applied to any kind of problem and how they gave their common consent to the solution obtained through the rigorous application of the positivist method. The solution was unimpeachable because nothing could contradict proven experience. Barreda, who taught the positivist method, insisted on its rigorous application. Barreda had the final word in every discussion. He ensured that his disciples followed his method.

In referring to Barreda's rigorous application of the positivist method, Parra said: ". . . we do not want to be affiliated with a particular system. The cultivation of the scientific method is our objective. All doctrines and opinions are to be submitted to its criterion. Those that it sanctions will become an integral part of our immutable credo. The contradictory ones will be condemned without mercy regardless of the sympathy they inspired in us before they were submitted to such a test."[11] The immutable credo of those doctrines that the method accepted or rejected was more important than sympathy and emotion. The rigorous application of the method provided the model to which every possible opinion should henceforth conform. Opinions, ideas, and beliefs that could not endure the tests of positivism "would be condemned without mercy," notwithstanding sympathy for them. The common fund of truths of which Barreda spoke would be obtained through the rigorous application of the method.

It was thus they tried to find an immutable credo, a credo that would make peace and order possible, a credo that would end the

10 Ibid., p. 7.
11 Ibid., p. 8.

existing crisis. A group of men terrified by past anarchy, who had no past and no guaranteed future, clung to what seemed to furnish them the basis for a new faith. They sacrificed every affection and sympathy for the security that the positivist method seemed to offer them. They continued to talk about a brilliant future nevertheless. Those who previously had felt that their future was insecure now felt that they had found a great future if they applied the positivist method thoroughly. Parra defended the positivists from the accusations made against them that they were unbelievers. On the contrary, he said, they have placed their certitude and faith in a guaranteed and great future. The positivist system, said Parra, was not discouraging, nor did it degrade human nature. On the contrary, it offered "a great theater . . . ; in the methodical study of natural phenomena, we promise you the scepter of the world; we can foresee the attractive perspective of progress whose limits no hand dares sketch today."[12]

Nevertheless, this idea of progress was vague to those men. They could not dare to sketch it, because they did not know it. They spoke of a great future but they had no idea of what this future was. Their immediate end was order. They conceived of progress in terms of social order. Order came before anything else. The application of the positivist method was directed toward this ideal, that is, order. Many years later, these same men believed that they had established this order and that they had found their basis in the work of Barreda. The rigor of the method was the application of a methodical distrust to everything that was not adapted to the common fund of truths that had been imposed on them. Everything that could not be reconciled with this common fund, that is, everything that did not fit into the new creed, was to be destroyed or eliminated. Its existence was dangerous. It would alter the order desired after so much difficulty.

Peace and order were possible only through ordered and uniform minds. In the future every possible idea, belief, and opinion was to be submitted to this uniformity. Otherwise, there would be a return to crisis, that is, to a feeling of insecurity. This mode of thought produced a society in which progress meant order. Fear of God was replaced by order and a fictitious peace. It

12 Ibid., p. 9.

was an order that was incapable of absorbing the ideas that more and more filled the spirits of Mexicans, to such a degree that there was moral and social nonconformity. But this nonconformity would delay until Mexican society felt the pressure of an order void of ideas, an order whose ultimate goal was order itself. In searching for unified minds and the possibility of a new society, the followers of Barreda made a series of studies and discussed diverse cultural and social problems. We will see who will most stand out and best represent the spirit that inspired their attackers.

II. The Application of the Positivist Method

§ 54. *The Application of the Positivist Method*
to Philosophical Problems

The method learned in Barreda's school was applied to diverse philosophical and social problems by the members of the Asociación. Barreda saw that they did not deviate from the strict application of the method. Among the philosophical works of Porfirio Parra, the one entitled "Las causas primeras" stands out. Parra tried to compare the history of first causes to the history of science. His objective was to criticize philosophy based on belief in first causes and to expound his own philosophy. In his exposition he compared two types of philosophy: one that supported first causes and one that supported demonstration. The former, said Parra, was based on the will; the latter on reality. We have already seen the social consequences of these philosophies in our study of Barreda. The former, which was based on the will, led to the imposition of ideas; the latter was accepted through demonstration.

Primitive man, said Parra, tried to explain natural phenomena through causality, that is, through the principle of a first cause, the only method then available. By observing nature, "he noted that the changes in nature proved that they were determined by an agent that appeared spontaneous and complete, namely, the will. On the basis of the iron law of logical reasoning, he applied this first causal notion to the exterior world whose phenomenal diversity he believed to be real. Thus he created as many independent wills as there were phenomena."[13] This was how fetishism originated. Then these apparently independent phenomena gradually were grouped together, reducing what was previously multiple wills, and thus polytheism originated. This is how man "explained the order of the universe, that is, as resulting from accord among the wills and divinities that govern it."[14] On the basis of this incomplete observation of nature, all physical phenomena were considered as upheavals of the general established order. Storms, earthquakes, and eclipses resulted, it was believed, from discord among the gods who animated nature. Later, said Parra, these wills were reduced until all phenomena originated from a single will, "which was considered the first and final cause of the universe."[15] According to Parra, this was how the philosophy of first causes originated.

There was another method by which man could know nature: the direct observation of facts. An example, according to Parra, was the Greek philosopher Aristotle, who "did not try to discover the first cause, but the most general fact, which included the largest possible number of individual facts. He did not, like Plato, launch into the sublime and unreal regions of a purely subjective world. Everything was submitted to examination by his perspicacious eye. One was elevated into heaven while still seeing the earth. His plan was that of science; his method the scientific."[16] Scientific philosophy was supported by real facts and experimentation.

Parra's work, of which a résumé has been given, was criticized by Barreda from the viewpoint of the strict application of the positivist method. Barreda said that he objected to the work because the author, instead of demonstrating according to the positivist method, merely affirmed the value of experience over knowledge supported by first causes. This work, said Barreda, appears

13 Porfirio Parra, "Las causas primeras," in *Anales de la Asociación Metodófila,* p. 53.

14 Ibid., p. 54.

15 Ibid., p. 54.

16 Ibid., p. 55.

to be that of a *sectarian*. Before affirming the value of a philosophy based on experimentation, one must convince nonbelievers through appropriate means. Barreda said: "A fundamental observation can be made that the work is *sectarian*. It will not be adequate to convince those who hold opposite opinions. . . . for us the truth that we profess is so obvious that appeal to memory is good enough. But, for those that do not have the same convictions it is inadequate. One must, as Mr. Parra has done, demonstrate that our doctrine is good and fertile and immediately prove that their doctrine is insufficient, infertile, and, therefore, bad. Thus, it is clear that our purpose is not to be a chorus for each other, but to win converts."[17] It was necessary to demonstrate the doctrine and convince nonpositivists of its excellence. Barreda was saying that affirmation provoked a negative reaction. Order was the ideal of the positivist doctrine; disorder must be eliminated. All Mexicans should think alike. This would be impossible if one affirmed, before he convinced, that a doctrine was good or bad. It was first necessary to convince others of the excellence of the first doctrine and the inadequacy of the second. This was the only way to give all Mexicans a common fund of truths.

Works that took into account the knowledge of only those who belonged to a particular school could only be sectarian. As such, only their converts accepted them without discussion. Barreda wanted converts. To get them one had to do more than affirm that a doctrine was good. One also had to demonstrate that it was a better doctrine than the one that the person one hoped to convert professed. Since the positivist method had a social function, it was necessary to attend first of all to those who did not share positivist views. It was necessary to convince them of the excellence of the positivist doctrine. The positivist philosophy was only an instrument to plan and order the Mexican mind. Hence, those charged with this planning must understand and use the doctrine as a tool of persuasion. They must know how to convince. Those charged with this task should select the truths that form part of the common fund in order to offer them to Mexican minds.

Therefore, Barreda wanted positivist truths to be explained as obvious truths for everyone, not just for those who professed them.

[17] Gabino Barreda, reply to the work of Porfirio Parra cited in *Anales de la Asociación Metodófila*, p. 71.

The important thing was to gain converts. Positivism, according to Barreda, should not be a sectarian philosophy, but one for society as a whole and, as such, obvious to everyone. Positive truths by their own worth should supplant other truths existent in society. However, in spite of the fact that the positivists did not want to attack any idea or doctrine, one of the requisites for the success of positivism as a social philosophy was that the positivists convince others that their truths were superior to the ideas and doctrine that they claimed they did not want to attack.

§ 55. *The Strict Application of the Positivist Method Independent of Emotion and Sympathy*

Among the works presented at the Asociación Metodófila was that of Pedro Noriega entitled *Consideraciones sobre la teoría de Darwin*. In discussing this work, Barreda expressed his own ideas, not so much about the Darwinian theory as about the place that theory might have within the positivist philosophy. Darwin was the pretext for a strict application of the positivist method. Barreda drew the conclusion that the Darwinian theory could not be supported by the scientific method. He said that it was not based on observation; it was based on a priori reasoning. "Whatever value is given to form and structure," said Barreda, in referring to the Darwinian theory, "it is not from them that we should derive the effective laws of reproduction and hereditary transmission; the study of the function itself in beings that possess them is certainly the only course that good method justifies. To infer those laws a priori with morphologic data instead of determining them a posteriori on the basis of observation is to return to metaphysics and pure intuition."[18]

Barreda used this discussion—that theories, ideas, and beliefs should not be accepted merely because they are attractive—to support Porfirio Parra's thesis. Only ideas that have been proven on the basis of the positivist method should be accepted. Referring to the reasons why the Darwinian theory was so widely accepted by young Mexicans, Barreda said, "It is easy to explain, in spite of its inadequate logic, why this theory is so generally accepted. It is believed that it symbolizes progress. That is why it is so at-

[18] Gabino Barreda replied to Pedro Noriega in an article entitled "Consideraciones sobre la Teoría de Darwin," in *Anales de la Asociación Metodófila*, p. 174.

tractive to the young. On the other hand, it has the great advantage of replacing theological cosmogony. That is why the partisans of Darwinism commonly believe that anyone who does not accept this theory necessarily believes in the biblical form of creation and is therefore accused of being reactionary and theological. They feel that they alone represent progress."[19]

From these ideas one could draw certain conclusions. Simply stating that a certain theory was opposed to certain prejudices did not make the theory good. That a theory such as that of Darwin was opposed to the theological ideas on creation was not enough to make that theory be considered sufficient to put an end to such prejudices. It was necessary to demonstrate through the positive method that the Darwinian theory of creation was true. It would be necessary to prove this by facts, that is, by experimentation. If this procedure were not followed, prejudices could not be eliminated. One prejudice could not be overcome by another. An a priori affirmation that man is the result of the evolution of the animal species could not disprove the a priori affirmation that man is a divine creation. The Darwinian theory could not be used to combat religious prejudices, because it lacks a demonstrable basis. The positive method does not use a priori affirmations; it demonstrates. Its affirmations are a posteriori. The affirmations of positive science can be proven by anyone. The Darwinian theory as it was applied by the young was an instrument of disharmony rather than persuasion. It was merely used to attack and combat the ideas of a particular group, but not to convince this group that its ideas were false.

In referring to the Darwinian theory, Barreda said: "They say that the theory leads us toward better rules of morality. That might be so, but I insist that we should limit ourselves to speak exclusively of method, that is, of the proofs, without worrying about the results. It is not logical to accept something as a fact because we sympathize with its results; we must demand proofs that support it."[20] The positivist method of demonstration should outweigh sympathy. Barreda wanted every affirmation to be supported by facts. Facts should prevail over sympathy. Sympathy, that is, the heart, can deceive, but the strict application of positivist logic can-

[19] Ibid., p. 102.
[20] Ibid., p. 106.

not deceive. These men tried to eliminate disharmony. But the best way to eliminate disharmony was to eliminate the heart. Harmony was no longer wanted, because where there was a heart there could also be disharmony. Order was all that was wanted. But order without a heart, that is, order that was not based on feeling, was merely physical order, an order based on natural facts. Sympathy and antipathy should be subordinated to this order. Since full harmony of human affections was no longer possible, the positivists desired harmony based on facts. Harmony based on the natural sciences was to replace the disharmony that originated in the human being.

This does not mean that Barreda had not spoken of the subordination of the mind to the heart. Remember that he said that the students should learn literature to balance the mind and the heart and prevent the heart from withering. In a speech honoring an artist, he said, "The heart, improved and perfected through the cultivation and growth of the benevolent inclinations, should command; the mind, fortified by science, should obey."[21] But at the same time what Barreda said about moral education should not be forgotten: through adequate training the sympathetic and altruistic acts should be repeated more frequently and, at the same time, the destructive and egoistic acts should be avoided. Thus, sympathy could be cultivated; it could be directed toward a determined end. This end was, of course, the objective of a rational appreciation. It was the mind that coldly calculated what was best for humanity. Sympathy would be guided according to this calculation. Sympathy was subordinate to the mind. The mind guided the affections by strictly applying the positivist method. The heart did not know which road to follow. It was cold reasoning that had found the road through its calculations. Thus reason should direct the heart. The mind knew what road humanity would follow in its progress. The heart should be subordinate to the mind and it would thus be the object of cultivation. It would go the way that the mind led it. This was how the positivists imposed their method of investigation of reality over sympathy and affection. Every doctrine and opinion that could not withstand the test "will be condemned without pity, no matter how much sympathy they in-

[21] Gabino Barreda, "Discurso de laudación del artista Juan Cordero," in *Opúsculos, discusiones y discursos*, p. 154. (Republished in *Estudios*.)

spired in us prior to this test." This is what a follower of Barreda said.

The new morality should be based on positivism. Morality cannot originate in sympathies or antipathies; it should be based on evidence. This is what the positivists attempted. They believed that they could in this way destroy the anarchy inherited, they thought, from the eighteenth century. In his Guanajuato speech Barreda blamed the clergy for causing disorder by its opposition to positivist progress. Ten years later he said that this anarchy originated in the eighteenth century, which produced the philosophic basis for liberalism. According to this criterion, positive morality would be the result of the evident necessity of imposing order over the disorder provoked by eighteenth-century ideas. "This systematization of morality on a positive and evident basis," said Barreda, "which has been demonstrated to be possible, is also an imperative necessity today. We must abolish, once and for all, anarchical and immoral scepticism, which was the necessary and immediate result of the rapid and growing discredit of Catholicism and, with greater reason, Protestantism, discredit that they have suffered since the apparition of the disunifying doctrines of the eighteenth century, and especially since the great French explosion of ideas."[22]

[22] Gabino Barreda, "De la educación moral," in *Opúsculos, discusiones y discursos*, p. 117.

III. The Theory of Some Positivists concerning the Social Order

§ 56. *The Relationship between Superiors and Inferiors*

Barreda's followers who belonged to the Asociación Metodófila also applied the positivist method to social problems. Among the essays published by the Asociación was one by Miguel S. Macedo, who later became one of the directors of the political party called Científicos. It was entitled "Ensayo sobre los deberes recíprocos de los superiores y de los inferiores."[23] His thesis concerned the relationship between superiors and inferiors. It established the social obligations of individuals toward each other. It contained the ideology of those who later assumed political power. Although only a sketch of the ideology is presented here, one can still get an idea of how those men conceived of society. We can see in this and another theory that will be presented later these men's justification for their social position or, at least, for the position to which they aspired. They justified themselves on the basis of the positivist method, which they applied to problems like the relationship between superiors and inferiors. As we will see later, they also applied the scientific method to the problems related to the right to social survival.

[23] Published in *Anales de la Asociación Metodófila.*

According to Macedo, only relationships of order fit into humanity. In humanity all men had a predetermined place. The relationship between men was predetermined by their place in society. By nature of one's position in society, one could only belong to one of two groups: superiors and inferiors. Society was a great ordered field in which some men were meant to command and others to obey. Each of these two groups had a series of duties and obligations in the relations between them. Macedo defined superiority as "the quality of possessing another quality in a greater degree than someone else."[24] Inferiority is considered as the lack of this quality. Superiority has diverse forms: superiority of feeling; of intelligence, wherein Macedo placed what he called the contemplative class; and of practical power. Macedo reduced the relationship between the superiors, who possessed any of these types of superiority, and the inferiors, who lacked them, to the following formula: "Self-denial of the superior for the inferior; respect and veneration of the inferior for the superior."[25]

Macedo considered superiority "of feeling" as the highest form, because the heart, he said, is the origin of every impulse toward humanity. Woman possessed this quality in its highest degree. In this field woman was superior to those who possessed physical and intellectual superiority. Man, said Macedo, because of his constant material and moral struggles, gradually lost feelings, and became socially useless because he was no longer capable of loving his fellowman. Thus, since woman was superior in this field, she had the duty to inspire in man the most elevated and moral acts. The obligation of man, who was inferior in feeling, was to venerate and respect woman. Regarding the relationship between man and woman, Macedo manifested a conception peculiar to the era: woman was the inspiration of lofty feats and man was a respectful admirer of woman.

Related to superiority "of feeling" is what Macedo called "energy and kindness of character." He considered it the most powerful element in the service of humanity. According to this kind of superiority it was the duty of its possessor to help humanity; the duty of the inferior was to venerate and feel gratitude toward him. In-

[24] Miguel S. Macedo, "Ensayo sobre los deberes recíprocos de los superiores y de los inferiores," in *Anales de la Asociación Metodófila*, p. 214.
[25] Ibid., p. 215.

feriors should not resist superiors who worked for the good of humanity. "They should have veneration and gratitude for them," said Macedo, "or they would be an obstacle toward the attainment of progress and well-being. Resistance, whether it be active or passive, will obligate the superior to lose time and energy in subduing it and, as a result, progress will be delayed."[26] In this thesis he outlined one of the arguments that would be used for political purposes: the promise to bring about certain social benefits and the obligation of those who benefited not to oppose their realization. This was the thesis of those who supported Porfirismo. No one should oppose a government whose end was progress and peace. Nothing should oppose a benevolent dictatorship whose end was social well-being. On the contrary, it was owed veneration and gratitude.

§ 57. *The Relationship between Rich and Poor*

Those who aspired toward material well-being, that is, those whose ultimate end was to obtain wealth, had to support a thesis that favored the wealthy. The wealth, as well as the social position that the rich would have in this society, had to be justified morally and socially. Macedo said that wealth was one of the types of social superiority. Society consisted of the rich and the poor. Through wealth, some are superior and some inferior. The rich, said Macedo, are an important part of the social machinery; they have certain obligations. The worth of this class is derived from "the powerful elements with which it deals and that it can use in the service of humanity."[27] The possession of wealth made it possible for this class to offer humanity great services. The wealthy, therefore, were in a position to produce social well-being. This was one reason why the rich were socially superior. They possessed a quality that the poor did not have, a quality that was derived from their wealth. Macedo said that whoever was superior by reason of his wealth could also be morally superior. "That superiority," said Macedo, "can easily lead to moral superiority: the rich need only to use their qualities to do good."[28] Later he added, "I do not

---

26 Ibid., p. 218.
27 Ibid., p. 219.
28 Ibid., p. 219.

hesitate to say that wealth constitutes, or can constitute, at least a moral superiority."[29]

The rich were not only economically, but also morally, superior to the poor. They not only possessed the goods necessary for their own well-being, but they also possessed more than they needed. On the other hand, the poor, "in order to procure a relative well-being that usually covers only the most pressing demands of life, must work."[30] When the poor do not work, neither do they have bread. Therefore, "science and morality are out of their reach: science, because one needs a peaceful mind and a rested body to cultivate it . . . morality, because misery . . . is not conscious of altruistic and elevated sentiments, because it spends all its cerebral activity in overcoming the present. It is impossible for them to think about the future or the present of others."[31]

Thus, wealth was an instrument that made one morally and intellectually superior to the poor. The rich, as possessors of wealth, had leisure, which made it possible for them to think about the good of humanity. Leisure made it possible for the rich to worry about the present and the future of others. Thus, what the socialists called surplus value made possible the well-being of society, according to Macedo. Without this increase in wealth, which made leisure possible, humanity could not progress. Wealth permitted the realization of altruistic acts and provided the tranquil mind necessary so that some men could concern themselves about the well-being of others. Thus, the rich were in a position to contribute to the well-being of society. Therefore, it was justifiable that wealth and its possessors be the superiors in society.

The rich, as the possessors of such an effective instrument of social well-being, had an obligation to protect the poor, "which," said Macedo, "was simply one of the many ways of serving humanity, that is, by using wealth as a basis of progress." This protection could take various forms, such as "supplying work—a just and equitable compensation for it . . . and also appreciation for the cooperation of the worker." Another thing that the rich could do was to carry out any of the "works that are purely charitable

29 Ibid., p. 219.
30 Ibid., p. 219.
31 Ibid., p. 220.

in every way."[32] Having explained the duties of the rich toward their inferiors, Macedo said, referring to the duties of the poor toward their benefactors, that the poor "have toward the rich not only a duty of gratitude that obligates them to return, whenever possible, service for service, but they also have the duty of respect and, furthermore, they have the duty of veneration."[33]

Respect, gratitude, and veneration toward the rich were, according to Macedo, the obligations of the inferior in wealth. But this positivist idea would be threatened by the liberal and democratic ideas becoming current in the period. "I believe," he said, "that the anarchy of modern societies has also invaded this area when they deny [through the democrats, he tells us in a note] that the poor have any obligations toward the rich."[34] Ignorance of these duties led only to social anarchy. In this thesis he boldly defended the rich by presenting them as possible social benefactors. It was enough that the rich could do good for them to be considered superior. The poor were not in a position to accomplish the good that humanity expected. On the other hand, it sufficed that the rich had the wealth that enabled them to accomplish this good. This was a defense of the class that would be sheltered by the protective wing of Porfirismo. It was a defense of the aristocracy of money. These aristocrats were able to do good and this ability justified them. There was concern for the problems of the poor, but nothing could be done about it, except to help the poor through work or alms. "The proletariat," said Macedo, "always has to exist in any population; but this should not prevent us from trying to better its condition. By improving its condition [we] will permit it to better fulfill its mission."[35]

Rich and poor had their place in society. Both were indispensable to society. The rich needed wealth for leisure, because leisure would allow them to have concern for others. For the poor was left the work, which was recognized to be so difficult that it left them no time for concern for their fellowman. The mission of the rich was to alleviate, as much as possible, the sad plight of

---

32 Ibid., p. 220.
33 Ibid., p. 221.
34 Ibid., p. 221. José C. Valadés, in his book *El porfirismo*, described this era in which the organization and propaganda of the workers were initiated.
35 Macedo, "Ensayo sobre los deberes recíprocos," p. 220.

the poor so that the poor could better fulfill their mission, that is, work. In summarizing the ideas of Macedo, one could say that the mission of the poor was to work for subsistence and to allow the rich the necessary leisure to worry about the present and future of humanity, and to give the rich the means to protect the poor by providing the poor with work for a just remuneration, or with charity. Thus, the well-being of the rich was the condition for the possible well-being of the poor. According to the thesis of Macedo, if the rich sacrificed their economic well-being, then the well-being and progress of humanity would be sacrificed. Remember how Barreda defended private property when he said that the rich man could not throw his own house through the window to be caught by idlers. Macedo concluded his thesis on the obligations of the poor and the rich by quoting a few words from Comte. "No society can subsist if inferiors do not respect superiors, and nothing will better confirm this law than the present degradation, in which, for lack of love, one obeys only force, even though revolutionary pride deplores the alleged servility of our forefathers, who knew how to love their superiors."[36] Macedo deplored the ignorance of the poor regarding their obligations. The poor refused to recognize the generosity of the rich man who offered them work and bread. Macedo felt that the poor would have no work or bread "if a benevolent hand did not offer it generously."[37]

§ 58. *The Relationship between Intellectual Superiors and Intellectual Inferiors*

Macedo also spoke of the superior and the inferior in respect to ability to command. Superiors, by virtue of their power of command, had the obligation to obtain benefits for their fellowmen by using their power in the service of humanity. On the other hand, it was the obligation of the inferior to obey and to respect the power of the superior.

Then Macedo spoke of the superiority of intelligence. The obligation of the intellectual, said Macedo, was to obtain the greatest good for humanity. "The intelligent man has the greatest obligation because he possesses the most powerful of all elements to improve social conditions and to serve humanity with dignity:

[36] Ibid., p. 221.
[37] Ibid., p. 219.

science."[38] The duty of the inferior was to revere him, to respect him, and to help him. By "revere" Macedo did not mean accept without argument; he believed that the inferior had a right to discuss whatever the intellectual superior affirmed. Respect did not imply *magister dixit*. It would be lack of respect and veneration if the one who argued was an inferior, that is, someone not capable of discussing the topic. But if the ideas of an intellectual were discussed by one who had the means or instruments necessary to arrive at opposite conclusions, then there was no lack of respect.

He who argues in this manner is, in fact, another intellectual, and cannot be failing in respect for his superior because "then superiority in science has disappeared and perhaps the respective situations have even been reversed."[39] This thesis is a logical consequence of the way in which intelligence was understood by the positivists. We have seen that, according to the positivist method, there can be no a priori affirmations, that is, affirmations that are made prior to demonstration. The positivists can accept nothing as truth that is not demonstrated by experience; they cannot accept affirmations that are based merely on the authority of intellectuals. Intellectuals have no more authority than that given them by the agreement between their affirmations and their demonstration of those affirmations. The superiority of an intellectual is his power to demonstrate what he affirms. If someone else can demonstrate that what the intellectual affirms is false, then superiority passes to him.

§ 59. *The Relationship between Sociology and Biology*

Manuel Ramos, another member of the Asociación Metodófila, presented a thesis that also tried to justify the social position acquired, or to be acquired, on the basis of ideas deduced from the positivist sciences. These sciences were used as an instrument to justify a certain way of thinking. These ideas concerning social problems were to be justified scientifically, as we will see in the work of Manuel Ramos entitled "Estudio de las relaciones entre la sociología y la biología."[40]

The theoretical problem that Ramos posed was the possibility of

[38] Ibid., p. 222.
[39] Ibid., p. 222.
[40] Published in *Anales de la Asociación Metodófila*.

the existence of a social science. He first criticized the theories that denied the existence of social science. He divided these theories into three groups: (1) the theory of immediate and continuous divine intervention in human events; (2) the theory that the history of society was the history of distinguished personages, that is, the theory of great men; and (3) the theory that denied the existence of social science, departing from the hypothesis that man was free. "If man is free to decide what he will do or not do, then man cannot be the object of the exact sciences. If there is an exact science there is no free will."[41]

Manuel Ramos opposed these theses when he said that social science can exist just as the biological sciences can. To make this affirmation, he established an analogy between the two sciences. "Social science should study the birth, development, structure, and functions of a society just as biology studies the birth, development, etc., of the individual. Social science should determine the characteristics common to all societies, the less general traits that pertain to certain groups, and, finally, the peculiarities of each one that correspond to individual characteristics, not forgetting, in any case, the circumstances under which those societies develop, that is, the influence of the surroundings."[42]

Ramos answered the objection that one might make to social science, that is, its degree of exactitude. Ramos said that if one expected rigorous exactitude from this science, equal to that obtained in the exact sciences, sociology would not be a science. But then one would also have to deny the name of science to those that seem most exact. "One has to consider the biographical phenomena in man that biology cannot foresee and that cannot be the object of science. But the phenomena of structure, development, and functions are within its domain. Also, within societies there are two orders of phenomena: some that are merely historical facts, which cannot be predicted by sociology; others, relative to their development, structure, and functions, that supply the materials of social science, which can predict the general march of social phenomena, without descending to its details." One can, said Ramos, "say that sociology is to history what biology is to biography."[43] Thus, just

41 Ramos, *El perfil del hombre y la cultura*, p. 263.
42 Ibid., p. 266.
43 Ibid., p. 268.

as the biographical events of man cannot be predicted, so the history of society cannot be predicted. On the other hand, if it is possible to predict the general characteristics of all men as living beings through the science of biology, then equally one can predict the characteristics that are common to all societies through the so-called social sciences.

From this analogy between biology and sociology Ramos derived an analogy between society and biological organisms. He said, ". . . nothing resembles a society as much as an organism. . . . Biological phenomena are, then, the best source of comparison for sociologists."[44] Besides, sociology could be compared with biology in the following aspects: First, the actions of a society depended on the actions of its individuals. Just as the actions of the individuals must conform to the laws of life, knowledge of the laws of biology is indispensable to the understanding of the actions of society. Second, society, considered as a whole, offers the phenomena of growth and other functions that are analogous to those presented in the life of individuals and studied by biology.

§ 60. *The Application of Social Science to Social Problems*

Ramos drew the conclusion that social science, whose possibilities he had demonstrated, should have a social application. This meant that those who governed should apply this science to every kind of problem. Social crises could be resolved through scientific research. If the governors would utilize social science and govern in conformance with the laws of society that have been discovered, they could resolve their social problems. The conclusions that Ramos drew anticipated the ideas of the Científicos, who, as the name implies, tried to govern, legislate, and guide the politics of the country according to laws they thought derived from science.

Ramos said that it was the obligation of every government to seek the well-being of society. To better attain this objective, it was necessary for government to conform to the laws that were discovered and demonstrated by social science. A government should seek the well-being of society without any sentimentalism. It governs to satisfy the special necessities of society as a whole rather than those of the individual. Hence, government should follow the

[44] Ibid., p. 270.

laws of social science and biology. Biological laws should be used to govern because they are valid for all men.

One of the biological laws that should be applied to the solution of the problems of society was that of the survival of the fittest. It was a law, said Ramos, that governments have not taken into account, and as a consequence society has been greatly injured. "An individual succumbs because he cannot resist the numerous causes of destruction with which we are all familiar, but resistance varies among individuals according to their constitution, character, social position, etc.; if one or more of the causes of destruction were suppressed, the number of the weak would increase and leave a posterity weak like them, and, by increasing at the same time the intensity of the causes of destruction that have subsisted, the human race would be more numerous but weaker."[45] Ramos cited the following biological law: "A faculty, whether it be corporal or intellectual, is developed by exercise; it weakens or disappears through inertia; and it is capable of transmitting itself by inheritance."[46]

Every man struggles with his immediate surroundings and in this struggle he develops his faculties; but if one should suppress the causes that threaten man's destruction, he would make the exercise of the defensive faculties unnecessary, and the result would be the atrophy of these faculties. "Lack of exercise," said Ramos, "weakens the faculties and finally destroys them completely."[47] Hence, the intervention of the state to help the individual in his struggle against his surroundings would be dangerous because this would weaken him. Instead, the defensive faculties should be stimulated so that they would not atrophy. "It is not a real advantage," said Ramos, "that certain causes of death are checked. One must always draw conclusions from the benefits obtained. If measures of this kind are multiplied, they might cause more harm than good in the long run. In general, they should accept as good all those measures that tend to suppress the evil in society, while not contributing to the inertia of the faculties that ennoble man, be they physical, intellectual, or moral."[48]

45 Ibid., p. 274.
46 Ibid., p. 273.
47 Ibid., p. 275.
48 Ibid., p. 275.

Ramos said that only the physically or intellectually strong should survive. The mission of the state was to stimulate these aptitudes and not weaken them by helping the individual. The state should not be concerned as to whether the weak perish, because their loss would redound to the well-being of society, since the unfit would not increase. To help the weak would harm society. "It will be clear how much harm can be caused by governmental measures, which, under the pretext of eliminating the sufferings of those who are incapable on their own to struggle against the difficulties of their existence, give them what they need, and thus prepare a sad legacy of ignorance, laziness, and criminality for posterity. Now one can understand how culpable are those who, for the pleasure of having done good, open their prodigal hands to pour their benefits over these germs of incalculable harm; one can understand how worthy of reprobation are those money wasters who, to avoid the eternal suffering that they fear in the other life, do not hesitate to inflict upon their fellowman a heavy and dangerous load like the one that is accumulating in those so-called asylums of charity."[49]

The most that one should do to help the socially unfit would be individual help, such as "the self-denial of a father and mother, the affection of the family, the sympathy of friends."[50] But never should society help. Society should not support institutions that protect the weak.

Ramos said that he had deduced his conclusions from science; he said that he had merely revealed the consequences of ignorance of a biological law. "The biological law of adaptation that is true for the other species is also true for the human species; the only thing necessary for its verification is the conservation of the general conditions that we have talked about, and legislative measures should be passed in this direction."[51] The proposed measures were of a scientific nature; they were presented as free from all sentiment born of a particular interest. What was proposed was the result of objective necessity, unmoved by sympathy or antipathy, or

[49] Ibid., p. 276. Remember when Barreda said, "The proprietors and rich perhaps would go to heaven, but the rest would remain in a true inferno," when he defended private property.

[50] Ramos, *El perfil del hombre y la cultura*, p. 277.

[51] Ibid., p. 278.

any other interests outside the positivist sciences. What Ramos said was merely the result of the application of positive science to a social problem. He justified his thesis when he said, "I attempt neither correction nor originality; everything or almost everything in this work has been expressed by the various authors of the positivist school who have been concerned with this same study."[52]

§ 61. *Positivism as the Justification for a Class Ideology*

In the essays of Macedo and Ramos, we saw the ideology of the class that was gaining social prominence and that reached its social peak during the Porfirian era. It was the ideology of that class that we traced from its beginnings, from its combative phase. Behind these ideas in positivist trappings was hidden the ideology of the Mexican bourgeoisie, which grew more and more powerful. These ideas were those of a class that was trying to strengthen its hold on power. José María Luis Mora expressed the ideas of the Mexican bourgeoisie in its combative phase. The bourgeoisie at that time had to adopt a combative, or destructive, ideology as opposed to the ideologies sustained by the class that previously held social power. Once the Mexican bourgeoisie acquired power, however, it gradually constricted the ideology that once had served it as an instrument. Liberalism was losing force and becoming a voice crying in the wilderness.[53] A philosophy of order was adopted. It was positivism, which was checked whenever it opposed the interests of the bourgeoisie.

The positivist philosophy was a basis on which the Mexican bourgeoisie could justify the new order. Every class has looked for an ideology that would justify its actions. The enemies of the bourgeoisie also justified their actions through a certain philosophy. The conservatives used a philosophy that the positivists called theology as a justification. It was the divinity of Christ that sustained mankind and the society that man had established. On the other hand, the liberals sustained the thesis of liberty in its widest sense, as they did the thesis of equality. Liberty was a natural right of all

---

[52] Ibid., p. 279.

[53] Valadés, *El porfirismo*, explains how liberalism loses force with the Porfirist regime, which looked for an equilibrium between all the political and social forces within the country.

men. The Mexican bourgeoisie needed a philosophy that would justify the order that it wanted to establish.

This justification would be found in the positive sciences. The sciences would justify the actions of the bourgeoisie and the social order that it wanted to establish. The Mexican bourgeoisie lacked a divine or heroic origin to justify itself in its claims to social primacy. It was necessary to have some justification for its right to this primacy. Its justification was the positivist philosophy. Justification that originated in what could not be demonstrated had no value. Every claim should be justified with positive facts. This was what the members of the Mexican bourgeoisie did. They demonstrated their right to social supremacy; that is, they justified their actions. The strength of this class lay in wealth. Thus, wealth was one of the instruments through which social well-being could be realized. In this way the bourgeoisie differed from the other classes, which did not possess it. Wealth made morality possible. Wealth provided a certain class with the leisure necessary for social concerns. This was the rich class, that is, the class of the leading members of the bourgeoisie. The rich, through their wealth, had more moral and intellectual capacities because wealth permitted them to concern themselves with such things. Therefore, the rich, that is, the Mexican bourgeoisie, had a right to the social preeminence that they acquired.

The other classes justified their rights as gifts from God, as the conservatives did, or, as the liberals did, as a benefit inherent in human nature. The bourgeoisie justified its rights by laws of science. The bourgeoisie had to justify its desire for wealth and power. One justification was found in the biological law of the survival of the fittest. The fittest is he who has the greatest resistance to the surroundings with which he struggles. This resistance, said Ramos, depended on character, social position, and so on.

Society was a battlefield in which the fittest triumphed. The fittest class in Mexican society was the bourgeoisie. The members of this class were those who had acquired the best social positions. The mission of the state was to protect them, not to stimulate the biologically inferior classes. The bourgeoisie, which was the class best adapted to the struggle against its surroundings, should have all the rights. The unfit do not deserve even public charity. The only task of the state was to protect the conquests of the Mexican bourgeoisie, because they were the result of personal efforts made by this class. Only in this way could one stimulate the best. This was the way by which the bourgeoisie attempted to justify itself as the privileged class, that is, by covering its actions with an ideology that boasted of being scientific and demonstrable.

IV. The Creation of the Social Order

§ 62. *The Social Consequences of Barreda's Work*

In 1880, a year before Barreda died, one of his followers and friends, José Díaz Covarrubias, published a pamphlet concerning the significance and future of Barreda's work as an educator.[54] "The works of Comte and the English positivists, such as Mill, Bain, Spencer, and Lewis, were familiar to the majority of Mexican youth. The purely negative doctrines of Voltaire and Rousseau had been replaced by ideas of Order and Progress based on Order."[55] Ideas of order replaced the combative ideas of the Mexican liberals. The mission of liberalism had come to an end. Mexican youth educated in positivist ideas wanted only order. The new generation, educated in the preparatory school founded by Barreda, were conscious of the need for order.

"The future of the country," said Díaz Covarrubias, "is tied to this great reform. Soon the youth educated under this regime will begin to take over, peacefully, the administration and politics. They will soon constitute an overwhelming majority and they

[54] [José Díaz Covarrubias], *Dr. Gabino Barreda, propagador del positivismo en México y fundador de la Escuela Nacional Preparatoria.*

[55] Ibid., p. 7.

will definitively eliminate any real influence of those superficial agitators who can see progress only through disorder, and of those reactionaries who cannot conceive of order except through degradation and reaction. . . . Thus, we hope," said Díaz Covarrubias, "to see in Mexico the beginning of an era of order, peace, and progress through the enlightenment and prudence of the new generation, which, upon entering political life, will replace the perpetual anarchists that have so discredited politics. It is everyone's opinion that this regeneration will be the work of Dr. Barreda."[56]

In fact, although the work of Barreda was strictly educational, it had important social consequences. Those educated in his school were influential in all fields: administrative, political, educational, economic. Barreda furnished the ideological basis for the triumphant Mexican bourgeoisie. The ideal of the bourgeoisie was a state that would serve its interests. To realize this ideal, it was necessary for those in government to think like the bourgeoisie; that is, those in public administration and in politics should profess the same ideology. Mora's thesis, which held that the state should not serve the interests of a particular social corps, was impossible, because the state would always be in the hands of a particular social body. The Mexican bourgeoisie, which, as long as it did not hold power, was opposed to the state's serving a particular corps, continued to take control of the state and use it for its own ends.

These men, whose ideology justified the order that they had established, entered fully into political life, carrying out the predictions of Díaz Covarrubias. In 1892 the Union Liberal party was founded. Its declaration was signed by distinguished followers of Barreda, such as Miguel S. Macedo, Justo Sierra, José Yves Limantour, and Joaquín D. Casasús. This was the first political declaration of the party that was later called the Científicos. The party's ideal was to use social order as a tool of progress. Regarding the scope of Barreda's work and its results, the engineer Agustín Aragón wrote in 1898: "En 1877, M. Telésforo García, écrivain vigoreux et adepte du Positivisme, fonda le journal *La Liberté*, qui intervint dans toutes les questions politiques palpitantes; c'est la première publication périodique dans laquelle on ait appliqué le critérium positif aux affaires publiques du Mexique. . . . Le Trésor

[56] Ibid., p. 11.

public avait toujours été en proie au plus grand désordre jusqu'à ce qu'un ancien élève de l'Ecole préparatoire, disciple de M. Barreda, M. l'avocat José Yves Limantour, ait accepté la charge du ministère des finances, qu'il dirige encore, et où sa gestion habile lui a conquis l'applaudissement unanime de ses compatriotes. Une haute moralité, une continuelle attention à sa tâche, et l'application du critérium positif à la résolution des questions, voilà les moyens employés par M. Limantour."[57] Another member of the cabinet to which Aragón referred was Manuel Fernández Leal, secretary of public works and instruction, who was also one of Barreda's collaborators in the preparatory. "Au Sénat, à la Chambre des Députés, les éléments constructeurs, plus ou moins affiliés au Positivisme, ont toujours prédominé et dominent encore."[58] Those educated in positivism were to constitute the principal governmental body. Porfirismo was the type of government adopted by the Mexican bourgeoisie. The ideology that sustained it was taken from and justified positivism. The ideal of order of the Mexican positivists was the ideal of peace maintained by the Porfirist regime.

§ 63. *The Meaning of Order to the Generation Educated by Barreda*

The need for order and its realization, which Barreda emphasized, influenced almost all his followers. The generation educated by Barreda knew and expressed the meaning of order. Both the direct and indirect followers of the Mexican teacher realized that, thanks to the work of Barreda, peace and order were possible in the Mexico in which they lived. During the Porfirian peace they recognized the educational work of Barreda that made this peace possible.

[57] "In 1877 M. Telésforo García, a forceful and expert writer on positivism, founded the newspaper *La Libertad*, which became involved in all the pressing political questions. It is the first periodical that has applied the positivist criterion to public affairs in Mexico. The Public Treasury had always been prey to the greatest disorder until a former preparatory school student, a follower of Barreda, the lawyer José Yves Limantour, accepted the position of minister of finance, which he still holds. His management has won him the unanimous applause of his compatriots. His high morality and continuous attention to his post and the application of the positivist criterion to resolve problems are the means used by M. Limantour" (Aragón, *Essai sur l'histoire*, p. 44).

[58] Ibid., p. 46.

In 1898, for the purpose of celebrating the seventeenth anniversary of the death of Gabino Barreda, his followers gave various speeches that reflected Barreda's ideas. The success of Barreda's educational work could be seen in these speeches. Order, an idea so dear to the Mexican teacher, served as a touchstone for his students. The new generation believed that it possessed an instrument of order, that is, an order that had been realized. Barreda's followers considered themselves to be members of a society where order reigned. They attributed this order to the educational work of Gabino Barreda.

"The admirable man who lies there," said lawyer D. Ezequiel A. Chávez, "saw in his youth and his maturity the torches of discord burning in the palaces and huts in his country. . . . Throughout the Republic, he heard the tragic outcry, that awful scream of anarchy, coming from innumerable mouths."[59] Barreda asked what was the origin of this anarchy and unleashed hatred. It was discovered that this hatred and anarchy resulted from the fact that "minds boiled, with opposing thoughts, spirits were overheated by contradictory emotions, impulsive wills were inflamed by contrary passions . . ."[60] Men fought among themselves because their ideas were contradictory. They could not understand each other. And this was the result of the diverse stages of cultural progress in Mexico. "Mexicans," said Chávez, "had contradictory ideas because each one's degree of culture was different; they were in diverse stages of progress and therefore each one harbored a different conception of the world."[61]

The disorder in Mexican society resulted from the cultural inequality of the Mexicans. Some were still in a theological stage, some in a metaphysical stage, and the best had reached a positivist stage. This diversity made social order impossible. "In the first, the theological stage, and in the second, the metaphysical stage," said Chávez in referring to the two important opposing groups, "each tried to impose its own faith, its own ideas, its conception of the universe on the other; and before this attack against the sanctuary

---

[59] Ezequiel A. Chávez, "Discurso," in *Discursos y poesía en honor del Dr. Gabino Barreda*, p. 8.

[60] Ibid., p. 8.

[61] Ibid., p. 9.

of consciences, each exploded with anger."[62] Disorder was the result of each group's trying to impose its ideas on the other. This intention provoked resistance and with it struggle and all its consequences. The disease lay in the varied stages of Mexican consciousness. Therefore, this disease had to be eliminated.

"The material anarchy of the revolution," said Chávez, "was merely a symptom, proof of a profounder illness, a profounder perturbation, a deeper insanity: the real disease was not there; it was something else. It was anarchy of thought."[63] Barreda attacked this disease by stressing orderly thinking, that is, an orderly mind. Mental order was necessary to eliminate material chaos. "It was Dr. Barreda," said Chávez, "who understood the real disease and who directly prescribed the sure remedy. If anarchy of thought made enemies among the Mexicans, it was necessary to destroy this anarchy; it was indispensable to subdue rebellious ideas, to channel them, and to discipline them."[64] It was necessary for Mexicans to understand each other so that they could work together and stop fighting among themselves. "Dr. Barreda said that Mexicans could unite and love each other and work together as brothers only if they understood each other. He was convinced that they must be compelled to draw closer together and to be side by side intellectually if their constant anarchy was to be destroyed. He saw that evil existed in Mexico because the people did not think alike and because they belonged to different centuries. He saw that in Mexico there were still prehistoric souls who belonged to the stone age, people who were restrained by secular tyrannies; souls of sixteenth-century conquistadores; spirits of the condottieri of the Middle Ages; and favorite sons of the nineteenth century. All these people existed simultaneously as the nebulous sons of the eighteenth century on whose thoughts the owl of negativism soared."[65]

The National Preparatory School was the melting pot for these contradictory spirits. There the minds of all Mexicans were made uniform. "The illustrious government of Juárez," said Chávez, "allowed Dr. Barreda extensive leeway to unite our compatriots

62 Ibid., p. 9.
63 Ibid., p. 9.
64 Ibid., p. 9.
65 Ibid., p. 9.

through the supreme virtue of science. He organized the National Preparatory School to teach the fundamentals of science and only science. He obliterated contradictions, disputes, anarchy for those who from near or from afar felt the harmonizing power of that school."[66]

Barreda tried in this way to eliminate what he considered to be the causes of national anarchy, that is, diverse ideologies. We have already seen how Barreda planned the educational program to establish a single ideology: an ideology valid for all Mexicans and independent of the ideology that each individual might profess. Individual ideologies were demoted in favor of an ideology with social scope. This was sufficient; it was enough that the ideology considered to be social have this scope in order to keep the particular ideologies from being dangerous. Those ideologies that did not take into consideration the positive order lost their social predominance. There was no need to deal with them if they remained in the place allotted to them by the positivist order: the realm of the particular. Therefore, said Chávez, Barreda "never tried to destroy any belief; he saw, however, that no one could impose one on others without enslaving consciences and thus stirring up anarchy."[67] Regarding Barreda's respect for the ideas of others, another follower, José Ramos, said, "The instruction of the teacher was purely scientific; never did I hear him, in class or in private, dwell on thorny subjects, which belong to the individual conscience."[68]

Barreda wanted to make every one think alike through an ideology that did not contradict the beliefs of each individual Mexican. We already know why: to attack an individual's beliefs would mean returning to anarchy. To openly attack another's beliefs would provoke resistance. The best thing to do was to convince, and this was possible only through an ideology with a scientific basis, because science did not affirm anything that could not be demonstrated. Science would provide the bond that would unite Mexicans. José Ramos said that Barreda spoke of the possibility that science would provide the bond that would unite the Mexi-

[66] Ibid., p. 10.

[67] Ibid., p. 10.

[68] José Ramos, "Discurso," in *Discursos y poesía en honor del Dr. Gabino Barreda*, p. 15.

cans. "Humanity is so divided," he said, "in respect to religious and political beliefs, that it seems impossible today to establish common ties by means of these beliefs. On the other hand, logically demonstrated scientific principles are, and always will be, the same for everyone; the sum of the three angles of a triangle is equal to 180 degrees; the square of the hypotenuse is equal to the sum of the squares of the other two sides. . . . These and other undeniable truths must be accepted by every enlightened man, be he republican or anarchist, aristocrat or democrat, believer or nonbeliever. You should be united by the bonds of science; everyone should participate in the communion of science, which neither excludes nor refuses anyone."[69]

Barreda tried to unite the Mexicans through bonds derived from the natural sciences; he wished to unite them in a way that was least human: through the physical sciences. He knew that it was impossible to unite them through the human side, through their beliefs or ideals. He recognized a field that was susceptible neither to planification nor to social ordering. Then he tried to make the least human science into the science that would serve the human order. The natural sciences were a neutral field where all Mexicans could be in accord. "We believe as you," said Chávez, "that there is a neutral field where all beliefs can coexist without conflict; that there is a common language that everyone can understand. We assure, as you have assured, that this promised land of human thought is that of science. We are certain that that superior language, in which there are no words for hate, is also science."[70]

The philosophy of Barreda was therefore not a combative philosophy, nor was it a philosophy of disorder. It was a philosophy whose ultimate end was order. Instead of attacking, it constructed. Anarchy was its only enemy. In another commemorative speech Miguel E. Schultz said that Barreda fought "against anarchy, the only enemy of human well-being, which it detests and attacks in every way."[71] Thanks to this constructive work, an era of peace was possible. Thus, his work would be considered patriotic. His work, said Schultz, was not only philosophic, but also patriotic,

---

[69] Ibid., p. 14.

[70] E. Chávez, "Discurso," p. 11.

[71] Miguel E. Schultz, "Discurso," in *Discursos y poesía en honor del Dr. Gabino Barreda*, p. 23.

because it prepared an era of peace and harmony, "by strengthening fraternity among the children of the same homeland through the conquest of uniformity or, at least, of a similarity of criteria."[72]

§ 64. *The Social Order that Resulted from the Educational Work of Barreda*

From what has been said, one will be aware of what the educational work realized by Barreda meant for the new generation. This generation felt that it had attained social equilibrium, that is, order, thanks to the previous labor of mental preparation. Pablo Macedo, brother of Miguel Macedo, who has already been mentioned, presented himself as living testimony of what Barreda's educational work represented as an instrument of order. Pablo Macedo was one of the Mexican positivists who, before he became a positivist, received the kind of education that Barreda was to reform. Macedo spoke of education prior to Barreda's reform. "According to the Plan of Lares, which was then in force, two years were dedicated to the study of Latin grammar before one could sign up for the 'philosophy' course. First one took logic or, rather, the three rules of the syllogism; then metaphysics, divided into three sections that dealt with 'the divinity,' 'the angels,' and 'the human soul'; and then morality. The second course in 'philosophy' was dedicated to the study of arithmetic, algebra (without passing beyond second-degree equations), plane and solid geometry, and rectilinear trigonometry. As a complementary course, we had a short treatment of geography, chronology, and French, which was necessary to translate the physics text book for the following year."[73] The lack of instruments for the study of physical phenomena added to this, said Macedo, was the reason why "we were almost always convinced by what the author affirmed, not because it was proven by our senses, but because of the teacher's authority and the pictures in the text book."[74] Once a person had completed those studies, the preparatory course was terminated.

The social results of this education, said Macedo, were twofold:

[72] Ibid., p. 19.
[73] Pablo Macedo, "Discurso," in *Discursos y poesía en honor del Dr. Gabino Barreda*, p. 26.
[74] Ibid., p. 27.

the first result was that the social classes who were to be influential in the destinies of the nation "would actually be very poorly educated. This class would not even understand its own ignorance but believe that it possessed wisdom."[75] But the second consequence was even graver; it was the cause of social anarchy. "What is there in common," asked Pablo Macedo, "between the lawyer, whose mind is nourished only on incoherent and incomplete metaphysical concepts, and the doctor, who has taken more or less but at least something from positive methods to reason in the field of the natural sciences? And what is there in common between the lawyer, the doctor, and the engineer, whose mind is almost closed to every horizon outside of the world of mathematics? Nothing, absolutely nothing!"[76]

Material disorder was, then, a result of the lack of educational uniformity. The Mexicans did not know one another; they were not capable of agreeing. Without this agreement social order was impossible. Without order society would result in chaos; lack of order nourished the anarchy to which society was a prisoner. Gabino Barreda came to establish order by changing education, that is, by making the studies the same for everyone and thereby making all Mexicans think alike. Barreda was, then, the one who brought about the peace that was so badly needed; thanks to his educational reform peace could be a fact. "Without him," said Macedo, "we probably would have belonged to that class of social epileptics who are unceasingly agitated by convulsions of vanity and ignorance, and who end up being victims of the moral hydrophobia that ambitious impotence determines and communicating the virus of their vilification and degradation to others."[77]

Thus, the peace and order that had been acquired had their origin in the work of Barreda. Gabino Barreda was the intellectual author of the new order, that of the Mexican bourgeoisie. Barreda fulfilled his mission: that of preparing the bourgeoisie to lead the country and to impose its own order. Macedo recognized other factors that made the new era of peace and order possible, such as the fact that Mexico hooked up to the "locomotive engine of Anglo-American progress," the political ability of General Porfirio Díaz,

[75] Ibid., p. 28.
[76] Ibid., p. 29.
[77] Ibid., p. 31.

the habit of profit, which diverted the energies of the Mexicans, replacing the previous revolts and violence. All these factors contributed, but one cannot deny, said Macedo, that "the respite from armed revolution that we are now enjoying"[78] is due to the educational work of Gabino Barreda.

§ 65. *The Order of the Mexican Bourgeoisie*

Thus, the education implanted by Gabino Barreda was a bond that unified the Mexicans. Those who could not agree on beliefs and ideas could agree on material consequences that came from an education that considered only material well-being and comfort. The bond that tied them together they called science. Science, they believed, was the field that united them; science made them understand each other. And the man who had shown Mexicans this field of union was Barreda. "Dr. Barreda was, therefore," said Don Ezequiel Chávez, "one of the most intelligent enemies of anarchy; he directly contributed to establishing the basis of Mexican fraternity on the firm foundations of science. Those of us who believe in science, those united by science, have come here today to render homage to this eminent founder. At this moment there are here around this sepulcher men with no religion, Catholics, loyal servants of the state, Mexicans without civil functions, many poor, and some rich; all are united to render a tribute of gratitude to the organizer of science in Mexico, the eminent intellectual who upon the darkness of antiquated ideas pronounced the sublime word of Genesis: let there be light, so that there would be light."[79]

The Mexican bourgeoisie's ideal of order was, therefore, the union of all with independence for the individuality of its members. Mexicans should no longer be separated from one another by their ideas or beliefs. Only one ideal should exist so that everyone could be united. Money is the only division that can exist. Some Mexicans might have more and others less, but money could not be a limited or closed boundary, because it was within the grasp of anyone who was capable of acquiring it through the means at his disposal. In this country, said Justo Sierra, "there are no closed classes, because those that are so called are only separated

---

[78] Ibid., p. 33.
[79] E. Chávez, "Discurso," p. 10.

among themselves through the movable boundaries of money and a good education; here there is no class on the move other than the bourgeoisie; it absorbs all the active elements from the inferior groups."[80]

The Mexican bourgeoisie educated by Barreda acquired order and peace. It assimilated the various groups of Mexicans who previously had conflicting interests. It succeeded in establishing a political and a social order into which the interests of all Mexicans apparently fitted, that is, strictly material interests, not ideological interests. The Mexican bourgeoisie succeeded in establishing a government into which all Mexicans seemed to fit. "The bourgeoisie," said Sierra, "was conscious of its being. It knew where it should go and what road it should follow to be master of itself. This would occur on the day that it felt governed by a character that would level everything to arrive at one result: peace. Army, clergy, religious reactionaries, liberals, reformers, sociologists, Jacobins, and, under the social aspect, capitalists and workers in both the intellectual and economic order formed the nucleus of a party that naturally took for its common denominator a name, a personality: Porfirio Díaz."[81] This was the new social order whose ideological basis was established by Gabino Barreda.

[80] Justo Sierra, *Evolución política del pueblo mexicano*, p. 444.
[81] Ibid., p. 445.

SECTION FIVE:
THE UTOPIA

I. Freedom of Conscience and Positivism

§ 66. *The Unconstitutionality of Positivist Education*

What has been shown up to this point is the adaptation of Mexican positivism to the circumstances current in Mexico when it was introduced as an instrument of order. We have also seen how positivism evolved into an ideology that justified the new order. We have seen how the social class called the Mexican bourgeoisie used positivism. Positivism for the bourgeoisie was merely an instrument in the service of its interests, as liberalism had been. In the step from liberalism to positivism, from an ideology of combat to an ideology of order, the Mexican bourgeoisie lost neither its characteristics nor its manner of feeling. The liberal mask, like the positivist mask, did not make the class known as the Mexican bourgeoisie abandon its ideas of material well-being and social comfort, and, consequently, it took great pains that the new order be unalterable. This class did not believe that physical force preserved order; it wanted to demonstrate that the order that it wanted to establish was the order that all Mexicans should want. The instrument that it used was persuasion. This ideal of order was expressed by a number of its members and was synthesized in the previous section. It was an order that contained all ideologies. It was an order to which all classes belonged. The aim of the bour-

geoisie was that this order, the place or social field in which everyone would fit, be none other than the order of the Mexican
bourgeoisie.

It has also been seen how the Mexican bourgeoisie passed from
a combative ideology, liberalism, to one of order, positivism. This
step was determined by the usefulness of these ideologies to it. Liberalism as a combative instrument had no reason to exist, once it
was triumphant. The Mexican bourgeoisie now possessed social
power. Now positivism, an ideology of order, as a constructive
ideology, an ideology of persuasion, should exist. But the bourgeoisie soon attacked positivism when positivism began to lean in
another direction and no longer served as an instrument in the
service of the bourgeoisie. This has been seen in a previous chapter.

All beliefs fit into the order desired by the Mexican bourgeoisie.
As an ideal order the bourgeoisie wanted the individual to enjoy
the freedom to think or believe what he wished, providing that
everyone be united by what the bourgeoisie referred to as the social
ideal of order, namely, one in which everyone worked and cooperated so that a great nation would arrive at its peak of material
progress. The bourgeoisie wanted a nation that would permit its
citizens to enrich themselves and to acquire the maximum amount
of material comfort. In this ideal nation there was no room for
sentimentalism or ideals, which were merely false pretexts for
acquiring power. The only ideal that one should take into account
was reality and not chimeras. By reality was meant everything
that referred to material well-being.[1]

Positivism was presented as a doctrine that synthesized the ideals
of the Mexican bourgeoisie. Positivism was presented as a doctrine
that justified the bourgeois ideal of order and, as such, the bourgeoisie accepted it, providing the doctrine did not alter its order.
Positivism was presented as an ideal social doctrine because it did
not seem to attack any doctrine, but respected all of them. Its
theories seemed to be only social and, therefore, it would not interfere with individual freedom. However, reality demonstrated that
the pretensions of this doctrine were only ideal theories. Reality
demonstrated that a great majority of the members of society that

---

[1] Remember when Mora said, ". . . it is not only important to check the rebels,
but a wise doctrine to banish chimerical projects from the mind is also necessary."

positivism wanted to unite did not accept the positivist ideology. Instead of establishing harmony among Mexicans, it had increased disharmony. Not all Mexicans agreed that the positivist doctrine was the doctrine of society. Positivism was attacked as a doctrine opposed to the ideas of the Constitution of 1857, then in force. It was said to be a doctrine opposed to the freedom of conscience upheld by this constitution. Two powerful groups, formerly antagonistic, liberals and Catholics, united and attacked positivism. The Mexican bourgeoisie was faced with a new enemy. Its members did not agree. It was a more dangerous battle than the armed one, because it was a spiritual battle. The spiritual power that the Catholic church had abdicated was disputed. This was a serious matter. The Mexican bourgeoisie wanted to leave this power a vacuum. It did not want any social group to have it, because it realized the danger of its possession. The Mexican bourgeoisie wanted to avoid the problem. It wanted neither to establish nor to allow the establishment of a spiritual power. Hence, it tried to convince the members of society that only social power that aimed to serve all the members of society was material. Therefore, in respect to spiritual power the bourgeoisie tried to be neutral.

But the doctrine adopted by the Mexican bourgeoisie to convince nonbourgeois members of society was now presented with claims that it had not made originally, such as this doctrine's claim to possess the spiritual power of society. Opposed to this claim were those whose doctrines, according to positivism, had been superseded: the Catholic ideology, called theological by the positivists, and the liberal ideology, called metaphysical by the positivists. These two ideologies were opposed to the positivists' attempt to take over spiritual power. But behind these two ideologies opposed to positivism was the Mexican bourgeoisie, which could not permit its social equilibrium to be upset. Positivism was now presented as dangerous, much more dangerous than conquered Catholicism and banished liberalism. Positivism threatened one of the main principles of the Mexican bourgeoisie: freedom of conscience. Instead of remaining neutral, as every spiritual ideology should, positivism tried to assume a power that should not exist if there were to be a permanent order. It tried to direct the conscience of the Mexicans. This teaching was unconstitutional and contrary to the interests of society. Here positivism was opposed to the interests of society, which it was supposed to serve. It was opposed to the class whose ideological tool it was supposed to be. The Mexican bourgeoisie differed from Mexican positivism. It is true that both progressed together, but only so long as the bourgeoisie used positivism for its own interests. They separated when the interests of the bourgeoisie were harmed. This explained the attacks and reforms suffered by the positivist educational system in Mexico. This also explained why Porfirismo, the political regime of the Mexican bourgeoisie, did not always support positivism, as it did not fully support liberalism or Catholicism. Porfirismo was a regime whose sole aim was to establish the order of the Mexican bourgeoisie, independent of any spiritual ideal. The only thing sought in this regime was an ideological equilibrium. It would not permit any particular ideology to acquire full social force. It would not permit anyone to acquire spiritual power. Positivism was a doctrine to justify order, but not a doctrine with enough spiritual power to obligate Mexicans to think in conformity with this doctrine. This was dangerous. It was against the interests of society. It was a kind of invitation to disorder.

§ 67. *Defense of the Constitutionality of Positivist Education*

The Mexican positivists defended themselves from the attacks that affirmed that positivism was opposed to the Constitution of 1857 and, therefore, society. The Mexican positivists tried to demonstrate that the educational reform of Gabino Barreda, based on positivism, was not unconstitutional. Horacio Barreda, son of the Mexican teacher, was one of the Mexican positivists who most intelligently defended the educational reform of his father. The writings of this little-known thinker show that he was one of the most intelligent Mexican positivists. In his work "La Escuela Nacional Preparatoria,"[2] Horacio Barreda refuted the most important attacks made against the educational reform of his father.

Horacio Barreda tried to prove the constitutionality of his father's reform by showing that, during the era in which his father was asked to collaborate in the educational reform, Mexico existed in a state of chaos. One of the tasks facing the new government

[2] Horacio Barreda, "La Escuela Nacional Preparatoria: Lo que se quería que fuese este plantel de educación y lo que hoy se quiere que sea," *Revista Positiva* 8 (1908).

was to prevent those who had been defeated from returning to the battle once they had recovered from their defeat. The conquerors knew from experience that, no matter how well the other side had been subjugated, it would renew its struggle for power at the first opportunity. The most intelligent thing to do was to convince those who were defeated to collaborate with the new regime. It was necessary to convince them, not subdue them. Violence had to be avoided, because it had been learned that violence only breeds more violence. "What was necessary was a fixed system of general ideas and common doctrines," said Horacio Barreda, which could be invoked at any critical moment "to obtain collective agreement."[3] The social postulates of the conquerors were the same as those sustained by republican institutions, those of liberalism. The new order had to be organized according to those principles. These principles were against all violence. Thus, if this party wished to organize the country on the basis of these principles, violence had to be avoided. The country had to be organized in this way so that no Mexican's interests would be attacked, in either the material or the spiritual sense. It was necessary to have a government that would govern for everybody and not just for a certain group, as other governments had done.

But to govern all Mexicans meant that all Mexicans should agree with each other. There was disharmony and disagreement among the Mexicans because of the disparity of their ideas and doctrines. Every Mexican tried to make his ideas those of society. A doctrine that would unify the Mexicans was needed. An ideology was needed that would be above individual ideologies; it should be a system of general ideas, a common doctrine, that would be valid for all citizens no matter what their particular ideas or doctrines. The establishment of such an ideology was possible only through an education that was the same for all Mexicans. An ideology was needed that could be instilled in all the members of Mexican society while still upholding republican ideals.

President Juárez, said Horacio Barreda, "knew that his glorious political work needed to be assured in the future by a radical reform in public education that would harmonize with the already conquered republican institutions."[4] It was necessary to have an

3 Ibid., p. 146.
4 Ibid., p. 146.

educational system that could be reconciled with republican ideals. We already know those ideals through the interpretation of José María Luis Mora. According to the ideas of this Mexican liberal, the state had a determined social mission, which consisted of protecting and serving the interests of society. The state should not be used as a tool by a certain body or faction. Its mission was to keep order. Once the liberals had won, they had to establish a government that would fulfill these postulates. Then, said Horacio Barreda, "if the supreme duty of every state consists in reconciling individual independence and social cooperation, in harmonizing order and liberty, in perfecting the control that the whole should exercise over its parts—either by imposing order on actions or by determining wills, depending on whether this state action is merely political in character, or is enclosed within a moral sphere so that its influence is spiritual—then, if all this is true, the social organization should eliminate from society every source of mental anarchy, whatever its form and origin, because all disharmony should yield before the supreme consideration of maintaining social existence."[5]

With these words Horacio Barreda tried to justify the necessity of an ideology that would eliminate spiritual, or mental, anarchy. To avoid this anarchy it was necessary to have a social doctrine that would reconcile the social order with individual freedom. This doctrine would have to predominate over the interests and ideas of the individual. This doctrine would establish mental order, that is, the order that would make freedom of conscience possible. For every individual to enjoy this freedom, it was necessary that every individual restrain himself, that is, submit to the general order. To make freedom of conscience possible, it would be necessary that every Mexican sacrifice his freedom to a determined limit, to order. Freedom of conscience should not be understood as the right to interfere with the freedom of others. To make this freedom possible a social doctrine was necessary that would not oppose this freedom and, at the same time, would be common to all Mexicans, no matter how much their individual beliefs differed. The theoretical basis for this social doctrine was provided by Gabino Barreda when he reformed public education according to the principles of positivism.

[5] Ibid., p. 149.

Horacio Barreda tried to demonstrate that the educational reform realized by his father could be reconciled with the principles of the Constitution of 1857, that is, that it could be reconciled with the ideals of the so-called revolution of Reform. The educational reform realized by Gabino Barreda meant for Horacio Barreda the "legal manifestation of the political constitution." The aim of this reform was to make possible the liberal ideal sustained in the Constitution of 1857. A doctrine that would carry out the ideals of this constitution was one whose principles would make all Mexicans agree by destroying their differences and every kind of mental anarchy. "Science alone . . . ," said Horacio Barreda, "can establish a communion of complete and lasting ideas when its theories are disseminated." The scientific method "is the only one . . . that has been able to destroy at the roots . . . offensive controversies and heated disputes that invariably result in adding the deepest hatreds and grudges to intellectual differences." Through science "criteria are unified and finally opinions are the same."[6] Positivists attributed a superhuman quality to science. They believed that through science it was possible to make all men think alike, something that neither religion nor metaphysics could do. Thus, science was the best instrument to make all Mexicans think alike. Everyone could agree with scientific truths because they are demonstrable truths. This could not be said about religious and metaphysical truths, and therefore, they could not serve as an instrument of mental unification for the establishment of the spiritual order.

Science could not clash with those who sustain theological or metaphysical principles, because science always abstains from affirming or denying principles that cannot be demonstrated through experience. Science neither affirms nor denies supernatural principles. An education based on science could not make judgments about supernatural principles, and thus it avoided useless arguments and anything that might cause disharmony and social disorder. A society educated in the principles of science cannot provoke disorder, for it is aware of the fact that any principle exposed to discussion or dispute must be relegated to the individual. In the new social order supernatural doctrines can be accepted only

6 Ibid., p. 150.

by the individual. The doctrine of society must be based on science. The new education has tried to abstain from intervening in individual ideas, and has taught ideas that belong to the public order. "The supernatural sciences," said Horacio Barreda, "the undemonstrable mysteries, are considered to be private, to belong to the individual. . . . They no longer are social; they no longer promote harmony; they promote disharmony. Therefore, they must fall back deep in the individual consciousness."[7] Theological and metaphysical principles only cause disorder in society. That is why they must be relegated to the depths of the individual consciousness. "On the contrary," he continued, "the doctrines of science, demonstrable beliefs, facts derived from observation, and the results of experience, have become part of the public order, because these things have proven to be the only effective means of destroying the roots of mental anarchy, the enemy of domestic and civil harmony."[8] The principles of science "thus form the general ideas that unite the various members of humanity in a common field of positive appreciation."[9] Ideologically, public order should be based on positive science, because disputes and discord do not enter into the realm of scientific principles, and because its principles are demonstrable. They are different from metaphysical and theological principles, which are not demonstrable. Therefore, positive science should be used as a doctrine to establish mental harmony among the Mexicans.

In this way, Horacio Barreda tried to show that the educational reform of his father was not opposed to the constitution. Instead, it tried to fulfill the legal provisions of the constitution, which declared the freedom of conscience. In other words, its purpose was to fulfill the precept that established the basis for the freedom of thought to which all Mexicans were entitled. Mexicans could think the way they pleased, but, since this freedom was a privilege of each individual Mexican, no one could impose his doctrines or ideas on anyone else. Therefore, this freedom could only be a privilege of each individual. Otherwise it would alter others' freedom of conscience. The positivist method, which aimed to fulfill this constitutional precept, proposed to banish "every metaphysical

[7] Ibid., p. 151.
[8] Ibid., p. 151.
[9] Ibid., p. 152.

speculation and every revolutionary tendency." Thanks to this type of education, freedom of conscience was possible. The individual conscience, applying the positivist method, had to determine what was obvious to every conscience, what all men should agree about. What could be demonstrated in this way would form the common fund of truths capable of establishing social order, that is, the mental agreement of all Mexicans. Only through this type of education was it possible to talk about true freedom of conscience. But this freedom, said Horacio Barreda, was not "the absolute, unlimited, anarchical, and disorderly intellectual freedom proclaimed by the metaphysicians of the eighteenth century. . . . The freedom here dealt with is organic and relative; it forbids us to violate the consciences of others by forcing them to accept our opinions; it forbids us to use any means other than persuasion to impose our beliefs on another."[10] The meaning of freedom in the constitution, according to the Mexican positivists, was ordered and limited freedom. Remember Gabino Barreda's thesis concerning freedom.

§ 68. *Freedom of Conscience Cannot Be Opposed to Social Order*

"Preparatory education," said Horacio Barreda, "by compelling the mind to accept what is necessary and justifiable, by leaving absolute freedom in doubtful areas, by training the mind to a reflective tolerance that inspires goodness rather than hate toward those who think differently, fully satisfies freedom of conscience."[11] In these words he made clear the social justification for the educational reform of Gabino Barreda. He pointed out that social order was possible through this education because it inspired tolerance and spurned violence. The individual was left free to think as he pleased, but, at the same time, he was convinced that there was a difference between what he wanted to think and what he should think. What he should think was what was demonstrated by science. Freedom of conscience did not imply a freedom that was opposed to the interests of society. One interpretation of freedom was that of the anarchic and metaphysical mind, and another interpretation was that of the ordered and positive mind. The former interpretation opposed the social order; the latter strengthened it.

10 Ibid., p. 153.
11 Ibid., p. 154.

The lawyer Eduardo Prado accused the positivists of having converted the National Preparatory School into an institution whose teachings attacked national principles, those that declared freedom of conscience. Horacio Barreda answered this accusation by pointing out that the opposite was true. He said that this institution as it was established supported, rather than opposed, the principle of freedom of conscience. Juárez, said Horacio Barreda, accepted the positivist doctrine as the official one because he recognized the fact that it would reconcile the interests of all Mexicans, and therefore "it was sufficient for the statesman to generally appreciate the new institution . . . which reconciled the conditions that guaranteed collective cooperation without sacrificing the independence of the individual; and which reconciled order, progress, and liberty."[12] Why then did Prado allege that the institution attacked freedom of conscience? Because he understood freedom in a metaphysical sense. He understood it as the right to disorder and as the right for the individual to think whatever he wanted. The individual could think as he pleased as an individual but not as a social subject. That which appeared good to the individual was not necessarily good for society. The conscience could not have the same freedom in social matters that it had in individual matters. Society was not a product of an individual whim, but of a social understanding at which all individuals in society arrived without being influenced by the whims of a few.

Society could not be conducted by principles that were valid for individuals only; it had to be conducted by principles that were valid for all its members, that is, demonstrable principles. These were the principles of science. Society should look to science for its guiding principles. From a social point of view, one spoke of freedom in the scientific sense, not in the metaphysical sense. In a scientific sense, freedom could not be opposed to order. "As if in the field of the well-established sciences of observation," said Horacio Barreda, "freedom in its absolute, anarchical, and revolutionary form . . . could ever reign!"[13] Absolute freedom was impossible in the sciences. One could never think that two and two equal five. Freedom cannot go so far. Likewise, in the political field one could not think that the doctrines of Mohammed or Christ

---

[12] Ibid., p. 156. Gabino Barreda talked of "liberty, order, and progress" (§ 23).
[13] Ibid., p. 157.

ought to govern society. This claim could not be demonstrated scientifically. It would be a dogmatic affirmation and, therefore, undemonstrable. The National Preparatory School could not accept this type of anarchical freedom. Its purpose was not to teach dogmas, but to "form true citizens, men fit for real life, who will be well prepared to perform their social obligations in conformity with the general interests of society." The aim of the educational reform carried out in the preparatory school was "to constitute a uniform and stable public opinion, which would cut the roots of the poisonous plant of intellectual disagreement. . . . The best [system of education]," said Horacio Barreda, "is the one that can best be reconciled with the social conditions of the historical moment through which the human mind is passing."[14]

In the individual field, conscience was completely free. But in the social field such freedom was anarchy. The Mexican positivists did not believe that the framers of the Constitution of 1857, in defending the idea of freedom of conscience, meant freedom to be understood in an anarchical sense, because such freedom would have been contrary to the constitution itself and would have been the seed of its own destruction. A school in which instruction agreed with the anarchical meaning of liberty would be contrary to the constitutional form that had given it life. And those who established the principles to guide the new society did not want this. Public education could not be a tool of the individual's egoism. It had to be a tool of society. "Every system of public education," said Horacio Barreda, "aims to prepare the individual for real life by supplying him with a fund of ideas, sentiments, habits, and opinions necessary for him to adapt himself to the social order in which he lives."[15] Public education aimed to teach the individual to live with his fellowman. It taught him to behave as a social subject. That is why this education could not interpret freedom in an anarchical and revolutionary sense. Freedom of conscience was interpreted as a freedom that had its limits in the principles of society itself. These principles were not based on a priori affirmations; they could be demonstrated. These principles, said Barreda, were demonstrable and, therefore, could be respected by everyone. They were scientific and therefore useful to society. Theological

14 Ibid., p. 164.
15 Ibid., p. 173.

and metaphysical principles were relegated to the individual conscience for approval or disapproval. They lost their social character, because they lacked the necessary qualifications to obtain
social acknowledgment, that is, they were not demonstrable or scientific.

§ 69. *The Enemies of Positivist Education*

The Mexican positivists wanted to attain an order based on a
natural equilibrium between the individual and society. They
wanted to divide the field in such a way that society arrived
neither at anarchy, through giving too much ground to the role
of the individual, nor to tyranny, through giving too much ground
to the social, or collective, role. However, this objective had inevitable enemies from the very beginning. When the Mexican positivists perfected a synthesis by which they attained an equilibrium
between the individual and society, they had to attack and be attacked by those who gave extreme importance to either of these
antithetical principles. The educational reform that was supposed
to be based on this social equilibrium was attacked from two sides:
by those Mexicans who wanted to return to the old order, that is,
the conservatives and the clergy, and by those Mexicans who
interpreted freedom of conscience in its absolute sense without
recognizing any limit, that is, the extreme liberals, or Jacobins.
But there was still another enemy, which was found among the
educators themselves. Horacio Barreda divided those who attacked
his father's educational reform into two big classes: "the one,
theological and metaphysical in nature, represented by the clergy,
the lawyers, and the lettered, attacked it in the name of morality,
classical education, and deposed entities. . . . The other appeared,
through a fatality worthy of lamentation . . . from the scientific
class itself. . . . Latent animosity was evidently provoked by specialist aims, by widely separated concepts, and by the concern
with mere detail that characterized the strictly scientific spirit."[16]

The clergy attacked the new school in the name of morality. It
said that the school was responsible for suicides, duels, and a multi-
tude of social evils.[17] "Regarding the metaphysical influence of

[16] Ibid., p. 307.

[17] Remember the decree to discontinue the logic text of Mill and Bain, replacing it by that of Tiberghien.

the lettered and the lawyers," said Barreda, "it was not the intellectual consistency of their attacks that made them dreadful, but the political position that their representatives enjoyed."[18] According to Horacio Barreda, the worst enemies were the men of science, because their attacks were clothed in scientific reasoning. To this was added the resistance of the politicians. "The political influence of the lawyers and literary men gave a great force to metaphysical defenders, who, whether in the press, in the parliamentary tribunal, or even in the very ministries, obstructed the organization of the school in a thousand ways. . . . The purely literary spirit of the time, as well as the Jacobinism that reigned supreme in philosophy, was the reason why many intellectuals could not understand the importance of an intellectual discipline that was capable of establishing a scientific and encyclopedic education. Nor could they understand why a doctor, a lawyer, or an engineer should acquire a complete knowledge about the world, man, and society. Had these talented men needed such a pile of scientific subjects to rise to their high social and political positions?"[19] They made the work of the school impossible by arbitrary reforms and by conceding "exemptions from studies." Therefore, it was impossible for the school to attain the intellectual order that its founder envisaged.

Nevertheless, it was the men of science who most harmed the new educational system by their narrow specialist point of view. "Sociology was omitted from the program," said Horacio Barreda, "and scientific morality was slipped in only under the protective wing of logic."[20] This evil was inevitable. Upon reforming public education on the basis of positivism, Gabino Barreda needed a teaching faculty that did not exist. It was necessary to use those professors whose background was most similar to the desired positivist education that they were to provide.[21] The teaching faculty was chosen from the men of science whom he could lay hands on. Men of science could best initiate the students into a positivist-type education, while professors capable of fully realizing this type of

18 H. Barreda, "La Escuela Nacional Preparatoria," p. 307.
19 Ibid., p. 309. See also § 50.
20 Ibid., p. 311.
21 A similar thing happened with socialist education; the lack of an adequate teaching faculty prevented its realization.

education were being prepared. However, these men of science lacked an overall vision; they could conceive neither of the unity nor of the importance of all the sciences. They believed that an education in which all the sciences were considered as a totality was a utopia. What was needed was what Horacio Barreda called a "philosophical spirit." Without a philosophical spirit it was "difficult to appreciate the essential nature and fundamental principles of each one of the sciences. Since they were concerned with specialization and, therefore, susceptible to the great specialist developments, they denied in all sincerity and good faith that it was possible for one to grasp all positive understanding in a few short years of study."[22] They said that this type of education made "Jacks-of-all-trades and masters of none." These men's spirit of specialization greatly hurt the new system of public education and prevented it from being more successful. The basis of positivist education, an organic education that included all the positive sciences in a hierarchical order, was considered an illusion by the men of science. They obstructed the plan because they considered it impossible. Each one placed emphasis on his own science to the detriment of the others.

[22] H. Barreda, "La Escuela Nacional Preparatoria," p. 314.

II. The Ideal of a New Positivist Spiritual Power

§ 70. *Society's Ideal of Accord among All Members of Society*

In spite of the fact that Mexican positivists wanted all members of
Mexican society to agree to self-evident, demonstrable principles,
their attempts were obstructed by other ideologies. Positivism had
been adopted as a tool for the establishment of social order. But
for this it was necessary that society accept its principles. First,
it was necessary that every member of society agree with these
principles. To obtain this agreement, positivism had to affirm that
it would respect the ideas and creeds of each individual, and that its
only interest was in the social field. It drew the line between the
individual and society. But, in spite of this precaution, meant to
avoid conflicts with the beliefs of the individual, the positivists
could not keep from invading the field of individual ideas and beliefs. To keep the individual from feeling attacked in this area,
they attempted to show that their affirmations were demonstrable
and therefore social in nature. Every positive affirmation was to be
demonstrated, and its end was to be social. The freedom of the
individual to think as he pleased was limited by social interests.
These interests were demonstrable; they were not based on a priori
considerations. The positivists had to convince the individual to
think in a certain way regarding social matters, not in whatever

way he pleased. But to do this meant to violate the individual's freedom of conscience, even though this might be socially justifiable. It could not have been otherwise, because it is impossible to say exactly what belongs to the individual field and what belongs to the social field. Positivism wanted to leave one field completely free and the other limited. But this was impossible because one cannot demonstrate with mathematical precision what belongs to one field and what belongs to the other. There are individual fields that can be part of the social field for some men and vice versa. The personality, that which makes one individual different from another, is both individual and social.

An education that tried to plan social life necessarily had to deal with the individual. To some, certain limits would appear to belong to the social orders; to others, they would seem to oppose individual freedom. Therefore, it was impossible to have an educational plan for society that all its members would respect. The positivists wanted to apply to the human being a plan that was successful in the physical field, that is, in the field of nature, but they did not realize that the human being was not nature even though he was part of it. Science was precise in mathematics and physics, but that did not mean that it was also precise in the field of human nature. Auguste Comte had already considered this problem when he established his hierarchy of the sciences. What was exact in mathematics was less exact in astronomy, physics, chemistry, and biology. This inexactitude reached its maximum in the science of humanity, that is, in sociology. However, it was natural for humans to strive toward extremes, to strive to be more than human, to dehumanize themselves. That is why the French philosopher reduced everything to science, in spite of the great difficulties that he had to deal with. Comte tried to make of the human being what he did of nature: a science, a social physics or sociology. He tried to make a science out of society as he had made a science out of nature. This was one utopia more in the history of mankind. But it was a necessary utopia, because it was natural for man to plan what reality destroyed. In Mexico, Comte's ideal was put into practice. The human being was submitted to exact measurements. There was an attempt to order society by ordering the individual. However, this ideal had to deal, as we have already seen, with the very nature of man, which could not be submitted to limits, even though man himself proposed it. Mexican positivism began to be aware of this fact.

§ 71. *Social Enforcement of the Principles of Positivism*

Horacio Barreda was fully aware of the reality with which an ideal positivist education had to wrangle. He was also aware of the revolutionary character of positivist education. He knew that the positivists would have to wrangle with Mexican society. He also knew that this plan of education would not be approved by all members of society, because it attacked their principles. He knew that positivism, willingly or unwillingly, had to enter into disputes and provoke discussion. This social doctrine was not fully accepted, because Mexicans did not wish to recognize the social enforcement of positivist principles and because many still upheld principles based on a priori affirmations. The Mexican mind had not yet reached its full development; it was still in the theological-metaphysical stage. The problems in the development of the stage that corresponds to modern society, the positive, were multiple. Therefore, many Mexicans disagreed with positivism because they felt that it interfered with the principles of the inferior stage to which they belonged. "What positive science," said Horacio Barreda, "does not interfere with some supernatural dogma?"[23] The privileges of the individual, which were supposed to be respected, suffered. The area that sheltered personal, nonpositive principles, which no longer were allowed to have any social force, had suffered. There is no doctrinal cleavage between the individual and the social in a society that has reached its full progress, that is, a society that has already reached its positive stage.

Theological-metaphysical principles have been relegated to the individual conscience. But this prevents social progress and order. The ideology of a progressive society should not abandon any area to nonpositivist principles. Every ideology is totalitarian and cannot yield ground to another ideology. Horacio Barreda wanted public education to be philosophic, that is, something similar to what today is known as ideology. "By a philosophical system is meant that the sum of human knowledge is coordinated on the basis of certain principles that tie them together and give them a common

---

[23] Ibid., p. 351.

goal."[24] It is an ideology that pursues specific ends in which, naturally, all society should participate. Every other existing ideology should subordinate itself to the ends pursued by the social ideology. If there is another ideology, it should not contradict the principles of positivism, because positivism has a social character, and the interests of society are more important than the interests of the individual. Other ideologies, theological as well as metaphysical, should submit to the principles of a social ideology. Therefore, an ideology with social ends necessarily has to injure those ideologies that have lost their social force in the course of the progress of society.

Thus, every society has an ideology that corresponds to its progress; it represents the spiritual power of that society. Did a spiritual power exist in Mexico that replaced the spiritual power of the Catholic church when it lost its social force? The state had separated from the Catholic church in Mexico, considering that church dogmas belonged to the individual conscience. The Mexican government did not interfere in the religious sphere, but neither did it permit the church to interfere in the material or political sphere. But, said Horacio Barreda, it was necessary to have a group charged with directing "the intellectual movement according to scientific doctrines that served as the basis of public, demonstrable, secular education."[25] The dogmas of the Catholic church were relegated to the individual. The church could not continue to hold spiritual power, because its beliefs, said Barreda, "are, socially speaking, part of the private order. But if spiritual power should rest on demonstrable doctrines there would be no incompatibility. Instead of being divorced, church and state would merely be independent, in order to better assure the unity of ends, designs, and aspirations that makes for the convergence of those two classes of activity, the speculative and the practical, that are one in interests and that complement each other."[26]

In these words one can see how Mexican positivism tried to gain spiritual power in Mexico, once the Catholic church had left a spiritual vacuum. The church had represented the spiritual power in Mexican society. Now, although it would continue to be a spir-

24 Ibid., p. 374.
25 Ibid., p. 392.
26 Ibid., p. 391.

itual doctrine, it had lost social force. Lacking that, its doctrines were incompatible with the mission of the state; hence, the necessity for church-state separation. To cooperate with the state and, at the same time, preserve its independence, it would have to have the same ideas as society. Mexico needed a spiritual power to guide the spiritual forces of the country in accordance with its own interests. To pursue these ends, the Junta Directiva de Instrucción Pública del Distrito Federal was created. It was endowed with the authority to recommend text books, make educational improvements, appoint Junta members, vote for professors, concede professional and titular degrees, examine and approve scholarships, make estimates, submit written proposals for the dismissal of professors, and appoint new professors. Gabino Barreda wanted the Junta to be independent of politics.[27] He wanted the Junta to be the spiritual power of Mexico. The ends pursued by the material and spiritual powers were the same, but their fields were different. Hence it was necessary that they be *independent*, but not *divorced*. In referring to the Junta de Instrucción Pública with regard to this matter, Horacio Barreda said: "that corporation could not immediately obtain the social influence that only time can bring, much less could it immediately enjoy complete *political independence*; however, the precedent was established that if civil power did not give up completely its right to exercise certain functions, which were actually foreign to it, it did in fact declare its incompetence in that field and recognize its need to receive help and counsel from a group of intellectuals specifically charged with proposing and considering measures concerning matters in which this group was considered competent."[28]

With reference to the formation of a spiritual power independent of material or political power, Gabino Barreda said the following in an invitation to the public school professors in 1874: "Everyone wants to form an association of those who have consecrated themselves to the noble teaching profession in order to use their talents to promote the progressive, yet gradual, intellectual and moral evolution of teachers, and their material and spiritual

---

[27] Agustín Aragón said that Gabino Barreda, "through the Junta Directiva de Institución [*sic*] Pública del Distrito Federal, provided for the progressive and complete independence of academic life from public power, temporal or political" ("Gabino Barreda y sus discípulos").

[28] H. Barreda, "La Escuela Nacional Preparatoria," p. 393.

independence of every outside and, therefore, degrading control."[29]
As can be seen, Mexican positivists tried to establish a power that
would give society spiritual leadership similar to the state's civil
leadership. They tried to establish a power which was independent
of civil and political power, but connected with the material power
in its final objective: to serve society. The objective was order,
peace. Both powers, the civil and the spiritual, could collaborate
in achieving this goal: the former could give Mexicans material
and political guidance, the latter spiritual and intellectual guidance. True peace and permanent order would be the result of the
efforts of both powers in their respective fields. It did not suffice
that one power attain order; it was necessary that both attain it.
The state and education should be the powers in charge of establishing political and intellectual order, but neither should interfere
in the other's sphere. Unfortunately, this condition was not fulfilled. Politicians continuously intervened in the Junta de Educación by making educational reforms and by eliminating examina-
tions in certain subjects.

§ 72. The New Spiritual Power

As can be seen, the Mexican positivists wanted to occupy the
spiritual vacuum left by the Catholic church. This idea conformed
with their doctrine. It has already been explained how it was impossible to introduce into Mexico, as was done in other countries of
Europe and America, Comte's religion of humanity, because of
the political and social circumstances. However, in the words of
Horacio Barreda and his father one can see how the Mexican
positivists aspired to become the spiritual leaders. The new spiritual
power was to be established on a demonstrable, scientific basis,
since it was now impossible to establish any power on a supernatural basis. It aspired to direct society intellectually. But, at the
same time, it tried not to serve as a tool of political power. When
metaphysical-theological ideas were confronted with the new spiritual power, they had no ground left but the private order. This new
spiritual power should be based on demonstration because this, said
Horacio Barreda, "neither violates the conscience by the imposition

---

[29] Ibid., p. 395.

of certain beliefs, nor does it try to win public confidence in any way other than by rigorous positivist demonstration."[30]

The spiritual leadership of society could not be achieved by supernatural principles. It must be achieved through the principles that invalidated supernatural ones, those of demonstrable positive science. Not faith, but demonstration, should be the basis of the spiritual leadership of society. The intellectual leaders of society should possess these principles, said Horacio Barreda, "once society can organize its relations on demonstrable principles, on foundations capable of being appreciated for their rational basis by competent intellectuals who furnish the leadership in society."[31] There is a class in Mexico capable of appreciating these principles. Society should depend on this class once those principles based on faith are no longer important. It is this group, that is, this social class, to which spiritual leadership should be entrusted.

§ 73. *Spiritual Power Cannot Be Neutral*

An education charged with realizing spiritual principles cannot be neutral. The Mexican positivists said that secular education was not neutral. An education that attempted to establish principles by which society should be directed intellectually and spiritually was not neutral, that is, it was not an education that could abstain from ideological interference. The constitutional precept that declares that education should be secular should not be interpreted this way. Secular does not mean that a certain ideology should not be taught; it means that an ideology that is considered necessary to establish social harmony should be taught. An education that tried to create social leadership necessarily had to hold principles valid for society; therefore, those principles must intervene against the ones that have lost their social leadership. This education will necessarily violate principles relegated to the private order, those over which there is a complete freedom of conscience. Positivism contradicts those principles relegated to the individual because positivism can advantageously replace them. Principles based on demonstration, said Horacio Barreda, "are actually not neutral,

---

[30] Ibid., p. 450.
[31] Ibid., p. 451.

as they would like to be, because they can advantageously replace
those principles that the progress of the human mind in its double
movement of assimilation and dissimulation has already separated
in order to replace them by new elements that verify positivist principles. . . . If one appraises the doctrine, one can see that all the
positive sciences, without exception, damage supernatural beliefs
by revealing the incompatibility between the fundamental dogmas
of supernatural faith and the demonstrable principles of the positive sciences."[32]

That is why the new education could not be neutral. It was based
on a new ideology, and, therefore, no other ideology could be allowed ground. Positivism tried to replace those ideologies that no
longer fulfilled their social mission. It desired the spiritual power
that they had abandoned; it attacked them where necessary. Secular education cannot be neutral. It must be demonstrable because
its principles are demonstrable. An education based on demonstration cannot be neutral, because these demonstrable principles must
attack principles that cannot be demonstrated, such as theological
and metaphysical principles. A public education that attempts to
direct Mexican minds must affirm or deny. "The positive system of
public education," said Horacio Barreda, "proposes to construct a
uniform and stable collective opinion that will assure social cooperation. At the same time, it proposes to institute a group of tendencies, habits, and customs no less opposed to debility or tyranny
than to rebellion or servility. One can express it by saying that its
purpose is to make the individual better fit to command and
obey."[33] If social order is desired, then it is necessary that positivism intervene affirmatively or negatively: it cannot be neutral. The
positivist doctrine is a constructive one. Therefore, it cannot be
neutral. It has to construct by overcoming every obstacle.

In order to make social order possible, it is necessary to teach the
individual how to command and obey. Those principles relegated
to the private order did not fulfill the necessary requisites for this
end. Theology led to servility and metaphysics to egoism. Neither
ideology left the individual any responsibility. He was not responsible for his acts. If he obeyed, he did it through fear or convenience:
"whether for reward or for dread of force or punishment," said

[32] Ibid., p. 452.
[33] Ibid., p. 458.

Horacio Barreda, "but always submitting temporarily and until a favorable occasion for rebellion presented itself."[34] No social order can be based on principles that do not hold the individual responsible for his acts. Order based on such principles is transitory, valid only so long as there is fear or reward. There must be an ideology that teaches the individual his duties and social obligations. An individual must accept the social order through conviction of its necessity, not because of the imposition of punishment or reward. Only a positivist education can give this conviction. "Only a positivist education," said Barreda, ". . . can worthily and efficaciously sanction the exercise of command and obedience."[35] Thus, positivist education was the only doctrine capable of establishing a true social order. Therefore, the new spiritual power must be established on the basis of positivism.

[34] Ibid., p. 469.
[35] Ibid., p. 469.

III. The Struggle for Spiritual Power

§ 74. *National Preparatory School Education*
Considered as Sectarian

In their desire to acquire the spiritual power of the nation, the positivists were opposed by the clergy, which was unwilling to give up its spiritual power, and the liberals, who were opposed to all spiritual power. The clergy, once it was conquered, could not openly attempt to recover the spiritual power that it had lost. But it did not want the positivists to have it, and justified this position with the liberal idea of freedom of conscience. The clergy and the liberals united against the Mexican positivists. No spiritual power should exist. The individual should have the right to think as he pleased. The secular school stood for the nonintervention of any power in the spiritual field. No doctrine should be imposed. No social group had the right to make its ideas the ideas of society. The positivist doctrine was merely one doctrine among many. It should not represent society. The positivists, just like the Catholic or any other church, had no right to impose their dogmas on Mexican society. Positivist education was sectarian. Positivism was a sect just like any other sect. Therefore, it had no right to claim to be the philosophy of society. The clergy and the liberals called for absolute freedom of conscience, and for absolute neutrality in the spiritual field. They did not want any spiritual power to be imposed. Since there was no doctrine with full social validity, none should be imposed.

The objections of "the tenacious adversaries of our preparatory education," said Horacio Barreda, "namely, the clergy and the Jacobin liberals," were based on two fundamental questions: "Is preparatory education in fact sectarian? Is public education a political or a social function?"[36] Clergy and liberals said that the educational reform was unconstitutional and sectarian and that it violated the freedom of conscience. This accusation, said Horacio Barreda, was based on the fact that preparatory education in Mexico embraced every aspect of human nature. Not a single crack was open to a supernatural, that is, a theological or metaphysical, interpretation. "Is it not possible that they want to eliminate an education that they fear because it embraces every aspect of human nature? Is it not possible that they want to exterminate it at its roots, clamoring that the school is sectarian and should not be tolerated, because it attacks freedom of conscience and because it does not maintain the neutrality that secular education should guarantee?"[37]

The clergy and the Jacobins feared an education that seized the spiritual dominion from them. According to Horacio Barreda, those groups opposed the educational reform because they felt that they ought to defend the spiritual power that they were losing. Both groups feared positivist education because it would put an end to any possible spiritual domination of a theological or metaphysical character. They were actually not so interested in defending freedom of conscience as they were in retaining the power that they were losing or, rather, of recovering a power that they had already lost. Freedom of conscience was used as a pretext to defend their power. It had nothing to do with actual freedom. The struggle, then, was not a struggle for freedom, but for spiritual power. It was a struggle between those groups that had lost spiritual power and the group that felt that it had a right to it. Clergy and liberals united to oppose a force that threatened to take their power. The argument on which they defended themselves was based on freedom of conscience. "The *trait-d'union* to which I refer," said Horacio Barreda, "proceeds from the opposition to the National Preparatory School; it was presented as a sectarian institution, as

[36] Horacio Barreda, "La enseñanza preparatoria ante el tribunal formado por el Bonete Negro y el Bonete Rojo," *Revista Positiva* 9 (1909): 398.
[37] Ibid., p. 397.

a *sui generis* plan of education that merely disseminates the ideas of a close intellectual group, that is, the doctrines of a philosophical conventicle, and it was considered as a seminary that confers the degree *prima tonsura* for entrance into a strange and exotic faith."[38] The instructors in the new school were considered as members of a sect, and not as possessors of truths that were valid for society as a whole. The philosophy taught in this school was not considered to be the one that should guide society. It was considered to be merely one among many philosophies; therefore, it had no right to social leadership.

To refute the liberal thesis concerning freedom of conscience, which was used to attack the new system of education, Horacio Barreda compared the meaning of freedom from a metaphysical and a positivist point of view. The freedom of conscience that they defended had an anachronistic and extinct meaning. "The liberals and freethinkers to whom I refer," said Barreda, "who interpret freedom of conscience in its metaphysical and absolute sense, which today results in positive anachronism, insist that everyone possesses the unalterable right to believe anything that he wants. Therefore, they consider as a violation of freedom any attempt to establish a system of common beliefs."[39] For the liberals, freedom meant the same regarding supernatural beliefs as it did regarding positive knowledge. In the uncertain realm of the supernatural one could choose what most pleased him. In the positive field one could not do this, because every affirmation could be demonstrated to be correct and unique. In the positive field freedom cannot be interpreted in an absolute sense. Freedom is limited by scientific demonstration. "Therefore," said Barreda, "these minds cannot distinguish the enormous difference between real science based on demonstration, that is, strict observation of the facts, and the supernatural, that is, undemonstrable doctrines based on divine revelation or theological faith. . . . Those freethinkers, who are most lamentably confused, indiscriminately invoke the principle of the freedom of conscience in its purest revolutionary sense, a principle that is opposed to those truths that can be scientifically demonstrated. Scientifically demonstrated truths can never oppress and tyrannize our intellect, as can those that are incapable of admitting this

[38] Ibid., p. 401.
[39] Ibid., p. 402.

kind of scientific evidence. That is the reason why they are obliged to impose themselves on the mind."[40] The liberals interpreted freedom of conscience in its absolute sense. They admitted no limits, not even the limits of science. But this was an error; it was opposed to reality.

Horacio Barreda defended positivist education. He said that positivism was valid for society as a whole. It was not sectarian, as some wished to present it. Positivist philosophy did not affirm the supernatural; it did not affirm anything that was valid for some and not for others. Its affirmations were valid for everyone, because they referred to reality, that is, to facts, and facts must be respected. This did not imply a violation of freedom of conscience, because this freedom had no place here. "The vain spirit that is always harbored under the revolutionary's red cap," said Horacio Barreda, "holds that no one has the right to unify public education, even on a scientific basis with no intention to impose any kind of theory or idea unless it can be demonstrated. Science has never tried to close the eyes of understanding by obliging one to accept that which has never been demonstrated, which cannot be verified, and which, therefore, contradicts the most obvious experience. Science does not conceive of spiritual freedom as consisting of the absence of a fixed system of beliefs, of amusement in the midst of scepticism and incredulity, of miserable enslavement to doubt, intellectual indiscipline, and moral anarchy. Furthermore, science does not believe that the individual conscience groans under the yoke of servitude when the intelligence acquires unshakeable convictions that remain in it, precisely because the latter does not possess that absurd faculty with which the Jacobin thinker wants to endow it, and because it cannot reject what has been demonstrated, cannot arbitrarily rebel against reasons that it has freely accepted, cannot cast away through its own caprice and will that which has already been observed as truth."[41] The scientific method demonstrates; it does not impose. But once something has been demonstrated, and is accepted by the individual; that is, once the mind has been convinced and has freely accepted the demonstrated truth, one cannot arbitrarily deny it. Thanks to the scientific method, intellectual, moral, and social order are possible. If this

[40] Ibid., p. 403.
[41] Ibid., p. 403.

were not true, if that which is demonstrated were arbitrarily denied, whenever the individual wished, then all certainty would be impossible. Everything could be reduced to an individual's capricious fantasy.

Freedom of conscience interpreted in an absolute sense would result in chaos, disorder, anarchy. "It is not in the dominion of the natural sciences," said Horacio Barreda, "where the great principle of freedom of conscience has its just application; for there, say what you will, no one tolerates the notion that everyone may think and opine as he pleases, although no one has the right to impose the conclusions of science by means that are not purely moral, rationally demonstrable, and persuasive."[42] Tolerance in an absolute sense can "be applied only to those doctrines that do not guarantee collective conformity, those that are no longer universally accepted, those that belong to the realm of the individual. Those doctrines no longer regulate public life, politics, industry, and war. They are applicable only to the realm of the supernatural, because in this area every one enjoys the inalienable right to believe what he pleases."[43] There is no room for tolerance and neutrality except with reference to ideas that do not influence public life. It would not be the same for those ideas whose validity have a social character. In this field conscience must limit itself to accepting that which every conscience accepts freely, through demonstration, which, once accepted, cannot be denied except by demonstration that what was accepted was incorrect. What is demonstrated not only is an integral part of the individual, but also must be accepted freely, without question, by everyone. Therefore, positive science, that is, science based on experience and demonstration, cannot be sectarian. This means that it is as valid for one group as it is for another. It is superior to every possible interpretation that originates in the arbitrary will of the individual. Thus, education that is based on positive science cannot be sectarian.

§ 75. *The Clergy and Freedom of Conscience*

What most attracted the attention of the Mexican positivists was the fact that the clergy advocated freedom of conscience. This was natural for the liberals, but for the clergy it was unusual. Barreda

[42] Ibid., p. 404.
[43] Ibid., p. 404.

said: "It is worthy of attention that Catholicism, which is opposed to the individual examination of conscience and which is a systematic partisan of the absolute subordination of reason to faith and revelation, proclaims a dogma of Protestant origin and adheres to a principle that it has always looked upon with horror."[44]

The concession made by the church to the liberal idea that everyone has the right to profess whatever supernatural beliefs that he wants to is "the most unnatural concession that the genuine theological spirit in its Catholic form can make."[45]

What attracted the attention of Horacio Barreda was a commonplace of human nature. Every individual or group claimed to possess the truth valid for everyone, that is, the common fund of truths. This common fund of truths can accept no other truths. This can be said of both Catholics and positivists. Both claimed to possess the truth. In other words, both claimed to possess the truths valid for all society. Both claimed the right to possess the spiritual power of society. Both theological and scientific truths were presented as beyond discussion. A revealed truth is beyond question, as is a demonstrated truth. What we have here is a dispute over who should possess spiritual power in society. Each claimed special rights. The clergy looked upon positivism just as the positivists looked upon the beliefs of the clergy, that is, as beliefs possessed by a certain sect and valid only for those who wished to accept them. The clergy, including all Catholics, had the same opinion of positivist education that the positivists had of Catholic education: an education that violated freedom of conscience because it was sectarian. Therefore, it was not valid for everyone. The Catholics looked at their religion just as the positivists looked at theirs: that their religion was the true one and, therefore, it was the only one that everyone should accept. Both Catholics and positivists believed that their truths should be accepted by everyone and that their truths had no other value than that given to them by the whim of their believers. The caprice of the individual was valid neither in the revealed truths of Catholicism nor in the truths demonstrated by positivism. Freedom of conscience is valid in all areas except these. The clergy might consider that its truths did not deny freedom of conscience because they were truths in which con-

---

[44] Ibid., p. 406.
[45] Ibid., p. 407.

science had no freedom. The same might be said for the positivists, who felt that their truths committed no transgression against the freedom of conscience, because freedom of conscience was not valid in this field. The clergy said that freedom of conscience was violated when another ideology, which was not its own, was imposed on individuals. The clergy felt that its truths were the only universally valid ones. It was the same with the positivists. They felt that other truths violated man's freedom of conscience. One can see that there was a struggle for spiritual power over society. Each ideology claimed to be the valid one for society and each denied this validity to any other ideology.

§ 76. *Defense of the Social Validity of Positivism*

In defending the social validity of positivism and its right to possess spiritual power, Horacio Barreda tried to show that everyone was more or less a positivist, but not everyone was a Catholic, a liberal, or anything else. In this way he tried to show that all ideologies, except positivism, were sectarian. Everyone, he said, was more or less positivist. Everyone followed positivist principles even though he did so unconsciously. All men applied these principles to their lives, some with more and some with less intensity, but nevertheless they applied them. But those facts were ignored. Some individuals were afraid of positivism without knowing its ideas. They were unaware of the fact that they continuously adhered to positivist principles. "Nothing," said Horacio Barreda, "justifies the declarations of those minds that are frightened by the sounds of certain words whose real meaning they are ignorant of. Under the pretext that positivism presents a double philosophical and religious meaning, they want to parrot the accusation that such a mental construction is the most perfect model of intolerance and tyranny."[46]

"Positivism," said Barreda, "in spite of the fact that it synthesizes the intellectual and moral nature of man, and in spite of the fact that it aspires to construct a philosophy and religion that include politics in their dominion, respects completely the great principle of freedom of conscience."[47] Our positivists did not feel that their philosophy needed to violate the freedom of conscience

[46] Ibid., p. 426.
[47] Ibid., p. 426.

because it imposed itself on its own merits. Its truths were self-evident, so there was no need for violence and intolerance. However, some men could not see the obviousness of positive truths, and our tolerant positivists were irritated because they could not understand such an absurdity. "Can you, my friend, conceive, by any chance," said Horacio Barreda, "that a moderately reasonable mind . . . , an understanding whose judgment has not been confused by passion, and a brain that has not been atrophied by the weight of a revolutionary's red cap or a cleric's black cap, can in good faith hold . . . that a scientific system of studies, which includes all those positive speculations that the most illustrious intelligences have contributed at all times and in all places . . . that such a system of education, that can take pride in having merited universal acceptance, because it has been able to make everyone think alike, and to establish a common criterion that can be honored by Buddhists, Mohammedans, Jews, and Christians, including Calvinists and Lutherans, a system of education that is interested only in knowledge that it can prove and demonstrate, should merit the name sectarian?"[48]

The positivists believed that a philosophy whose fundamentals have a universal character cannot be sectarian. This type of ideology is superior to any individual opinion or religion. It is the only type of ideology that can establish a common criterion, independent of any individual criterion. This philosophy cannot attack freedom of conscience and, therefore, it cannot be unconstitutional, because this ideology, "by strictly discarding," said Horacio Barreda, "every supernatural dogma that produces disharmony, attacks mental anarchy at its roots, and realizes in the order of ideas, which is the basis of political and social order, the supreme aspiration of our Magna Carta."[49] By fully realizing an educational system based on positivist principles, the attainment of full national unity, different from that attained by an education based on theology or metaphysics, could be accomplished. If positivist morality were fully realized through education, said Horacio Barreda, one would not have "to join the files of young students who view the world as an evil exile." The world would not be seen as something "that inspires contempt

---

[48] Ibid., p. 431.
[49] Ibid., p. 432.

and horror until the blessed hour to abandon it forever arrives."
The hour of death is seen as blessed by those who believe in a doctrine "that obliges the human being to look upon worldly bonds as
obstacles to future happiness, and who continuously emit . . . that
terrible scream that provokes the most painful fright and suffocates
in the breast every generous impulse, every concern for the wel-
fare of others, a terrible cry that we obey, filled with a sudden
egoistic explosion, a terrible cry that makes us forget human soli-
darity when it says: Save yourself if you can!" Nor, if positivist
morality were fully realized, he continued, would we see "the
young generations leave school with their hearts impregnated with
revolutionary ideas, with minds crammed with negative and metaphysical principles. We would not see them enter into public life
viewing veneration and respect for superiors as stupid prejudices
and considering the principle of authority, and social hierarchy,
like so many other things, as incompatible with the sacred Jacobin
dogma of social equality."[50] Men educated in such principles cannot be good citizens. Neither can they feel love for their fellowmen,
their country, or society. They can only egoistically defend their
own interests. They care about nothing but their soul or, rather,
about the interest represented by a freedom full of egoism. Men
educated in theological and metaphysical principles cannot be good
citizens. They are truly sectarian. Their interests are particular
rather than social. Therefore, individuals educated in these prejudices have no right to be the spiritual mentors of the nation, because their interests are contrary to those of the nation.

The Jacobins are no more than "talents swollen with vanity and
complacency," said Horacio Barreda, "thanks to the leavening of
personal infallibility that fermented a mass of intelligence, poor in
scientific culture but rich in classical literature, in the culture of
the dead languages, and in abstruse dissertations concerning the *ego*
and the *nonego*, which do not even leave a crack open to the *us*.
With no more religion than an accommodating deism, they are
always ready to defend personal rights and much too slow to pre-
scribe duties and obligations."[51] Therefore, the clergy, said Barreda,
are men who are totally ignorant of the world, their families, and
their country. Barreda recalled the words of the gospel in which

50 Ibid., p. 434.
51 Ibid., p. 434.

Christ asked: "Who is my mother? Who are my brothers?" How is it possible to expect anyone who thinks this way to care about society and his fellowmen? Opposed to this egoistic way of thinking, said Horacio Barreda, is the positivist philosophy, which is concerned about the world and humanity. What is important for positivism is the family, country, and humanity. The young people educated in the positivist school "will not label their patriotic love and civic duties as petty sentiments," as they are labeled by those who are concerned only about the things of the other world. "Our novices, instead of beatifically lifting themselves to heaven, will remain nailed to the earth to study the structure of societies, to appreciate better the importance that human feelings have in the economy of those societies."[52] Positivism "awakens in them the desire to serve their country and to die for it if necessary."[53] Those educated in positivism tend to "coordinate their sentiments, their thoughts, and their acts around the family, country, and humanity."[54] As one can see, it is impossible to accuse of being sectarian an educational system whose ultimate goal is humanity. It is a philosophy in the service of all men and not simply in the service of an individual or a group.

As a religion, positivism is also superior to all others. Nor is it sectarian. It is the true religion of humanity. The adherents of other religions can be counted. Those belonging to the religion of humanity cannot, because it is a religion valid for all men. "If today," said Horacio Barreda, "all the revealed religions could count their adherents and distinguish all of them with a particular name, the Religion of Humanity, by virtue of its very spontaneity, would find adherents in every human breast, and it has no more apparatus than the nature of the organization of man, which endowed it with sentiments that cannot remain indifferent to domestic, civil, and universal aspects. If these are the differences noted today between a supernatural religion and one that is purely human, tell me in good Castilian, my friend, with your hand on your heart, which of these can be considered sectarian?"[55] Revealed religions cannot unify men. On the contrary, they separate them into sects.

[52] Ibid., p. 436.
[53] Ibid., p. 436.
[54] Ibid., p. 437.
[55] Ibid., p. 443.

This is not the case with the religion of humanity, which is concerned with all men and is recognized by all. "If we ask Christians or Buddhists about their supernatural beliefs, none will be the least ashamed to reject those dogmas that are not of their theology. But ask adherents of any religious communion if they feel in their hearts love of family and country, and veneration and gratitude for our human benefactors, and you will see that they will be proud that they practice those dogmas and that cult, and they will be anxious to remove any contrary idea from your mind."[56] Thus, men are separated by their dogmas, but, on the other hand, they are united by what is referred to as properly human. Dogmas are proper to supernatural doctrines. That which is peculiar to man is proper to positivist philosophy. Hence, the reason why those religions that are based on the supernatural cannot unify man. The religion of humanity is different because its principles come directly from man himself, from the reality of man. All men can see in it something that is proper to them.

Everyone is in some way a positivist, because positivism originates in the reality proper to the human being. Positivism, said Horacio Barreda, in its twofold aspect of philosophy and religion, is not sectarian. Everyone is in some way a positivist—from primitive man, who made and used instruments to confront nature, trying to decipher nature's laws through close observation, to modern man, whose motto is *Foresee in order to act*. All men have utilized observation, all have fulfilled to some extent the positivist idea, *Foresee in order to act*, even though afterwards they used nonpositivist means, perhaps because they were not able immediately to find the means that they needed. "There is not a single intelligence that does not acknowledge in certain cases positivist tendencies in thought and action. This is true even if we see the intelligence, in other and more complicated orders of speculation, throw itself into the realm of the mysterious and unknowable. This happens when, for lack of real theories to guide the individual in practical life, the intelligence is impelled to seek the aid of ultraterrestrial influences; finally these influences will change the intelligence's own activity into a kind of inertia that waits for the action of a supernatural driving force to impel it to

[56] Ibid., p. 446.

movement."[57] Thus, everyone in some measure is a positivist. However, not everyone who has pursued the positivist sciences has reached the height of progress achieved by the positivist sciences. Those who still trust in theological and metaphysical doctrines are reactionary. They are more or less incomplete positivists, depending on the degree to which they have accepted nonpositivist explanations. A theological or metaphysical explanation is merely a transitory solution, which originated from the urgent need to solve certain problems quickly. But these solutions are merely provisional in character. They are used only until man succeeds in acquiring true solutions, that is, positivist ones. However, inertia, or mental negligence, causes many men to accept solutions that should be merely transitory. According to Mexican positivists, the clergy and the Jacobins belonged to this group. "By a complete positivist," said Horacio Barreda, "one should understand the spirit that is free from the prejudices of the revolutionaries and the anarchists, the spirit that is free from reactionary predilections for the mysterious and unknowable. This spirit is neither frightened nor offended by the logical conclusions derived from applying the same methods of reasoning, from guiding beliefs toward the demonstrable, from taking a single decisive criterion to judge in our own acts and others' conduct what is susceptible to verification and proof in this world rather than what can be justified or condemned only by virtue of supernatural judgments."[58] To be a complete positivist it is not necessary blindly to follow Comte or other positivists, but rather one can criticize them on those points in which their method was not strictly positive. Positivism, unlike supernatural doctrines, cannot be tied to a name or to a particular person. That is why one can say that positivism is not sectarian. A positivist education is valid for all society. It is superior to supernatural dogma. If it attacks these dogmas, it is for the good of society. A positivist education cannot be opposed to freedom of conscience, because freedom of conscience in its unlimited interpretation has no place in the social field. Hence, positivist education, instead of being opposed to the constitution, supported it, since the spirit that ruled positivism recognized the need to establish order. This is how Mexican positivists defended their right to possess the spiritual

[57] Ibid., p. 470.
[58] Ibid., p. 473.

power of the Mexican nation. Horacio Barreda demolished the attack against the educational reform, which accused positivist education of being sectarian.

§ 77. *The Utopia of the Mexican Positivists*

Now our positivists are going to answer the second objection made by the clergy-Jacobin coalition, which Horacio Barreda sums up as follows: "Is public education a social function of the state or of a theoretical body dedicated to study and to purely intellectual speculations, without direct interference by the state?"[59] To this question, said Horacio Barreda, they responded as follows:

The clergy felt that, "since public education is a social function rather than a political function, it should generally be organized by the family and commended to the private initiative of the individual."[60] Regarding the Jacobins, "boasting about those tendencies toward disorder and anarchy that harmonize so well with their invincible predilections toward individualism and lack of discipline . . . they also proclaim that one should leave the direction and reorganization of public education to private initiative."[61] Clergy and liberals alike agree that education should be taken from the state and given to private initiative. But, said Horacio Barreda, the clergy has in this way laid a trap. The clergy uses liberal ideas to recover its lost spiritual power. And into this trap the liberals have ingenuously fallen. The clergy, through private education, tried to seize its lost spiritual power. Its defense of freedom of conscience was designed to eliminate the obstacles that the state might present. It wanted the state, through its neutrality, to abandon to it the Mexican mind. Once it had succeeded, said Barreda, its first victims would be the ingenuous liberals, because the freedom of conscience in its absolute sense for which they fought would be completely eliminated and every mind would be used as a tool of theological dogmas.

Another response was given by those scientists who had not yet attained full positivist development. Horacio Barreda called them incomplete positivists. "The incomplete positivists . . . view it as normal that the state indefinitely keep in its hands the organiza-

[59] Ibid., p. 477.
[60] Ibid., p. 478.
[61] Ibid., p. 478.

tion of public education as they conceive it, that is, as special, and these incomplete positivists do not object to abandoning the cultivation of the mind and heart to theological influence."[62] What interests this group is that the state supply the student, not with an ideology, but with a series of special branches of knowledge. Education should be neutral with respect to ideologies, which would be abandoned to outside influences.

Our positivists accurately see the danger of both positions. Both abandon spiritual power through a supposed neutrality. Our positivists see that this can only benefit the clergy, which had always had this power. Publicly the existence of spiritual power is not recognized. It should be left to the individual. The real enemy of our positivists, as for Comte, was the Catholic church. This had to be so because the positivists wanted to occupy the position that was once held by the Catholic church. Mexico was no exception. Here, also, our positivists aspired to occupy the place that the Catholic church once held. They attempted to be the spiritual leaders of Mexico. They did not agree that there was no spiritual power in Mexico. They did not agree that education should be secular, that is, neutral. They wanted a positivist education, one that would conform to their principles.

Our positivists had their own answer as to who should be in charge of education. "The complete positivists," said Barreda, "who always take a sociological point of view, accept the independence of church and state (not the divorce that exists between the two today, when political power is obliged to base its acts on positive and demonstrable notions, and not on incomprehensible mysteries). They see as the consequence and a necessary condition of the separation between *theory*, ideas, and opinions, on the one hand, and practice, acts, and execution, on the other, the organization of a spiritual power, namely, a competent body of theorists dedicated to the study of all the abstract positive sciences; this body, through its influence, was to complete and aid the political power."[63] Our positivists talk about the independence of both church and state, but by church they do not mean the Catholic church, as might be supposed—not the church of those so-called representatives of supernatural believers—but the positivist church.

[62] Ibid., p. 479.
[63] Ibid., p. 479.

They spoke of a positivist church, a church that should aid political power, not of a divorced church. The positivists aspired to possess the power left by the Catholic church upon its divorce from the state. Mexican positivists wanted their church to help the state, but they also wanted it to keep its independence. This idea was never more than an ideal, in other words, a utopia. Mexican reality would not permit the realization of this idea. Although Mexican positivists saw this, they did not give up hope. They knew that they were up against a reality that they could not avoid. Therefore, Barreda said, "while societies are organized in the normal way demanded by the needs of progress, the complete positivists recognize a condition for the future rise and organization of that new spiritual power: that for the time being public education be coordinated and disseminated by the state."[64]

The reality that Mexican positivists had to face was considered transitory. They knew that for the time being they could not do anything about the reality in which they lived, but they did not give up hope. They temporarily accepted the fact that civil power should direct education, because this was the best guarantee that education would not fall into the hands of any outside force. Meanwhile, Mexican positivists would work to establish the basis for the new power. "Only an education in harmony with the most urgent needs of modern society," said Barreda, "can little by little improve knowledge so that there will arise from those secular schools the organs that will later organize the desired spiritual power. In turn, this spiritual power, once formed, will organize public education according to the requirements of civilization."[65] Regarding secular education, Mexican positivists said that in form it too was transitory. But, as we have already seen, by education they did not mean neutral education. They meant a preparatory education that would replace education based on the supernatural. "The complete positivists," said Barreda, "accepted the only solution to the problem. Today they support secular education while striving for free discussion of educational material and the free individual initiative of competent people, aiming toward the enlightenment of the state."[66]

[64] Ibid., p. 480.
[65] Ibid., p. 480.
[66] Ibid., p. 480.

In summary, the ideal of Mexican positivists was to be the spiritual leaders of Mexico. This ideal, like others, was not realistic. Reality was contrary to their aspirations. Do not forget that the positivist philosophy was brought to Mexico to serve the interests of a class that we have labeled the bourgeoisie. The interests of this class would not have permitted the establishment of this power. In their own interests, the bourgeoisie wanted this power to remain leaderless. Society and the powers that represented it had to remain neutral toward ideas, beliefs, and opinions. To impose an idea or an ideology on someone was to try to destroy the equilibrium that had been established. Mexican positivists were conscious of this reality, but they considered it transitory. Meanwhile, they worked to acquire spiritual power in the future and, with it, the realization of a society in accord with the positivist ideal and the ideal of the religion of humanity. This was the utopia of Mexican positivists, which, like every ideology, was opposed to reality, of which the positivists were no more than instruments. José Torres was right when he asserted that positivism was not to blame for the evils of Mexico. The positivist ideal was one thing and the reality called Porfirismo was another. But, if it is true that one thing was the ideal and another thing was the reality, one cannot deny that positivism, as the generation of the Athenaeum saw it, was used as a tool for the reality called Porfirismo. Positivism provided the weapon by which to justify a series of acts contrary to the positivist ideal.

BIBLIOGRAPHY

Anales de la Asociación Metodófila "Gabino Barreda." Mexico City: Imprenta del Comercio de Dublán y Chávez, 1877.

Aragón, Agustín. *Essai sur l'histoire du positivisme au Mexique.* Preface by M. Pierre Laffitte, Director of *Positivisme.* Paris: Société Positiviste, 1898.

———. "Gabino Barreda y sus discípulos." Speech read before the Mexican Athenaeum on March 8, 1938.

Arnáiz y Freg, Arturo. Prologue to *Ensayos, ideas y retratos,* by José María Luis Mora, Biblioteca del Estudiante Universitario. Mexico City: Ediciones de la Universidad Nacional Autónoma de México, 1941.

Bancroft, Hubert Howe. *Vida de Porfirio Díaz.* San Francisco: History Company, 1887.

Barreda, Gabino. "Instrucción pública." *Revista Positiva* 1 (1901).

———. *Opúsculos, discusiones y discursos.* Mexico City: Imprenta del Comercio de Dublán y Chávez, 1877.

Barreda, Horacio. "La enseñanza preparatoria ante el tribunal formado por el Bonete Negro y el Bonete Rojo." *Revista Positiva* 9 (1909).

———. "La Escuela Nacional Preparatoria: Lo que se quería que fuese este plantel de educación y lo que hoy se quiere que sea." *Revista Positiva* 8 (1908).

Batres, Leopoldo. *Historia administrativa del Sr. General Porfirio Díaz.* Mexico City, 1920.

Bernheim, Ernst. *Introducción al estudio de la historia.* Translated by Pascual Galindo Romeo. Barcelona: Editorial Labor, 1937.

Boletín de Instrucción Pública. Mexico City: Tipografía Económica, 1903.

Boletín de la Escuela Nacional Preparatoria. Mexico City: Tipografía Económica, 1908. [Director: Porfirio Parra.]

Bréhier, Émile. *Historia de la filosofía*. Translated by Demetrio Náñez. Buenos Aires: Editorial Sudamericana, 1942.

Bremauntz, Alberto. *La educación socialista en México*. Mexico City, 1943.

Calero, Manuel. *Un decenio de política mexicana*. New York, 1920.

Caso, Antonio. "La filosofía moral de don Eugenio M. de Hostos." In *Conferencias del Ateneo de la Juventud*. Mexico City: Imprenta Lacaud, 1910.

―――. *Filósofos y doctrinas morales*. Mexico City: Librería Porrúa Hnos., 1915.

Ceballos, Ciro B. *Aurora y ocaso* (1867–1906). Mexico City: Imprenta Central, 1907. [Historical essay on contemporary politics.]

Centinela Español, El. Mexico City, 1879–1881. [Biweekly publication of political information. Director: Telésforo García.]

Chávez, Ezequiel A.; José Ramos; Miguel E. Schultz; Pablo Macedo; Jesús Urueta; and Porfirio Parra. *Discursos y poesía en honor del Dr. Gabino Barreda*. Mexico City: Tipografía T. González Sucs., 1898.

Comte, Auguste. *Catéchisme positiviste*. Paris, 1892.

―――. *Cours de philosophie positive*. 6 vols. Paris, 1830–1842.

―――. *Discurso sobre el espíritu positivo*. Translated by Julián Marías. Madrid: Revista de Occidente, 1934.

―――. *Primeros ensayos*. Translated by Francisco Giner de los Ríos. Mexico City: Fondo de Cultura Económica, 1942.

―――. *Système de politique positive*. 4 vols. Paris, 1851–1854.

Conferencias del Ateneo de la Juventud. Mexico City: Imprenta Lacaud, 1910.

Croce, Benedetto. *La historia como hazaña de la libertad*. Translated by Enrique Díez-Canedo. Mexico City: Fondo de Cultura Económica, 1942.

Davis, Harold Eugene. "La historia de las ideas en Latinoamérica." In *Latinoamérica anuario de estudios latinoamericanos*. Vol. 2. Mexico City: Universidad Nacional Autónoma de México, 1969. [Also in English in *Latin American Research Review* 3, no. 4 (1968): 23–44.]

[Díaz Covarrubias, José]. *Dr. Gabino Barreda, propagador del positivismo en México y fundador de la Escuela Nacional Preparatoria*. Appendix by Manuel Flores. [Biographical annotations taken from *Extrait de l'histoire général des hommes du XIX siècle vivants ou morts de toutes les nations*. Mexico City: Tipografía de Gonzalo A. Esteva, 1880.]

Fuentes Mares, José. Prologue to *Estudios de Gabino Barreda*, by

Biblioteca del Estudiante Universitario. Mexico City: Ediciones de la Universidad Nacional Autónoma de México, 1941.

Gabilondo, Hilario. "La *Lógica* de Tiberghien en la Escuela Nacional Preparatoria." *La República* (1880).

Gamboa, Ignacio. *El positivismo y su influencia en el estado actual de la sociedad mexicana.* Mérida, Yuc.: Imprenta Loret, 1899.

García, Genaro. *La educación nacional en México.* Mexico City: Tipografía Económica, 1903.

García Bacca, Juan David. *Introducción al filosofar.* Tucumán: Universidad Nacional de Tucumán, 1939.

Gaupp, Otto. *Spencer.* Translated by J. González. Madrid: Revista de Occidente, 1930.

Gooch, G. P. *La historia y los historiadores en el siglo XIX.* Translated by Ernestina de Champourcin and Ramón Iglesia. Mexico City: Fondo de Cultura Económica, 1942.

Groethuysen, Bernhard. *El origen de la burguesía.* Translated by José Gaos. Mexico City: Fondo de Cultura Económica, 1943.

Hale, Charles A. "Sustancia y método en el pensamiento de Leopoldo Zea." *Historia Mexicana* 20 (October–December 1970): 285–304.

Hammeken Mexia, Jorge. "La filosofía positiva y la filosofía metafísica." *La Libertad* (1880).

Hazard, Paul. *La crisis de la conciencia europea.* Translated by Julián Marías. Madrid: Pegaso, 1941.

Henríquez Ureña, Pedro. "La cultura de las humanidades." *Revista Bimestre Cubana* 9, no. 4 (1914).

———. *Horas de estudio.* Paris: Sociedad de Ediciones Literarias y Artísticas, 1911.

———. "La obra de José Enrique Rodó." In *Conferencias del Ateneo de la Juventud.* Mexico City: Imprenta Lacaud, 1910.

Heráclito. *Fragmentos.* Translated from Greek by José Gaos. Mexico City: Alcancía, 1939. Republished in *Antología filosófica. I. La filosofía griega.* Mexico City: La Casa de España en México, 1941.

Jullian, C. Introduction to *Extraits des historiens français du XIX siècle.* Paris: Librairie Hachette, 1898.

Libertad, La. Mexico City, 1878–1884. [Political periodical. Editors: Francisco G. Cosmes, Eduardo Garay, Telésforo García, Justo Sierra, and Santiago Sierra.]

Lombardo Toledano, Vicente. "El sentido humanista de la Revolución Mexicana." *Revista de la Universidad de México* 1, no. 2 (December 1930).

López-Portillo y Rojas, José. *Elevación y caída de Porfirio Díaz.* Mexico City: Librería Española, 1921.

Macedo, Miguel. "Ensayo sobre los deberes recíprocos de los superiores y de los inferiores." In *Anales de la Asociación Metodófila "Gabino Barreda,"* pp. 213–228. Mexico City: Imprenta del Comercio de Dublán y Chávez, 1877.

Manero, Antonio. *El antiguo régimen y la Revolución.* Mexico City: Tipográfica y Litográfica "La Europea," 1911.

————. *¿Qué es la Revolución?* Veracruz: Tipografía "La Heroica," 1915.

Mannheim, Karl. *Ideología y utopía.* Prologue by L. Wirth; translated by Salvador Echavarría. Mexico City: Fondo de Cultura Económica, 1941.

————. *Libertad y planificación social.* Translated by Rubén Landa. Mexico City: Fondo de Cultura Económica, 1942.

Marvin, F. S. *Comte.* Translated by Salvador Echavarría. Mexico City: Fondo de Cultura Económica, 1941.

Messer, Augusto. *La filosofía en el siglo XIX: Empirismo y naturalismo.* Translated by José Gaos. Madrid: Revista de Occidente, 1926.

México, su evolución social. Edited by J. Ballescá and his successor. 3 vols. Mexico City, 1900–1902.

Mill, John Stuart. *Sistema de lógica.* Translated by Eduardo Ovejero y Maury. Madrid: Daniel Jorro, Editor, 1917.

————. *Utilitarianism, Liberty and Representative Government.* London: J. M. Dent and Sons, 1940.

Monitor Republicano, El. Mexico City, 1867–1888. [Editor: José María Vigil.]

Mora, José María Luis. *Ensayos, ideas y retratos.* Prologue and selection by Arturo Arnáiz y Freg. Biblioteca del Estudiante Universitario. Mexico City: Ediciones de la Universidad Nacional Autónoma de México, 1941.

————. *Obras sueltas.* Paris: Librería de Rosa, 1837.

Nacional, El. Mexico City, 1880–1900. [Political periodical. Director: Gonzalo N. Esteva.]

Ortega y Gasset, José. *Esquema de las crisis.* Madrid: Revista de Occidente, 1942.

————. *Historia como sistema.* Madrid: Revista de Occidente, 1941.

————. "Ideas para una historia de la filosofía." Prologue to *Historia de la filosofía,* by Émile Bréhier. Buenos Aires: Editorial Sudamericana, 1942.

————. *Obras.* Madrid: Espasa Calpe, 1936.

País, El. Mexico City, 1899–1914. [Daily newspaper of general interest. Director: Trinidad Sánchez Santos.]

Parra, Melesio. *El señor general Porfirio Díaz juzgado en el extranjero.* Mexico City: Tipografía de la Secretaría de Fomento, 1900.

Parra, Porfirio. "Las causas primeras." In *Anales de la Asociación Metodófila "Gabino Barreda,"* pp. 49–67. Mexico City: Imprenta del Comercio de Dublán y Chávez, 1877.

———. "La educación intelectual." *La Libertad* (1881–1882).

———. "Importancia de los estudios lógicos." *La Libertad* (1881).

———. Introduction to *Anales de la Asociación Metodófila "Gabino Barreda,"* pp. 5–10. Mexico City: Imprenta del Comercio de Dublán y Chávez, 1877.

———. *Lógica inductiva y deductiva.* Mexico City: Tipografía Económica, 1903.

———. "La reforma en México." *Gaceta de Guadalajara* (1906).

Patria, La. Mexico City, 1887–1914. [Political daily newspaper. Director: Ireneo Paz.]

Portugal, José M. de Jesús. *El positivismo, su historia y sus errores.* Barcelona: Imprenta Eugenio Subirana, 1908.

Quevedo y Subieta, Salvador. *El caudillo.* Mexico City: Librería de la Vda. de Ch. Bouret, 1909. [Essay on historical psychology.]

———. *El general González y su gobierno en México.* Mexico City, 1884.

Raat, William D. "Ideas and History in Mexico: An Essay on Methodology." In *Investigaciones contemporáneas sobre historia de México,* pp. 687–699. Austin: University of Texas Press, 1971. [Memoria of the Third Reunion of Mexican and North American Historians in Oaxtepec, Morelos, November 4–7, 1969.]

———. "Leopoldo Zea and Mexican Positivism: A Reappraisal." *Hispanic American Historical Review* 48 (1968): 1–18.

Rabasa, Emilio. *La evolución histórica de México.* Mexico City: Librería de la Vda. de Ch. Bouret, 1920.

Ramos, Manuel. "Estudio de las relaciones entre la sociología y la biología." In *Anales de la Asociación Metodófila "Gabino Barreda,"* pp. 255–279. Mexico City, 1877.

Ramos, Samuel. *Historia del pensamiento filosófico en México.* Mexico City: Universidad Nacional Autónoma de México, 1943.

———. *El perfil del hombre y la cultura en México.* Mexico City: Editorial Pedro Robredo, 1938.

Rava, Adolfo. *La filosofía europea en el siglo XIX.* Translated by Oberdan Caletty. Buenos Aires: Editorial Depalma, 1943.

República, La. Mexico City, 1880–1885. [Literary and political daily newspaper. Director: Ignacio M. Altamirano.]

Revista de la Instrucción Pública Mexicana. Mexico City, 1896–1910. [Director: Ezequiel A. Chávez.]

Revista Nacional de Letras y Ciencias. Mexico City, 1889–1890. [Directors: Justo Sierra, Francisco Sosa, Manuel Gutiérrez Nájera, and Jesús E. Valenzuela.]

Revista Positiva. Mexico City: Tipografía Económica, 1901–1914. [Editor: Agustín Aragón.]

Reyes, Alfonso. *Pasado inmediato.* Mexico City: El Colegio de México, 1941.

Ruiz, Luis E. *Elementos de ciencia.* Mexico City: Editorial La Libertad, 1883.

———. *Nociones de lógica.* Mexico City: Editorial La Libertad, 1882.

———. *Nociones de lógica.* Mexico City: Oficina Tipográfica de la Secretaría de Fomento, 1890.

Saenger, Samuel. *Stuart Mill.* Translated by José Gaos. Madrid: Revista de Occidente, 1930.

Salazar, R., and J. G. Escobedo. *Las pugnas de la gleba.* Mexico City: Editorial Avante, 1923.

Scheler, Max. *Sociología del saber.* Translated by José Gaos. Madrid: Revista de Occidente, 1935.

Shotwell, James T. *Historia de la historia en el Mundo Antiguo.* Translated by Ramón Iglesia. Mexico City: Fondo de Cultura Económica, 1940.

Sierra, Justo. *Evolución política del pueblo mexicano.* Prologue by Alfonso Reyes. Mexico City: La Casa de España en México, 1940.

———. "México social y político." *Revista Nacional de Letras y Ciencias* (1889–1890).

———. *Prosas.* Prologue by Antonio Caso, Biblioteca del Estudiante Universitario. Mexico City: Ediciones de la Universidad Nacional Autónoma de México, 1939.

Spencer, Herbert. *La beneficencia.* Translated by Miguel A. Unamuno. Madrid: La España Moderna.

———. *El individuo contra el Estado.* Barcelona: Editorial Bauzá, 1930.

———. *Inducciones de la sociología.* Madrid: La España Moderna.

———. *El organismo social.* Madrid: La España Moderna.

———. *El progreso, su ley y su causa.* Madrid: La España Moderna.

———. *Sociología.* Madrid: La España Moderna.

Tiberghien, G. *Lógica: La ciencia del conocimiento.* Translated by José M. de Castillo Velasco. Mexico City: Librería Madrileña, Vol. 1, 1875; Vol. 2, 1878.

Torres, José. "La crisis del positivismo." [Unedited manuscript; courtesy of Professor Samuel Ramos.]

Valadés, José C. *El porfirismo: Historia de un régimen, 1876 a 1884.* Mexico City: José Porrúa e Hijos, 1941.

Valverde Téllez, Emeterio. *Bibliografía filosófica mexicana.* Vol. 2. León Gto.: Imprenta Jesús Rodríguez, 1913.

Vasconcelos, José. "Don Gabino Barreda y las ideas contemporáneas." In *Conferencias del Ateneo de la Juventud.* Mexico City: Imprenta Lacaud, 1910.

Vigil, José María. *Revista filosófica.* Mexico City, 1882.

———, and Rafael Ángel de la Peña. *Discurso sobre las antinomias y deficiencias del positivismo con motivo del texto para lógica.* Mexico City: Imprenta del Gobierno, 1885.

Voz de México, La. Mexico City, 1870–1908. [Political, religious, and scientific daily newspaper of the "Sociedad Católica." Director: José Joaquín Arriaga.]

Wilson, Irma. *Mexico: A Century of Educational Thought.* New York: Hispanic Institute in the United States, 1941.

Windelband, Wilhelm. *Historia de la filosofía.* Translated by Francisco Larroyo. Mexico City: Antigua Librería de Robredo, 1943.

Zea, Leopoldo. *El apogeo y decadencia del positivismo en México.* Mexico City: El Colegio de México, 1944.

Zubiri, Xavier. "Sobre el problema de la filosofía." *Revista de Occidente* (Madrid) 11, nos. 115 and 116 (1933).

INDEX

Catholic church: 104, 128, 135, 219, 220; and Comtian doctrine, 28, 29; control of education by, 131; denied material power, 55, 56; erosion of spiritual power of, 200–201, 202; gains in strength, 123–124; and human progress, 41; Jacobin attack on, 102–103; and mental emancipation, 41–44; opposes positivist concept of freedom, 98, 100; opposes positivist spiritual order, 130, 134; opposes preparatory school reorganization, 110; Porfirist stance toward, 186; protection of individual rights from, 71; rocks bourgeois boat, 185; sows seeds of own destruction, 44; spiritual authority of, uncontested, 85; as viewed by second-generation positivists, 144. *See also* clergy, the

Catholics: as critics of positivism, 14, 17

caudillos: 48, 49; as agents of tyranny, 74, 77; and freedom, 80; and the theological phase, 33. *See also* military, the

Chávez, D. Ezequiel A.: on anarchy in Mexican society, 172–173; on educational method, 173–174; on founding of scientific order, 178; on scientific method, 175

Chevalier, ———: 133

Chile: Comtism in, 56

China: static religion of, 100

Christ: 104, 192, 215

Christianity: and the Comtian order, 29; loss of faith in, 28

Christians: and positivism, 213, 216

Científicos: 155, 163, 170; abuse of positivism by, 22; use of positivism by, 16

circumstances: vs. ideals, 34–35; relationship of, to ideas, 6–7

cívicos: opposition of, to corps, 67

Civiles: defined, 63

clergy, the: 89; accused of sectarianism, 213–215, 217; advocates freedom of conscience, 210–211; and bourgeois interests, 68; as component of conservative class, 32; confiscation of property of, 108–109; contests positivist control of education, 206–207; designs of, on spiritual power, 218; as enemy of bourgeoisie, 80; as enemy of progress, 45, 52, 53, 93, 94, 154; identified with reaction, 62, 63–65; and ideology, 24; interests of, 65–67; and mental emancipation, 41–44; and Mexican education, 50–51; opposed to positivist education, 194; opposes liberals, 47, 48–49; and the Porfirist regime, 179; and redistribution of privilege, 84; reeducation of, 81–82, 83; rights of, 87; sows seeds of own destruction, 44; and the theological phase, 33; views positivism as sectarian, 57. *See also* Catholic church

colonialism: end of, xi; varieties of, xviii–xix

Comte, Auguste: 15, 18, 32, 34, 40, 54, 61, 97, 140, 169, 202, 217; anticlericalism of, 41, 219; antiliberalism of, 41; attempts of, to reconcile order and liberty, 25–27; as class spokesman, 23–25; ecclesiastical rites in philosophy of, 56; on foresight, 82–83; as instrument of culture, 4; interpretation of history of, 52–53; new order envisioned by, 27–29; as originator of positivism, xi, xii; on relationship of inferiors to superiors, 160; sociology of, 198–199; and the three phases of progress, 33

Comtism: Mexican vs. European application of, 30, 31–32

Condorcet, Marie Jean Antoine Nicolas de Caritat, Marquis: on morality, 97

conscience, freedom of: Catholic defense of, 210–212; interpretations